Britain: The Unauthorised Biography

DAVE REAR

FOR TOMO AND EMI

CONTENTS

ACKNOWLEDGMENTS

Many thanks to my wife and family, and everyone who offered help on early drafts of the manuscript. Thanks also to my brilliant cover designer, Guus Floor.

1. PREHISTORIC BRITAIN (700,000 BC – 55 BC)

Prehistory is the name given to the long period of time before societies developed writing systems. The prehistory of Britain began with the migration of primitive man from mainland Europe and ended with the arrival of the Romans. Over this long and difficult period, Britain gradually progressed from being a bleak and inhospitable land, in which people were locked in a grim battle with mother nature, into being a bleak and inhospitable land, in which people were locked in a grim battle with each other. Along the way, the country passed through the Ice Age, the Stone Age, the Bronze Age and the Iron Age, ending the period under the sway of the mysterious Druids.

The Stone Age

The Britain of a million years ago was a cold and barren wasteland, a windswept tundra where life was a constant struggle against freezing vicious weather. In other words, pretty much the same as today. The only difference was that a million years ago, she was in the grip of an ice age, which left the land buried under thick layers of impenetrable glaciers. Fortunately for future historians, however, the ice age did not continue unbroken. In between the cold spells, there were periods when the climate warmed and the ice sheets retreated. During one of these interglacials between 700,000 and 900,000 years ago, it is thought that the first people arrived in Britain.

At this time, Britain was still joined to the European continent by land, and so the first settlers crossed the English Channel on foot. These people were not *homo sapiens*, as they hadn't been invented yet, but their more primitive ancestors, *homo erectus*. According to archaeological evidence, these brave, or perhaps just lost, men and women lived as hunter-gatherers in groups of around

25 people. A scattering of 78 sharpened flints dating back at least eight millennia are the oldest artifacts that have ever been found in Britain. Their discovery in Norfolk in 2010 revealed that the first humans had arrived here a full 250,000 years earlier than previously thought.

Around 15,000 years ago, the weather finally began to warm up permanently, heralding the end of the ice age at last. More people began arriving overland from the continent, perhaps as many as 20,000 in total. The warmer temperatures led to rising sea levels, which gradually began to separate Britain from the continent. The coup de grace is believed to have been delivered in 6000 BC by a tsunami, triggered by massive landslides in Norway. A ten metre high wave swept 25 miles inshore, turning low-lying plains in the east into the North Sea and marshlands in the south into the Channel. All of a sudden, the 20,000 hunter-gatherers found themselves stuck here for good.

Luckily, with the end of the ice age, life was getting easier. As temperatures soared to significantly higher levels than today, the land became covered in great forests, which attracted animals like pigs, cattle, deer and even elephants. Over time, the settlers' hunting tools became more sophisticated. Instead of the old method of chasing animals until they collapsed in exhaustion, Stone Age hunters developed weapons that could take them down on the run. Throwing spears, harpoons and even bows and arrows all came into use, not only giving people in Britain the edge over their larger prey but also suggesting a way they would eventually be able to kill lots and lots of French people. Suddenly evolution was beginning to make sense at last.

The Neolithic Age

The idea that, instead of chasing around the wild for a few hours hunting pigs and deer, people should toil away from dawn till dusk clearing land, ploughing soil and shovelling cow dung began in the Middle East in 8000 BC. Eventually by around 4000 BC, the first farmers crossed by boat into the British Isles, bringing with them the rudimentary tools of farming, such as spades and sickles. Making their way from the coast, they soon encountered local tribes of hunters and gatherers, to whom the newcomers introduced themselves with a traditional hearty farming welcome: "Get off my laaaaaand."

We know very little about early interactions between farmers and hunter-gatherers, though it is unlikely to have been entirely peaceful. However, DNA evidence suggests that over time, probably a period of several centuries, the hunters were gradually incorporated into agricultural communities. As farming spread across the land, the great forests were cut down to create fields and grasslands, and permanent stone or wooden houses took the place of caves and shelters. The farmers cultivated crops of wheat and barley and domesticated cattle and pigs. Sheep, not native to Britain, were brought over on ships, sustaining a population that by 2000 BC had reached around 300,000.

As permanent communities grew, farmers began to band together for joint construction projects. They built miles of wooden pathways through boggy areas, piled up circular earth banks as enclosures for their animals, and even dug opencast mines to reach supplies of stone and flint. They also held communal ceremonies to commemorate special occasions and began building primitive megaliths like Pentre Ifan in Wales.

The Bronze Age
The next big thing that happened in Britain was the Bronze Age. This landmark development was, again, hastened by new migrants arriving from the continent. The invention of bronze was a huge step forward, for it allowed the creation of sharp and durable tools that transformed people's everyday lives. Archeologists have found the remains of axes, knives, chisels, buckets, swords, shields, skewers and even razors, all molded from the new metal. For some reason, however, it was the discovery of bronze beakers that

impressed the archeologists the most, and so they decided to call the new migrants the Beaker People. It was probably not the name they'd have chosen themselves.

To be fair, though, the Beaker People did not waste their beaker-making prowess. There is evidence to suggest they were the first people to introduce alcoholic drinks to Britain in the form of the sweet honey wine known as mead. In time, they also began to brew beer from grains like wheat and barley, which at last made the backbreaking hell of farming seem worthwhile. The bronze beakers gave the new drinks a nice metallic tang.

As well as drinking heavily, or more likely as a result of drinking heavily, Bronze Age Britons also began engaging in massive work projects like Stonehenge. The stone circle we see today was constructed in around 2200 BC, though a wooden circle is thought to have existed at least 500 years previously. Its giant bluestones were transported 200 miles from the Preseli Hills in south-west Wales and must have required literally millions of hours of labour.

The current consensus is that the circle was built to celebrate the changing of the seasons, since many of the stones were arranged to point to the sun at important times of the year. It was also used as a burial ground. One thing we have learned from the tombs discovered around the site was the tragically short lives Bronze Age people led. Most were dead by the age of thirty, and practically all the skeletons found at Stonehenge over the age of 25 had severe arthritis. Dragging around massive bluestones probably hadn't helped.

The Age of People Not Liking Each Other Very Much
As the centuries went by, farming still remained the occupation of most people in Britain. However, it was trade with the tribes of mainland Europe that attracted the brightest and best. Tin was the major commodity Britain had to offer, mined in remote and inhospitable wildernesses like Cornwall. The major additive in the

creation of bronze, tin was a valuable export, and it soon led to an influx of gold and precious metals into the country. The gold was molded into expensive fashion accessories, such as hair ornaments, broaches and bracelets, which reflected the high status of those who wore them. Unfortunately, however, this soon lead to jealousy among the rival clans:

"Ooh, doesn't Alaric the Death-Giver have beautiful hair ornaments?" warriors would exclaim to one another enviously. "And where did he get that *gorgeous* broach?"

Often these tensions spilled over into war, conflict and face slapping. To make matters worse, the climate in Britain was changing, turning two degrees colder over the course of several centuries. Wind and rainfall increased, leading to ruined harvests and widespread flooding. The upshot was that in the years following 1000 BC, everyone was feeling pretty miserable and fed-up. Instead of working together to construct megaliths, clans began to raid each other's territories. They built fortified enclosures on top of hills to keep their enemies out, herding their livestock inside when raids threatened. All in all, Britain was becoming a very nasty and violent place, an environment in which brawn triumphed over brain and brutishness beat back culture. In other words, it seemed like just the kind of place the Celts might feel at home.

Iron and Celts

The Celts are terrifying in appearance, mad keen on war and quick to begin a fight. They are boasters and threateners, full of rage, and often drunk. They use few words and turn violent at the slightest provocation.

So wrote the Greek historian Strabo after a night out in Glasgow in 1986. But the Celts were also pretty shirty 3000 years ago as well. Named by the Greeks, they appeared in Western Europe around 700 BC as a plethora of warring tribes probably originating from around the Rhine (though there is also evidence they may have come from Spain). The largest tribes made their home in Gaul, where they eventually came up against the Romans, while others crossed the sea and arrived in Britain and Ireland. They traded with each other over large distances, brought together by shared legends and dialects of a common language. Occasionally they even stopped fighting each other long enough to use it.

In Britain, the Celts arrived not as an invasion but as a gradual infiltration from the continent, no different from the migrations that had been going on for thousands of years. Nobody called our island dwellers Celts at the time – the Romans knew us as Britons, a name attributed to the Greek explorer Pytheas who arrived on our shores in 325 BC. However, it seems that by the 6th century BC most of the inhabitants of the British Isles were speaking varieties of Celtic languages. They were also molding iron, which required much higher temperatures to extract and manipulate than the softer bronze. The ancient Britons found iron extremely useful, since it hurt a lot more when they hit each other with it. They used it to make everything from swords and battle axes to everyday peaceful items like flails and spiked war hammers.

Bards and Druids

According to the Romans, the culture of ancient Britain revolved around two major activities, fighting and drinking, generally conducted at the same time. There was, however, more to Iron Age society than this. For instance, there was storytelling. Despite having no written texts, the Britons were huge fans of poetry, the recital of which was the preserve of a specialist class of storytellers known as bards. A trainee bard spent as many as twelve years learning the techniques of the trade and memorising the some 350 Celtic story-poems. Once qualified, he could be hired out for feasts, where he would entertain the revellers with slow, theatrical renditions of these epic poems, thus allowing the host to sneak out halfway through and burn down his guests' hillforts. He was therefore an integral part of Iron Age culture.

Another integral part of culture were the Druids, who had control of religious and legal matters. The Iron Age Britons were animists who believed that gods and spirits resided in the objects all around them. Sources of water like springs and pools were considered particularly sacred, as was the oak tree and the mistletoe that grew upon it. This is the origin of kissing under the mistletoe, which must have been just as embarrassing to the ancient Britons as it is to us today, particularly since they lived in extended families, meaning there were always lots of aunts around.

The spirits had to be provided with offerings and sacrifices to keep them happy. Along with gold and precious metals, they also demanded blood, including that of human beings. The most famous example of human sacrifice was Lindow Man, found in a peat bog in Cheshire in 1984. An examination of his well-preserved remains revealed that his assailants had first knocked him unconscious with an axe, then strangled him to death with a cord, and finally cut his throat. Such a death, archaeologists surmised, was so interesting it could only have been for ceremonial purposes.

The people responsible for carrying out these sacrifices were the Druids. Almost uniquely in Britain at the time, Druids could read and write, but they wisely refused to pass on this skill to the rest of the population in case people realised they were frauds. Armed with secret and arcane knowledge they had just made up, the Druids had a variety of important roles within society. As well as deciding who should be thrown into which peat bog on which particular day – not an easy choice considering the number of bogs in Britain there were to choose from – they also acted as advisers to chieftains and kings and as judges and arbiters of the law.

Iron Age law was surprisingly flexible, with execution rarely used as a standard form of punishment. Instead the system was largely based on fines, or 'honour-prices'. The higher the social standing of the victim of the crime, the more honour they were said to have. The more honour they had, the higher the fine the wrongdoer had to pay. Killing a tribal chieftain would, therefore, lead to the highest fine possible, whereas hacking to death a landless peasant would just be a pretty cheap way to let off some steam. The catch to this system was that if you could not afford to pay the fine, the kin of the victim had the right to do anything they liked to you, from selling you into slavery to gutting you open like a pig. Furthermore, if the wrongdoer escaped for some reason, then the victim's kin was obliged – not permitted, you understand, *obliged* – to carry out a blood feud with the renegade's family until it was decided the crime had been properly revenged. Because, why the heck not?

2. ROMAN BRITAIN (55 BC – 410 AD)

In 43 AD, the history of Britain officially began. For thousands of years, from primitive hunter-gatherers to axe-wielding warriors, the inhabitants of Britain had got by without taking note of a single thing that happened to them. With the coming of the Romans, however, this all changed. Thrust into the civilised world, the Britons celebrated their newfound sophistication by painting themselves purple and shrieking a lot. For the next 400 years or so, this remained their dominant pattern of behaviour in both good times and bad, though it never seemed to succeed in getting rid of the Romans. Their overlords, in the meantime, had built towns, roads, aqueducts and baths, determined not to let their stay in Britain be spoiled by the presence of British people.

The Coming of Julius Caesar

In 55 BC, the Roman Republic, entering the final thirty years of its long existence, was dominated by three powerful men, who formed a ruling triumvirate across the ever-expanding empire. These were Marcus Crassus, scourge of rebels and conqueror of Spartacus, Gnaeus Pompey, scourge of pirates and conqueror of the east, and Julius Caesar, scourge of Gaul and conqueror of Pompey's and Crassus's wives. Battling each other for preeminence in the republic, each man was determined to do whatever he could to win fame and glory for himself and his legions. Only one of them, however, was crazy enough to try and do this in Britain.

Gaul had still not been entirely subdued when Caesar turned his thoughts toward the small island across the water. Rumours abounded that the Celtic Gauls were being aided by their British cousins, and Caesar decided it was time to learn more about them. There was also something strangely alluring about the little-known isles of Britannia. Cut off from the continent and permanently shrouded in fog, many Romans believed them to lie on the edge of the world. For an adventurer like Caesar, this was too great a temptation to resist.

We are fortunate in that Julius Caesar was not only a brilliant general but also a meticulous narrator of great historical deeds, particularly his own. We thus have a first-hand account of his first forays into Britannia. In 55 BC, he assembled 12,000 troops in eighty ships and sailed north toward the white cliffs of Dover. By the time of his arrival, there were at least fifteen large tribes in England with a total population of around two million. It was in many respects a thriving country, with an abundant grain supply and coinage that bore the stamp of tribal kings, hallmarks of a relatively advanced civilisation.

Unfortunately for Caesar, the southern tribes of England had already been warned of the invasion to come. When Caesar attempted to land his ships, he was met by a shrieking horde of naked warriors whose bodies were pierced with tattoos and covered from head to toe in purple woad. Not *that* advanced a civilisation then, thought Caesar. When the general finally did manage to land his troops further up the coast, he found himself embroiled in a series of pitched battles. Many of the Britons fought skillfully on chariots, and although Caesar proceeded to win a handful of battles, the fight was never easy and he soon decided to leave. Plus there was the terrible weather, the desperate excuse for food, the appalling public transport etc.

However, if there was one thing you could say about Julius Caesar, it was that he always came back for more. The following year, he arrived on the shores of Kent again, this time with 25,000 infantry, 2000 cavalry and a war elephant. His army marched inland as far as Hertfordshire and defeated a combined British force under the leadership of Cassivellaunus, the king of one of the dominant tribes of south-east England. But just as glory beckoned, Caesar received news of yet another revolt in Gaul that required his presence. It seemed the pesky Gauls simply would not lie down and surrender, which was strange considering Gaul was just another name for France. Back across the Channel Caesar's army sailed, leaving not a soul behind. It would be almost a century before any Roman was brave enough to step foot on British soil once more.

The Conquest of Claudius

Blessed with ninety years free of war from overseas, the tribes of Britain were determined not to waste the chance that had been presented to them and quickly declared war on each other instead. Powerful tribes expanded their territory at the expense of their neighbours and grew rich from trade with the Romanised peoples of Gaul. Some of the weaker southern tribes even volunteered to pay taxes to Rome in return for protection, which the Romans promised to provide just as soon as they returned to Britain in about, say, never. Finally in 40 AD, fed up of being ignored, the king of one of these tribes, Verica of the Atrebates, decided to travel to Rome to ask for help in person. Enduring cold, hunger and discomfort of every sort along the way, he was determined that this time he wouldn't take no for an answer.

"No," said the Emperor Caligula.

This was the same Emperor Caligula that had slept with his three sisters, made his horse a consul, and thrown a whole section of spectators into the arena to fight lions. But still, he told Verica sternly, he wasn't crazy enough to go to Britain. Fortunately, just a year after this Caligula was assassinated by his army, who appointed a new emperor called Claudius. Claudius immediately announced his intention to send the army to Britain, which wasn't much of a way of thanking them but they were kind of stuck with him now. The new emperor needed a cause to curry favour with the people, and this was the only one he could think of at short notice other than throwing the whole lot of them to the lions.

The emperor was smart enough, however, not to go himself, at least at first. Instead he sent his shrewd general Plautius along with 40,000 troops. Landing in Kent, the legions marched as far as the River Medway, where they found the powerful Catuvellauni tribe waiting for them on the other side, under the command of their king Caratacus. While the armies prepared for battle by refining their tactics and sharpening their swords, or in the Britons' case by standing around and getting noisily drunk, Plautius secretly sent a team of crack troops downstream. Swimming quietly across the river on horseback, they launched a surprise attack on the Britons. At the same time, the rest of Plautius's army crossed the river upstream and attacked the Catuvellauni from behind. The result was a decisive Roman victory.

Free of substantial opposition, the Romans advanced along the south coast and laid siege to dozens of British hillforts, which didn't seem quite as impregnable as they once did. Finally, once most of the south was in Roman hands, the emperor Claudius arrived. He brought with him huge war elephants to scare away any final resistance, and the defeat of the Britons was soon complete. Barely four months after the invasion had begun, the emperor and his legions captured the Catuvellauni stronghold at Colchester, where he received the public submission of ten kings and one queen.

Just two weeks later, Claudius returned to Rome to the joyous cheers of the populace. Making a triumphant procession through the city, the emperor had Caratacus of the Catuvellauni paraded through the streets in chains, a common fate for defeated kings and usually the prelude to a quick death by strangling. But the people of Rome were so taken by the Briton's cheeky Essex-boy charm that Claudius decided to grant him his freedom. It was a decision he soon lived to regret, when Caratacus took over a nice piece of land near the forum and started selling crack.

The Revolt of Boudica
Over the next twenty years, the Romans took control over most of

southern England. But they often met fierce opposition from the tribes they conquered. In the year 60 AD, they faced an uprising so serious it almost spelled the end of Roman rule.

Ironically, spelling the end of anything was the last thing that sprung to mind when it came to the revolt of Queen Boudica / Boudicca / Boudicea / Boudicia etc. Boudica was the wife of one of the British kings who was loyal to the Romans, Prasutagus, leader of the Iceni tribe in East Anglia. On his deathbed, he made a deal with the Roman governor to divide his kingdom up between his two daughters and the Roman emperor Nero. Prasutagus knew the arrangement was safe because if there was one thing you could say about the Romans, it was that they always kept their word. And indeed, the Romans did keep their word right up to the moment Prasutagus died, at which point they seized his lands, subjected his wife Boudica to a public whipping, and raped his daughters. Boudica was absolutely outraged. How could the Romans be so savage as to seize her husband's lands?

Red-haired with a harsh voice and a piercing glare, according to Roman chroniclers, Boudica set about raising a vast army of men, women and children, all desperate to drive out the Romans or at the very least to stop Boudica shouting at them. They headed for Colchester, the Roman capital, and ransacked the city. Then they turned on the cities of Londinium (London) and Verulamium (St Albans). The chariot-riding Boudica and her army massacred all before them, perhaps as many as 80,000 people. She was particularly harsh on Roman noblewomen, impaling them on stakes and cutting off their breasts, especially the ones that were prettier than her. Meanwhile, most of the Roman army was hundreds of miles away in northern Wales, where they were fighting another rebellious group of nutters, the Druids.

Back in Rome, Emperor Nero, who had been enjoying his usual afternoon pastime of feeding his pet lions with martyrs, considered pulling out of Britain altogether. Fortunately, however, the Roman governor Paulinus had an alternative plan:

"Why don't we just kill them all instead, sire?"

Now that he thought about it, this was just the kind of thing Nero enjoyed, and so the Roman legions marched back from Wales and began to hunt the Britons down. Boudica's army of 200,000 vastly outnumbered the 10,000 Romans. However, they were no match for the discipline of the highly-trained legions. They met at the Battle of Watling Street in the Midlands. When the Romans advanced in a tight formation and began to cut through the chaotic mass of Britons, Boudica and her army turned and fled, running into their own families who had been stationed behind with wagons. With no way of escape, they were massacred in their tens of thousands. Boudica and her unfortunate daughters poisoned themselves with hemlock to avoid capture, and that was the end of that.

The Romans Go to Scotland And Then Leave Soon Afterwards

Once Boudica's rebellion had been put down, the Romans declared that there weren't to be any more for a while, allowing their new territory to fall under the famous *pax Romana*, Latin for 'Roman just settle down and do what you're told already, okay?' But Latin was never a strong point of the Britons, and soon there was trouble brewing up north.

Unlike the south, the north of England had been largely untouched by the Roman occupation. In 71 AD, the dominant northern tribe, the Brigantes, began to create unrest under the leadership of their king Venutius. The Romans, who had been looking to expand their rule, reacted quickly and managed to push the Brigantes back to their lands in Yorkshire. Along the way they constructed forts, including in Mancunium (the Roman name for Manchester), from which the modern inhabitants of the city take their nickname. The forts gave the Romans the perfect base to launch a campaign into the wild, untouched land of Scotland.

In 77, the arrival of an ambitious Roman governor named Agricola heralded the first advance into Scotland. Coordinating his forces by land and sea, he led a series of bold campaigns, making good use of native English warriors who, in a development that would change British history forever, realised just how much fun it was to kill Scottish people. In 83, they won a decisive victory in the northeast and secured their control over a large area of the country. Suddenly, Agricola was dreaming not only of Scotland but also across the sea to Ireland, a land the Roman world knew nothing about other than its famously large concentration of ire.

Fortunately, the emperor Domitian recalled Agricola to Rome before it was too late. Domitian had come to the conclusion that the Roman Empire was becoming too large and unwieldy, and frankly didn't it have enough red-haired people in it already? Roman ambitions to conquer these wild lands ended with Agricola's recall, and from then on the imperial strategy was based not on how to get the Roman Empire inside Scotland but how to stop Scotland from getting inside the Roman Empire. It involved the construction of a very large wall.

Keeping the Peace
In 122 AD, the emperor Hadrian visited Britain, determined to build a grand and ambitious monument that would serve to divert attention away from his slightly girly-sounding name. In the end he couldn't think of anything more manly than a wall, and he wisely elected to build it across Scotland where the country was not so wide. Even so, it was big: 75 miles long and up to six metres high in some parts.

"We'll call it Hadrian's Wall," said the emperor. "That's *H*adrian with an H."

Despite the wall, Britain still proved a tough place to govern. Taking up as many as ten percent of the empire's troops, it required more soldiers than any other province. The Romans were forced to put fortifications around major towns, something not necessary in larger but more submissive provinces like Gaul. The tribes of Scotland were a constant menace, prompting Hadrian's successor Antoninus to build a second wall further inside the country, which he proudly called the Antonine Wall. Unfortunately, it was made of blocks of turf rather than stone, and now barely anybody bothers to go to see it.

Peace of a sort reigned until 192 when the assassination of a rubbish emperor named Commodus, played by Joaquin Phoenix, triggered a long period of instability as various rivals competed for the top job. Britain, with its large number of troops, was suddenly an important place for aspiring tyrants, and in fact it was the British governor, Clodius Albinus, who put himself forward. Albinus meant 'pale' in Latin, which happened to everyone who spent too much time in Britain, and it wasn't long before he was defeated in battle by a much more tanned rival from Africa, Septimus Severus, a cooler name by far. Severus arrived in Britain in 208, determined to make sure no British governor ever got so cocky again. He split the province into two parts: Britannia Superior and Britannia Inferior. Only one of these names referred to the south.

After Severus died, however, civil war and anarchy followed for the next fifty years. It got so bad that in 273 Britain, Gaul, Spain and lower Germany were able to break away from the Roman Empire and form their own independent Gallic empire. The empire lasted for fourteen years but after the death of its first emperor, Postumus, its unity began to crumble. A strong Roman emperor named Aurelian took advantage and, to the relief of just about everyone, the Romans resumed control.

Towns and Roads

The most noticeable difference in Britain between the time before the Roman invasion and after the Roman invasion was the presence of towns. Before the Romans, the Britons had never bothered with towns as they correctly surmised this would involve living in fairly close proximity to other Britons. But through a combination of Roman ingenuity and slave labour, Britain was soon dotted with dozens of towns with all sorts of bewildering innovations, including stone arches, window glass, sewage systems and under-floor heating. The most important were London, Colchester, York, Lincoln and Gloucester, which served as regional capitals for the unruly province.

The Romans connected their towns together with networks of roads, which they always built in a perfectly straight line in order to prevent local outbreaks of imagination. Several of the most important main roads in Britain today still follow the routes of the original Roman ones. Watling Street became the A2 and A5 in the Midlands; Pye Road became the A140 in East Anglia; Dere Street in the north became the A59 and M1. Not all the Roman roads were original, however. Some, like Watling Street, had existed as wellworn tracks from Bronze Age times. The Romans just made them look better and took the credit.

Towns and roads led to an economic boom in the country as craftsmen and merchants rushed to meet demand for new products from around the Roman Empire. Both national and international trade flourished. British products could now be transported as far away as Africa and the Middle East, and then they could be transported back around three days later when they broke down under warranty. The most popular export was the *birrus Britannicus*, a kind of rainproof cloak and hood. Nobody did rain products better than the British.

Cultural Pastimes

As well as technology and engineering, the Romans also brought many important cultural developments to the people of Britain. Chief among these was, of course, the tactical chunder, carried out during a banquet to allow you to continue eating and drinking long past the moment when you would normally stop. The British took to this practice so easily it was almost as if they had invented it themselves. Then there was the Roman concept of bathtime. When they first set foot in Britain, the Romans had been shocked by the almost total absence of naked collective bathing. Soon, however, the public bathhouse became the focus of social life in every town in Britain. The bathing ritual began with a dip in the tepid pool, then moved on to the steamy hot tub, before ending with a refreshing swim in the cold outdoor pool. Despite their reputation for dirt and smelliness, the natives actually took to the pastime of bathing quite readily, and some people in Britain continue to bathe regularly to this day.

Along with bathing and barfing, the third major cultural activity in Roman Britain was the public show. The shows were held in purpose-built stadiums on the edge of towns, which often had enough seats to hold the entire local population. They staged animal fights, wrestling matches, chariot races and, of course, gladiator combats. In many ways, they were the forerunners of modern reality shows, except that in the Roman version the contestants could actually die on the show rather than the audience simply wishing they would.

Of all the different shows, chariot racing was the one at which Britons most excelled. Racing around the track at breakneck speeds, the top charioteers were the Formula 1 drivers of their day, feted throughout the land. After the races, vicious fights commonly broke out between the fans of rival teams, resulting in mass brawls that wrecked property for miles around. In all the chaos that came with the fall of the Roman Empire and the centuries of war and oppression that followed, this was the one custom the people of Britain never allowed to perish.

The Beginnings of Christianity

Of the many things the Roman Empire was renowned for, tolerance was not one of them. But in religious matters, they were surprisingly open-minded. They allowed conquered peoples to continue worshipping their own gods just so long as they made room in their pantheon for Roman ones too. But in the province of Judea a young man called Jesus came along, who preached a doctrine of a single deity. At first, the Roman authorities did not take this obscure Jewish sect seriously, but as the faith spread through the empire, they decided they'd better start getting rid of them. This led to martyrs.

The first martyr we know of in Britain was a Roman soldier by the name of Albinus, who was beheaded early in the 3rd century after giving shelter to a Christian priest. Many years later, Albinus was declared a saint, and the town where he lived was renamed St Albans in his honour. When the persecution of Christians ended with the accession of Emperor Constantine in 306 AD, Christianity in Britain could be practised more openly. Evidence of a small cathedral has been excavated near Tower Hill which dates back to the 4th century.

Christianity in England did not really took off until the arrival of charismatic missionaries like Augustine in the late 6th century. Ireland, however, got an early taste of what was in store when St Patrick strode ashore over a hundred years earlier. Despite his stereotypically Irish name, Patrick was actually born in England. At the age of sixteen he was carried off by slavers to Ireland, but managed to escape back to England six years later, where he became a bishop. Returning to Ireland, he began to convert the natives to Christianity, baptising thousands including princes and nobles. According to legend, of course, Patrick also drove out all the snakes, a neat trick since it's pretty certain there weren't any snakes in Ireland to begin with. A more probable explanation for the legend is that the snakes represented the religion of the Druids, who used serpents as their chief symbol.

The Decline and Fall of the Roman Empire

Towards the end of the 3rd century, Britain began to come under pirate attack from tribesmen in northern Germany called Saxons. To keep the marauders out, the Romano-Britons, as the more optimistic inhabitants now saw themselves, built large forts along the southern and eastern coasts. They called these fortified areas the Saxon shore, apparently unaware that the Saxons might rather seriously misconstrue its meaning.

Unfortunately for Europe, the Germans did not restrict their attacks to Britain. They were also discovering the delights of invading Gaul and Italy too. In response to the threat, the Romans began to withdraw troops from Britain, leaving the Romano-Britons feeling a trifle exposed. In 367, wild Caledonians and Picts from Scotland swept over Hadrian's Wall and laid siege to York, while on the south coast the Saxons began to make sure their shore lived up to its name.

In desperation, the Welsh monk Gildas wrote to Emperor Honorius pleading for his help:

The barbarians are driving us into the sea and the sea is driving us back to the barbarians. Two forms of death wait for us, to be slaughtered or drowned.

By this time, however, Rome herself was being overrun by Visigoths and Vandals, who were finding more whitewashed marble walls to graffiti than they ever dreamed possible. Northern England was the first to suffer from the Roman loss of power. Tribal leaders reasserted their influence, while the remaining Roman armies (who had long been made up of native Britons) re-organised themselves under chieftains, including one named Coelius of Old King Cole fame.

In 410 AD, Rome's 600 year reign over the West came to an end. Britain was left adrift in a sea of angry Germans, the centuries of comparative peace and prosperity about to reach a nasty and distinctively Teutonic conclusion. Although the Roman way of life in Britain did not die out immediately, two centuries of Saxon, Angle and Jute invasions eventually took its toll on the infrastructure they had left behind. It marked the beginning of a new age for the islands of Britain. Not a good new age, obviously, but a new one. It would be known, cheerfully, as the Dark Ages.

3. THE DARK AGES (410 – 1066)

The fall of the Roman Empire brought slavery, death and misery to millions of people throughout the Western world, which was unfortunate because that's largely what the rise of the Roman Empire had brought too. The difference during the Dark Ages was that hardly anybody kept a record of it. There didn't seem much point since manuscripts were so easily set on fire, the predominant cultural activity of this period. Britain attempted to get through this flammable period of history by being so permanently damp that nothing would ever stay lit. But the one thing you could never accuse Germanic or Viking invaders of was a lack of persistence. For 500 years, they burned and pillaged their way through the British Isles, leaving behind for posterity nothing of any value except most of the language, customs and heritage of modern Britain. More than 1500 years later, they still haven't apologised.

The Anglo-Saxon Invasion

As the Roman legions sheepishly left town, promising to be back just as soon as things calmed down a bit, the way was clear for German and Scandinavian tribes to move in. These tribes were roughly divided into three groups: Saxons, Angles and Jutes. The Saxons spread out in the south and west of the country; the Angles settled in the east; while the Jutes carved out their own impressive empire on the Isle of Wight[*]. Each group lent their names to the places they occupied: East Anglia for the Angles, Wessex for the West Saxons, Sussex for the South Saxons, and Essex for the East Saxons.

According to the Venerable Bede, writing about 300 years after the event, the Saxons were led by a pair of brothers named Hengist

---

[*] This is why it's not known as the Anglo-Saxon-Jute invasion.

and Horsa, 'stallion' and 'horse' in Old English, who had been invited to the country as mercenaries by a British warlord named Vortigern. The two brothers found they quite liked Britain and, turning against their benefactor, sent word back to their friends in Germany to come and join them. It was from this unfortunate episode, Bede says, that the Germanic migration began in earnest.

Apart from Bede's unreliable testimony, we have very little information about the Anglo-Saxon invasion. The only source available from the time was the Welsh monk Gildas, who wrote an extended sermon called *The Ruin of Britain*, which gives you some idea as to what he thought about it. Gildas paints a picture of horror as the German tribes spread up through the south-west:

A number of the wretched survivors were caught in the mountains and butchered wholesale. Others, their spirits broken by hunger, went to surrender to the enemy; they were fated to be slaves for ever, if indeed they were not killed straight away, the best outcome.

As a good Christian, Gildas may have exaggerated the brutality of the heathen invasion of his land. While there were certainly battles, most of them fairly one-sided affairs, it was hardly a genocide. Modern DNA records combined with evidence from contemporary graves suggests the numbers of incomers to have been relatively small, somewhere between 100,000 and 200,000 out of a total population of around 2 million. These numbers were, however, enough to ensure the almost total capitulation of the Britons, at least in the south and east. In these areas, the Saxon warriors took control, leaving the natives either willingly or unwillingly to accept a new class of overlords, albeit ones slightly less sophisticated than the Romans.

The invasion didn't get as far, however, as Wales, Cornwall and northern England, while some Britons also sailed across the Channel to Brittany. The modern Breton language can be traced back to the Celtic languages of Cornish and Welsh. The Anglo-Saxon advance into the west might have been quicker were it not for a battle fought around 500 AD at a location called Mount Badon, probably somewhere in Somerset. Gildas tells us of a Romano-British commander who led the Britons to a great victory, temporarily halting the Saxon progress. And therein began the strange, made-up legend of King Arthur.

The Legend of King Arthur

'No figure on the borderline of history and mythology has wasted more of the historian's time,' wrote the historian Noel Myers, momentarily forgetting about figures like Jesus Christ. The only evidence of Arthur's existence was Gildas's reference to the British warlord at Mount Badon. Gildas named him Ambrosius Aurelianus, which contains some of the same letters that Arthur does. Gildas says he 'won some battles and lost others', which is hardly a ringing endorsement of our nation's most famous hero, but to be fair it wasn't really a winning time for the Britons.

Other than that, we don't have much until in 830 the Christian monk Nennius of Wales suddenly started writing about 'Arthur' as a great leader who had fought twelve battles against the Saxons. Then in 1130 another Welshman with too much time on his hands, Geoffrey of Monmouth, wrote in the legend of Merlin the Magician. After that, the Norman French added a few more details, before finally an English writer named Sir Thomas Mallory completed the whole story in 1485, creating one of the first books to be printed in Britain.

Despite its almost completely fictional foundations, the power of Arthur's legend was extraordinary. Henry Tudor even claimed to be descended from Arthur in order to prove his right to the English throne, which gives you a clue as to how little right he *actually* had. Edward III constructed a circular table and considered re-creating the fellowship of King Arthur's knights. Then Hollywood turned Camelot into a musical, and suddenly

Gildas was very much regretting the whole thing.

Anglo-Saxon Society

The hub of Anglo-Saxon society was the great hall, where the great, if not necessarily the good, would gather for long nights of drinking, feasting and endless recitals of Beowulf. The great hall would have been owned by a land-owning chief, or thegn, who himself owed allegiance to a king. The Germanic kings were perpetually at war with one another, because no matter how much land they stole from the Britons they always had another towel they wanted to lay down.

Despite their differences, however, the tribes shared a common culture. They were pagans, worshipping Norse gods but with slightly different names that could conveniently be made into weekdays, such as Tiw, Woden, Thunor and Frige. Death for the Anglo-Saxons meant setting out on a journey, and so they were buried with the things they would need with them, like weapons, clothes and jewelry. The most famous burial site discovered so far was the tomb of King Raewald of East Anglia, dating from the early 7th century and unearthed in Sutton Hoo in 1939. Despite being one of the first Saxon converts to Christianity, Raewald wisely hedged his bets when it came to death, having his longboat buried alongside him just in case heaven was a bit wet.

As the naming of the weekdays suggested, the Germanic tongue of the Anglo-Saxons gradually evolved into the English spoken today, though not without a few bumps along the way. What we now know as Old English would be mostly unrecognisable to a modern speaker, though the grammar would be disturbingly familiar to a contemporary German. Some words, however, have largely maintained their form and meaning, such as *faeder* (father), *modor* (mother), *sunu* (son), *dohtor* (daughter) *mann* (man), *sweord* (sword), and *hus* (house). Many of the place names are also largely intact. *Ham* was a village or estate, *ton* was a farm and a group of Roman buildings a *caester*.

The Conversion of Britain

By the late 6th century, the Anglo-Saxon kingdoms were getting more settled. One thing, however, was still a constant annoyance. That was the insistence of the Anglo-Saxon kings on worshipping ridiculous, made-up deities like Woden and Thunor. This was quite out of step with the rest of Western Europe, which preferred rational, easily understood deities like the Holy Trinity instead. Fledgling bishops in Ireland and Rome made a decision, therefore, to send over missionaries to sort things out.

Considering that almost every aspect of Anglo-Saxon culture was pretty much guaranteed to land them in hell, the conversion of the Anglo-Saxons was remarkably straightforward. The kings appreciated the fact that the monks could read and write, because it made promulgating laws a whole lot easier. One of the first to arrive was an Irish missionary called Columba who, having tired of people constantly assuming he was a woman, set up a strictly male-only monastery on the tiny island of Iona off the northwest coast. He was soon followed by other Irish monks, who founded monasteries all over the country and said that sure they wouldn't mind writing out the king's latest tyrannical promulgation just as soon as he waded into this river here and let them pour cold water on his head for some reason. It seemed like a reasonable quid pro quo.

Meanwhile, in far-off Rome Pope Gregory the Great was thinking his missionaries better get in on the act too and he sent his top man, St Augustine, off to Kent to meet King Aethelbert. As the story goes, Augustine actually got his first sight of Anglo-Saxon people at a slave market for young boys in Rome[*]. Seeing the fair skin and golden hair of the boys, Augustine exclaimed, 'These are not Angles but angels!', shortly before he turned round and

---

[*] Augustine was not, of course, planning to buy any of these young slave boys himself, because that was not the direction the Catholic Church had moved in as yet.

25

realised they had snaffled his wallet.

King Aethelbert took to Christianity quite easily and made Augustine the first Archbishop of Canterbury, which sounded a lot grander than it probably was at the time. By the late 7th century, the faith had spread across Britain like wild fire and there were monasteries and churches everywhere. Things were going very well, except for the inevitable fights that broke out between Irish and Roman monks about how best to teach the pagans about the limitless love and patience of Jesus Christ. Principal among these fights was the argument over how to fix the date for Easter each year.

Eventually, in 664 the King of Northumberland called for a synod of bishops at Whitby Abbey in order to settle the differences. According to contemporary sources, the king's decision-making process went something like this:

King:	So, when was this Jesus Christ crucified anyway?
Advisers:	Nobody has any idea, sire.
King:	So why are they arguing about it?
Advisers:	Because they're Irish and Italian, sire.
King:	Christ. Is it always going to be like this?
Advisers:	Of course not, sire! Eventually the Irish will start arguing amongst themselves as well.
King:	Best go with the Italians then?
Advisers:	Good choice.

As Christians across Britain agreed to be guided by the teachings of the Roman Pope, the Irish bishops went home in a huff, from which they never really recovered. Nobody ever did succeed, however, in fixing a date for Easter.

The Rise of Mercia

The Anglo-Saxon kings were firmly Christian by now, but continued to use ruthless violence to enrich themselves and extend

26

their power, something strictly forbidden by the Church's teachings unless you were pretty high up in the hierarchy. Of all the kings, King Aethelbald of Mercia was the most ambitious. A devout and prayerful man who devoted himself to religious pursuits like Bible-reading, monastic reform and nun seduction, he began calling himself not only King of Mercia but also King of the South English. This naturally came as a bit of a shock to the other kings in the south, not least because none of them had even realised they *were* English. It turned out that the Venerable Bede had used the term in his ecclesiastical history and it had kind of stuck.

Aethalbald's successor, Offa, went even further. In his reign from 757 to 796, he captured all the English kingdoms except Northumbria and Wessex, plucking out the eyes of the king of Kent and making vassals of many others. He also tried to conquer the people of Wales, until their inhospitable terrain and fierce mountain singing drove him off. In the end, he constructed a vast wall and ditch along the border to keep them out, or perhaps himself in. Known as Offa's Dyke, it was 2.5 metres deep and up to 20 metres wide. Much of it is still visible today, though it is far less effective at keeping out the Welsh than it once was.

Mercia's reign as the preeminent power in England was brief. By the 820s, its empire had collapsed, driven back by unhappy vassals and internal squabbles. The future lay with Wessex, which controlled the southern ports and the mineral resources of the west. Still, the Mercian rise had coincided with a growing level of cultural sophistication in Britain. Offa had minted his own coins and had even communicated in Latin with the great emperor Charlemagne on the continent. The Celts of Ireland, Cornwall, Wales and Scotland, meanwhile, were also in close contact with each other, united by their common language of bitching about the English. Trade was beginning to flourish and the monasteries were spreading literacy, at least to each other. At last, after 400 years of hardship, things were finally looking up. What could possibly go wrong?

Raiders from the Sea

In 789, three long, low ships appeared off the coast of Dorset. As they came into shore, the local reeve rode out to greet them, delighted because nothing this exciting had ever happened in Dorset before[*]. "Hello there, strangers!" he shouted jovially, shortly before the men from the ships drew their battleaxes and chopped him into little pieces.

This was the first of many interactions the English were to enjoy with the people known as Vikings. For the next sixty years or so, shiploads of these Scandinavian hunks would pop up every spring and summer, murder all the locals in sight and steal anything that would fit on their boats. What they couldn't fit on their boats, they wrecked or burned down to make sure there'd be nothing left there to steal when they came back a year later. They were fearsome these Vikings, but not necessarily bright.

The poor Anglo-Saxons complained bitterly at this brutal invasion of Britain, a sense of irony not being one of the things Germanic tribes were renowned for. They called the Vikings 'wolves to be feared' and 'stinging hornets', while the Irish named them 'ruthless, angry, foreign, purely pagan people', which was more accurate but a bit of a mouthful for the look-outs.

The hapless English had no idea how to stop these vicious raiders. They couldn't gather an army to fight them, because no-one knew where or when the next raid might be. Nor could they mount a defence of the beaches, since there was too much coastline to cover. So they tried doing the thing that over the years they had become best at: praying.

This, however, didn't seem to help. In fact, the Vikings often targeted churches and monasteries since, in line with the humble teachings of Jesus, these were the places that always had the most

---

[*] or since

gold. In 793, they ransacked the monastery of Lindisfarne, killing all the monks and burning their books. A year later they hit Jarrow, where the Venerable Bede had penned his works. The attacks horrified all good Christians. People began to wonder if God had forsaken Britain, while others, like the monk Alcuin of York, blamed the Anglo-Saxons themselves for years of sinful behaviour:

Consider carefully, brothers, and examine diligently, lest perchance this unaccustomed and unheard-of evil was merited by some unheard-of evil practice....Consider the dress, the way of wearing the hair, the luxurious habits of the princes and people.

The Vikings Decide to Stay

Then in 851 things changed. For the first time the Vikings didn't sail away at the end of the summer. Instead, they hung around in camps for the winter, living off the spoils of their incessant raids. As the weeks lengthened into months, the English started dropping subtle hints about it perhaps being time to go home: early start in the morning, work to catch up on, local population to re-grow, that sort of thing. But the Vikings had decided that living in Britain would be better than living in Denmark, Norway or Sweden, which gives you some idea of just how bad *those* places were.

By the mid-860s, their thinking had changed again. Now the Vikings figured that if they were going to stay in Britain for a while, they may as well *own* the place too. A huge Danish army under three brothers named Halfdan, Ubbe and Ivar the Boneless ripped through Northumbria and East Anglia and wrecked half of Mercia. Showing little respect for Christian virtues, they killed King Edmund of East Anglia by tying him naked to a tree and shooting him full of arrows, an act that left Edmund so holy he had to be made a saint.

In just a few years, the Danes had conquered much of Britain. They settled quickly, thanks to the simple, easy-to-assemble furniture they had got from their friends in Sweden, and built a base in York, which they re-named Jorvik in honour of the local Viking museum. Soon they were turning their greedy Scandinavian eyes towards Wessex, the richest and most powerful of all the kingdoms that had sex in the name. Little did they realise, however, that in Wessex there was a new sheriff coming to town, who went by the very impressive name of –

Alfred the Great

On a frosty winter's day in January 871, Aethelred, King of Wessex, rode out to meet the vicious Viking horde who were poised to attack on the Berkshire Downs. Waiting a few hundred metres behind him was his younger brother Alfred, and, fortunately enough, an army. The battle that followed was long and bloody, but somehow the men of Wessex came out on top. It marked, however, only the beginning of the fight.

A few months later, a new army of Vikings arrived from Denmark and Aethelred promptly died of illness, leaving his 22 year-old brother Alfred as king. For the first year Alfred valiantly succeeded in losing battle after battle before he made the first of many intelligent decisions during his reign and paid the Vikings a huge sum of money to go away and attack Mercia instead. Miraculously the Vikings obeyed, and for the next five years Alfred watched in an almost constant state of amusement as the rival English kingdom burned repeatedly. In the meantime, he himself concentrated on building up a large navy for Wessex just in case the Danes ever came to their senses and returned.

In 876, when they finally did return under a new leader called Guthrum, Alfred was ready for them, destroying their fleet of 120 ships in the English Channel. Two years later, however, things did not go quite so well. Alfred and his followers had been enjoying their usual Christmas festivities in Somerset, when Guthrum and his forces suddenly burst upon them. The English were taken completely off-guard and Alfred was forced to flee into marshland with only a handful of men. For the next five months he remained in hiding, testing the hospitality of the marsh dwellers by continually burning their cakes yet insisting they still call him Alfred the Great[*].

By May, however, he was ready to go back to war. He sent out messages that all loyal Englishmen should meet him at Egbert's Stone, and people were so amazed that their king had managed to survive the entire winter in Somerset without dying of boredom that they rallied to his side. This time it was the Vikings who were caught unawares and Alfred dealt them a decisive defeat at the Battle of Edington. With the enemy at his mercy, Alfred was determined to impose harsh conditions on their surrender. The Vikings were to leave Wessex immediately and jolly well not come back, and what's more Guthrum had to get baptised.

"Okay," said the Vikings, not sure whether the last bit was a joke or not. "And what else?"

"Erm... that's it."

"And... er... what's to stop us breaking our promise the moment we feel like it?"

"You'll go to hell," said Alfred.

Privately, the Vikings were fairly sure they were heading to hell anyway, judging by the number of arrows they had lodged in St Edmund's body. But for now at least a deal was a deal. Alfred and his new godson Guthrum drew a line from London to Chester with everything to the west going to Alfred and everything to the east to the Vikings. The Viking part of England became known as the Danelaw, while to the west Wessex helped itself to London and the smouldering remains of Mercia. Slowly the nation of England was beginning to take shape.

---

[*] The cakes story, inevitably, was a myth, probably copied by Alfred's biographers from an earlier Norse saga. In reality, Alfred never even went near a stove.

Aethelred the Unready and the Viking Return

From 959, Edgar ruled England for over twenty years and was so successful he ended up being called Edgar the Peaceful, not the kind of nickname that came around very often during the Viking era. But when he died in 975, things quickly went back to normal. He left two young sons by different mothers, Edward and Aethelred, aged twelve and eight, and, inspired by their father's strong and fearless example, they too were determined to have memorable nicknames. Unfortunately, Edward's nickname turned out to be Edward the Martyr when he was murdered by his younger brother's supporters just three years into his reign. Aethelred then became king, but since he was only around eleven years-old it was pretty clear he wasn't really – how can we put it? – *prepared* for kingship.

Sure enough, things went badly from the start. Being too young to rule alone, Aethelred had to rely on grown-up advisers, whom he chose, naturally enough, on the basis of who gave him the most sweets that day. But this soon led to rot and decay[*]. It was made even worse by his murdered brother being declared a saint, a decision based mainly on the fact that compared to Aethelred just about anybody was.

As if this was not bad enough, in 991 a massive fleet of Viking ships suddenly turned up on the Essex coast, even though Aethelred hadn't invited them or anything and wasn't in fact dressed yet. Despite their best efforts, the English were defeated and in desperation Aethelred paid the Vikings a huge sum of money to leave. This money became known as the Danegeld, and it soon put a severe dent in Aethelred's pocket money.

Inevitably, the Vikings kept coming back and demanding more,

---

[*] It is a fascinating historical footnote that Aethelred the Unready is actually a mistranslation from the Old English, which really meant Aethelred the Ill-Counseled. It was a joke, you see, because Aethelred itself meant Noble-Counsel, so his nickname was really a clever pun based on the irony of a king named Noble-Counsel being so badly..... Oh, forget it.

which Aethelred duly paid. Eventually, however, his allowance ran out and he started to get desperate. In 1002, he spread a proclamation that all the Danes in England were to be murdered on the same day, even those who had lived in the country for generations and had passed the citizenship test and everything. The St Brice's Day Massacre of November 13 was shameful even by Aethelred's standards, and it was also stupid because what the king really should have done, of course, was murder all the Danes in *Denmark* as well. As it was, all he succeeded in doing was making them mad. The king of Denmark, Swein Forkbeard, whose sister may have been among the victims of the massacre, immediately sailed to England with a vast army, determined to take bloody revenge on the monster who had perpetrated this horrible and vicious crime. There was nothing that could possibly slake his righteous fury.

"Would it help if I gave you £36,000?" said Aethelred.

"That'll do nicely."

But he was soon back, this time with even more men and his son Canute. In 1013, after years of fighting and quite a bit more attempted bribery, he forced Aethelred into exile in Normandy and declared himself King of England.

King Canute

Swein's reign lasted just a few months before, having realised there wasn't any point in killing English people now that he was in charge of them all, he died. His army proclaimed his son Canute king, but the English nobles were determined that a good English monarch should be on the throne instead. Unfortunately, there weren't any good English monarchs around, so they had to plump for Aethelred again, inviting him back from Normandy but only on the condition that he stop being so unready[*] all the time. Aethelred agreed and for once succeeded in catching the Vikings off-guard.

---

[*] Ill-Counseled

Canute fled back to Denmark in surprise.

But Aethelred's new reign fared no better than his old one. In 1015, he faced a massive rebellion from Danish descendants in the north led by, of all people, his own son Edmund, who was upset at the amount of corruption in his father's court in the sense that he quite fancied being king. Then Canute invaded again and Edmund decided he wouldn't like to be king *just* yet, only for his father, in true Aethelred style, to die on him almost immediately, putting him in charge anyway.

For several months, the twenty year-old Edmund resisted the invasion pretty well, earning himself the best nickname yet, Edmund Ironsides. In October 1016, however, he was defeated by Canute in a major battle at Assandun, putting him at the great Dane's mercy.

Now, up until this point, the Vikings had never been known for what you might call subtle diplomacy. But the new master of England proved he was as canny a canute as there ever had been. Wary of angering Edmund's many supporters, he agreed to split the country with the young pup and even suggested that when one of them died the other should inherit the whole kingdom. Of course, there was no way Canute could possibly have known that just one month later Edmund would indeed meet a premature death, and if some people suggested that an assassin had secretly hidden inside Edmund's privy hole and stabbed him up the buttocks as he toileted, that had nothing to do with Canute, who had no idea what Edmund's buttocks even looked like from underneath.

Not surprisingly, it took a while for people to accept Canute's rule. But gradually, thanks to the king's fair nature and just laws, the English came to respect their Danish ruler. Canute went on to inherit the kingdom of Denmark too, giving him territory that stretched over Norway and much of Sweden. So large was Canute's empire that some claimed the sun never set on it, though, to be fair, for six months of the year it never rose on it either.

Last but not least, Canute was also responsible for one of the most famous anecdotes of English history. In order to prove to his fawning court that he was not a god, he set his chair in the sea and ordered the tide to turn back. When the sea failed to obey his command, he exclaimed dramatically, "Let all men know how empty and worthless is the power of kings." To which his followers responded, "Brilliant, sire! And, sorry, you gain from this experiment... what exactly?"

Edward the Confessor

Canute ruled for twenty years, but his death in 1035 precipitated a succession crisis so desperate it would eventually leave England under the rule of a Frenchman. The first problem was the general uselessness of Canute's two sons. Canute had wanted his throne passed to Harthacanute when he died, but there was some confusion about whether half-a-canute would be strong enough to carry such a heavy load, particularly as he was stuck in Denmark at the time. Instead his half-brother Harald got the job. Needless to say, Harthacanute was not at all happy about this, and when he was finally able to extricate himself from Denmark, he sailed over with the full intention of starting a civil war.

Luckily, Harald did the sensible thing and died before his brother could get to him, but even so Harthacanute was so angry he ordered his body to be disinterred and thrown into a bog. Unfortunately, that was just about the only thing Harthacanute did during his three-year reign, and when he died there was no-one to succeed him other than Edward, the son of Aethelred, who had grown up in exile in Normandy. Edward had the support of the powerful Godwin family of Wessex, but as his reign went on it was Edward's French-speaking Norman friends who assumed greater influence. Some historians argue, in fact, that Edward was the first *de facto* Norman king of England.

Apart from stirring up tensions with the Godwins, Edward did very little with his time on the throne, except pray a lot and go to church. He even had a new church built for himself, the Norman-style Westminster Abbey, where everybody looked forward to him being buried. Other than that, his only other notable act was to sell off England's navy, because, really, what were the chances that England would get invaded by anyone soon? Frankly, there was nothing else to do but declare him a saint.

Now if Edward had been as dedicated in the bedroom as he was in the confessional, things might have turned out differently for England in 1066. But there was only one kind of hole that Edward was interested in and that was the kind found in crucifixes. For the last decade of the reign, most of the ruling was done by Harold Godwinson, offspring of the Godwins who had reasserted his influence over the Norman faction at court. When the king finally died in 1066, there no heirs or close relatives to inherit the throne, leaving an almighty power vacuum that somebody was certain to try and fill.

There were three contenders: Harold Godwinson, the favourite of the Saxon nobles; William the Bastard, Duke of Normandy; and Harald Hardrada, King of Norway. If only Edward could have said which one he preferred, things might have been okay. But he was as vague on that as he was on everything. William claimed he had promised the throne to him during a visit to London, but Harold Godwinson was sure he had offered the kingdom to him on his deathbed. Or had he said Harald? It was a terrible mess and soon there would be swords flashing and arrows flying. It was only a matter of time before somebody got one in the eye.

4. THE EARLY MIDDLE AGES (1066 – 1216)

Edward the Confessor's untimely death from a surfeit of holiness left his kingdom at the mercy of William the Conqueror and his ruthless band of Norman embroiderers, who were determined to turn the whole place into a badly-done tapestry. Under the Normans, Britain moved out of the Dark Ages and into the so-called Feudal Age. Feudalism brought with it exciting developments like barons, knights, castles and crusades, making life so miserable for the general populace that when the Bubonic plague finally put paid to it several centuries later by dealing an agonising death to one-third of the population, people felt it was a fairly reasonable quid-pro-quo. At the end of the period, after years of tyranny and misrule, the king was forced to sign the Magna Carta, a document so desperate it suggested the formation of a parliament might actually make England better run.

The Battle of Hastings

After the death of Edward the Confessor in 1066, Harold Godwinson was crowned King of England with the approval of the witan, the semi-formal assembly of English nobles. Across the English Channel, however, there were disturbing rumours that William, Duke of Normandy, had decided that he was the rightful king. William had become duke at the age of eight after the death of his father, despite having being born out of wedlock[*]. Since then he had survived numerous plots and assassination attempts to grow into a strong, cunning and increasingly enormous man, described by chroniclers later in his life as having the physique of a pregnant woman, as well as the unpredictable mood swings.

He claimed his right to the English throne because Edward had apparently once offered it to him during a visit to London in 1051

---

[*] a misfortune that led him to be nicknamed William the Bastard, sometimes shortened to 'the bastard' or later 'that Norman bastard'.

out of gratitude for the kindly treatment he had received during his exile in Normandy. And if that wasn't enough, Harold Godwinson had apparently sworn allegiance to him in 1064 when he washed up on the Norman shore after a shipwreck. And if *that* wasn't enough, well, William had an army.

With these stories in mind, Harold Godwinson was understandably wary of the threat from Normandy, and he stationed his army and navy on the south coast as a precaution. After eight months, however, there was no sight of any Norman conquerors at all and Harold's men were starting to become restless. The king was about to disband them when he suddenly received news that Harald Hardrada of Norway had invaded from the north and was camped out at Stamford Bridge. His men were absolutely aghast: 'But there's a game on this Saturday!' But Harold knew it was a different Stamford Bridge and he rushed up there in just four days, catching the Norwegians off-side and dispatching Harald Hardrada from the penalty spot.

His men were still celebrating when they got news that William had landed his army on the south coast. Muttering darkly about the crowded fixture list, Harold gathered up his army and rushed them back down south to Hastings, where William had set up camp. As they marched in double-quick time, it was said that they looked up and saw Halley's Comet streaking across the sky. Everyone decided this was definitely an omen, if only they could remember which kind.

The battle with the Normans raged all day. Three times William had his horse killed beneath him, possibly out of sympathy for the horse, but three times he was able to kick his knights off theirs and mount back up again. Finally, as the English army began to tire, Harold was shot through the eye by an arrow and cut down by William's knights. Seeing their king fall, the stricken English turned and fled, crying as they ran that it would have been far better to have lost to Norway instead.

William marched his army to London and was crowned at

Westminster Abbey on Christmas Day, which even God found pretty offensive. The ceremony did not go well, however. When Archbishop Aldred said, 'Will you take this prince to be your king?', the assembled throng in the abbey let out a great roar of agreement. But since agreement had never really been part of the Norman plan, William's guards stationed outside misunderstood what the noise was. Assuming the English were revolting, they proceeded to set fire to the surrounding houses. The throng from the church then rushed outside and, according to contemporary accounts, some started to fight the fires, some started to fight the Normans, while the rest spotted the opportunity and went looting. 1066 was a seminal date for the English in more ways than one.

All these events were faithfully recorded in the Bayeux tapestry, which was woven in England a few years later. Probably commissioned by William's half-brother Odo, it was likely intended as propaganda for the Norman invasion, the new rulers clearly feeling that sewing pictures of great English heroes with arrows sticking out of their eyes would somehow cause people to hate them less. It was hung, however, not in England but in Odo's bishopric of Bayeux in France, where it remains to this day.

The Harrying of the North
Once his position in the south was secured, William was determined to establish his rule across the whole of Britain, including the areas most English kings had decided were pretty much unruleable, like the north. The people of the north, however, had never been keen on the rule of anyone but themselves, and when they discovered that not only was William not a northerner but from a place even further south than the south itself, they were not going to lie down quietly. William's response in the winter of 1069 was to march his army to York, where he issued a typically ruthless order:

"Harry the north!" he yelled.

"Right!" shouted his men in unison. "We'll... er... what?"

"It's a lot worse than it sounds," explained William.

Indeed, the so-called Harrying of the North was shocking even by the standards of the time. William's troops went on the rampage, burning villages, slaughtering farm animals, raping women and stealing crops. Sometimes, in the frenzy of killing, they got confused and found themselves stealing villages, slaughtering crops, burning women and raping farm animals, and then they had to go back and do it all over again, which just made things worse. When they left an area, they sowed salt into the ground to prevent its rebirth, leaving the few survivors to starve in the harsh winter cold. Some even resorted to cannibalism. Over 100,000 are said to have perished.

When it was over, William replaced the local Anglo-Danish lords with Normans, who built castles from which to rule over their new lands. The north of England secured, William now turned his attention to Scotland, a place even the Romans had given up trying to conquer. In 1072, he took an army and fleet to Abernethy, where he met the Scottish king Malcolm Canmore and casually suggested what might happen to the future Scottish whiskey industry if the only thing they could grow from now on was salt. The Scots submitted without a murmur. Canmore's sons took English wives, and gradually English replaced Gaelic as the language of government, though, as a concession, they were permitted to speak it in an incomprehensible dialect.

As for Wales, William made a very sensible decision. Rather than trying to control the five unruly Welsh kingdoms himself, he posted his most loyal and capable lords on the borders, giving them the freedom to be as mean and oppressive as they liked without his direct say-so. Allowed to keep their own private armies, the so-called marcher lords succeeded in building several castles in Wales, keeping rebellions in check while providing the locals with much-needed infrastructure to throw rocks against.

The Feudal System

With his new kingdom secure, William set about bringing modernity and progress to Britain by fixing it to an archaic system that was designed never to change ever. It was known as feudalism and had existed in Normandy for over a hundred years, where it had brought unparalleled wealth and prosperity, at least to William and his friends if not to many others.

The first rule of feudalism was that all the land belonged to the king. In William's case, he kept one quarter of it for his own personal use while he leased out the rest to his barons, bishops and abbots as a reward for their cruelty to the local population. Almost all of these new landowners were Normans, some 200 of them controlling 95 percent of the land. In return for his king's generousity, the baron would bow down before him and swear to 'become his man'. Becoming a king's man meant you had to supply him with knights and funds whenever he required and swear not to become anybody else's man at the same time, no matter how nice he smelled.

The baron was free to do anything he liked with his land: farming crops, dispensing justice and raising his own taxes. Like the king, he would keep a certain portion for himself and then lease the rest out to his knights. The land was divided into manors, farmed by freeholders, serfs and slaves in ascending order of filthy impoverishment and descending order of life expectancy. Serfs were not permitted to leave the manor and were required to work not only on their own small plot of land but also the somewhat larger plot of the local lord. They also had to pay taxes: one-tenth of their produce or a *tithe* to the Church and the rest to the lord at whatever he decided would be an amusingly unpayable rate.

Despite its inequality, however, the feudal system brought much-needed order and stability to medieval society. It gave barons time to rule, knights time to fight, bishops time to pray, and peasants time to wish barons, knights and bishops would stop ruling, fighting and praying all the time and do a bit of work for a change.

The Domesday Book

It was while spending Christmas 1085 in Gloucester that William had the idea of carrying out a massive detailed survey of all the property, wealth and livestock of the people of England. "Well, what the hell else are we going to do while we're in Gloucester?" he said. All his counsellors agreed that it was an absolutely fantastic idea and immediately set out to ready the king's horse, asking casually how long he thought he'd be away, until William pointed out that he didn't actually intend to carry out this survey himself but was in fact intending that they should do it.

"Oh," said the counsellors, less keen on the idea now. "And what's the point in surveying everybody's wealth and livestock then?"

"So that we can tax it all away from them," replied William.

"We'll get right on it!"

Astonishingly, the survey was completed in little more than a year. Royal officials were sent out to almost every shire of England, where they held assemblies in which the local officials were required to list every possession on their land. The final product was compiled into two books, Little Domesday and Great Domesday, which ran to 913 pages and contained two million words in Latin. Little Domesday, covering the most populous region of East Anglia, was actually the longer of the two because it contained more detail, down to precise numbers of livestock. It was called Little Domesday because it was in a physically smaller format. By the time the counsellors got round to doing Great Domesday for the rest of the country, they had understandably lost a bit of interest and the level of detail dropped considerably. It seems to have been written by one single clerk. The information contained in the books was used for taxation. People called it Domesday because, like the Day of Judgement, there was no appeal to its decisions. Unlike any other nation in Europe, still largely made up of confederacies of dukedoms, it laid the foundations for England to become a fully-fledged administrative state.

William II: Most Unpopular Man in England

After twenty years under Norman rule, the English had gradually begun to accept the new order of things. French had replaced English as the language of the ruling classes, and a huge influx of French words began to enter the English language, including – to take examples entirely at random – *bile*, *piss*, *phlegm*, *fart*, *crap*, *incontinence* and *urine*. French names like William, Richard and Henry came into fashion, taking over from perfectly decent English names like Egbert, Aethelred and Eadwig.

Fortunately, there was some good news on the way because in 1087 William I finally died. He was so obese by the time of his death that his corpse wouldn't fit into the coffin during the funeral. When the chief mourners tried to force it in, his body exploded like a water bomb, spraying rotten innards all over the cathedral. The bloated king was survived by his three sons, Robert, William and Henry, who immediately began to bicker and fight, primarily over whose job it was to clean the cathedral. Fortunately, their father had thought carefully about how to ensure each son got his fair share of the inheritance. To his eldest son Robert, he entrusted the powerful Duchy of Normandy. To his middle son William he awarded the throne of England. Finally to his youngest son Henry, he left a sum of money and a large dollop of nothing at all.

Strangely, this did not go down well. As it turned out, each of the three sons was quite keen to have Normandy, England *and* the cash all to himself, leading to a great deal of fraternal squabbling, generally conducted by other people with swords. But, despite the early battles, the arrangement stayed as it was, which meant that England had the misfortune to have their second King William in a row. The new king called himself William II, but everybody else knew him as William Rufus owing to his ruddy complexion.

William was so unpopular during his thirteen year reign that it was said he was hated by every person in England. Greedy, vain and irreligious, he imposed heavy taxes on his subjects to pay for wars in a rebellious Scotland, appropriated revenues meant for the church, and once had an opponent blinded and castrated for suspected treachery. Even his own barons hated him and they normally loved that kind of thing. Probably gay, he bore no children and kept a dissolute and frivolous court, openly expressing his contempt for the English and their way of life.

The only positive thing William II achieved was to die violently in 1100. Hunting in the New Forest with a group of friends, including his younger brother Henry, he was hit by an arrow that was supposedly meant for a stag. The shot was fired by Sir Walter Tyrell, renowned throughout England – accurately as it turned out – as a deadly shot. Sir Walter immediately fled to France, leading to persistent rumours that the shot had been no accident. Henry, meanwhile, maintained his own innocence in the matter, protesting that he couldn't possibly have been involved since he had nothing at all to gain from his brother's untimely death, except... er... ah yes, that. He was crowned King of England three days later.

Henry I: Blood-Sucking Eel

Henry was fortunate that his elder brother Robert was on the First Crusade at the time of his coronation, otherwise he might have had to take Sir Walter hunting a second time. But when Robert did return, Henry quickly disposed of him in battle, adding the Duchy of Normandy to his now well-rounded inheritance. He kept Robert in prison for the next 28 years, first in the Tower of London and then in Cardiff, where he died.

Henry was almost unique among the Normans, and the French generally, in that he didn't actively hate the English – which is to say he didn't hate the English *ladies*. Over the course of his reign, he produced over twenty illegitimate children, a record for any British monarch before or since. He even married an English girl, the great-granddaughter of Edmund Ironside who went by the homely name of Edith. This pleased his English subjects greatly but angered his fellow Normans, who forced Edith to change her name to the much saucier Matilda.

Literate and prayerful, Henry devoted himself to administrative and legal reform, which, up until now, hadn't been considered a particularly kingly thing to do. He granted the barons a Charter of Liberties, which made them happy, and sent itinerant officials around the country to curb abuses in the provinces, which made them less happy. He also founded the Exchequer to administer tax revenue and came up with a new way of accounting using tally sticks. He allowed these to be used for paying taxes, creating such a demand for them they began to be used as currency. (Tally sticks remained in use for the next 700 years, until they were eventually taken out of circulation and stored in the Houses of Parliament. In 1834 the authorities decided they were taking up too much space and ordered them to be burned. Unfortunately, the fire got out of control and the resulting conflagration burned down the Houses of Parliament.)

For 35 years, Henry ruled wisely and fairly, bringing peace and prosperity to the kingdom, as well as a good deal more toddlers. Unfortunately, having fathered so many illegitimate sons, what Henry forgot to do was have any legitimate ones, except for one unfortunate boy who got himself drowned in a shipwreck. When he died in 1135 after eating 'a surfeit of lampreys', a kind of blood-sucking parasitical eel that Henry was reputedly obsessed by[*], he ended up with only his eldest daughter Matilda. Although he had taken the unprecedented step of having his barons swear to accept her as heir, there was another claimant lurking, a grandson of William the Conqueror named Stephen. The result? Anarchy.

The Anarchy: Stephen and Matilda

---

[*] possibly because they reminded him so much of his tax-collecting

Stephen was in Boulogne when he heard that Henry had been at the lampreys again, but he rushed over to London while Matilda was still in France with her husband Geoffrey Plantagenet, Count of Anjou. His sudden arrival put Henry's barons in a bit of a quandary. On the one hand, they had sworn an oath to accept Matilda as heir. But on the other hand, she was not there and, well, let's face it, she was a girl. So the barons happily broke their oaths and crowned the interloper instead.

Despite this straightforward beginning, it was clear from very early on that Stephen wasn't going to get a very smooth ride as king. For one thing, he really wasn't interested in the business of being a monarch, which his barons kind of wished he'd mentioned before they broke all their oaths. He hated the administration and legal work, which people had rather got used to the king taking care of now; he didn't give out enough land to his friends; he kept taking counsel from the wrong kind of people; he couldn't stop the Welsh and the Scottish invading his territory; and, well, you could shorten his name to Steve, for heaven's sake.

Things really fell apart in 1139 when Matilda had finally managed to extricate herself from her business in Anjou and led an invasion fleet across the English Channel. For the next nine years, she and Stephen fought a series of battles up and down the country, with neither side ever managing to finish the other one off. In 1141, Matilda defeated Stephen at Lincoln and prepared to have herself crowned in London, only for the Londoners to shut their gates to her when she refused to halve their taxes. Then later in the year Stephen captured her twice, only for Matilda to escape both times, first by wearing a white dress in the snow and then by disguising herself as a corpse.

The so-called Anarchy wreaked havoc upon the good people of England. With the food supply devastated, thousands died of starvation, while thousands more were eaten alive by marauding Yorkshiremen. With no central authority to control them, the barons were more beastly than ever. Serfs were often pulled from their land and forced to build castles for the controlling forces, only to be tortured and executed for treason when the opposition turned up. As usual, the Anglo-Saxon Chronicle had the exclusive story, reporting that Christ and all his saints were 'asleep'.

By 1148, Stephen had finally got the upper hand, and Matilda retreated to France. But four years later, Stephen's son and heir died of illness. As war broke out once more, Stephen finally got the message that in the end the woman will always win. He signed a treaty that would see Matilda's son Henry inherit the throne after his death. A year later, without any help from Sir Walter Tyrell, Stephen duly obliged.

Henry II: Strong, Stable, Stark Naked

Henry Plantagenet was already Duke of Normandy, Duke of Aquitaine, Duke of Gascony and Duke of Anjou by the time he became King of England at the age of 21. He had achieved this by being related to every noble family in France or by marrying into them, or – since this is the aristocracy we're talking about – more likely both. Chief among his assets was his marriage to the formidable Eleanor of Aquitaine, the ex-wife of Louis VII of France[*], who, though nine years his senior, had attracted the virile young Henry because she was endowed with an absolutely enormous pair of duchies in south-west France.

As King of England, Henry II brought peace and stability for 35 years, at least to England if not to the countries nearby. After the long Anarchy of Stephen's reign, he felt he needed to restore royal authority throughout the land. Scotland went easily, with Malcolm IV ceding control of Northumbria and slinking back to the highlands in a skirt. Wales, however, put up more of a fight, forcing Henry's army of armoured knights to abandon their invasion by being relentlessly wet and slippy.

---

[*] Louis had divorced Eleanor for being barren, whereupon she married Henry and bore five sons and three daughters. So that was awkward.

Then there was Ireland. Medieval Ireland was divided into many small kingdoms which spent most of their time at war with each other. When one of these kingdoms appealed to Henry for help, the ambitious young monarch jumped at the chance of sending a bunch of displaced nobles from Wales he wanted to get rid of. Led by Richard "Strongbow" de Clare, the Earl of Pembroke, the English nobles crushed the rebels and then, for lack of anywhere better to go, decided to hang around. By 1171 when they still hadn't returned, Henry decided he'd better go and investigate. Warning them that next time he might send Eleanor instead, he quickly got the errant nobles to bend the knee. The English-owned lands in Ireland became known as the Pale, from the Latin word *palus* meaning stake or boundary. Soon the phrase 'beyond the pale' came into use, eventually taking on its modern meaning of 'being from Ireland'.

If he had only done this much, Henry would already have gone down in history as a powerful monarch. But the young man had energy to burn. As he watched his rival go back and forth to his lands in France, Louis VII remarked: 'Now in England, now in Normandy, he must fly rather than travel by horse or ship.' Not content simply with military campaigning, Henry was also a skilled administrator, and not only that but also a tireless murderer of archbishops. Unfortunately, as it turned out, murdering archbishops was not considered a strength in medieval England and it got the all-powerful monarch into a bit of trouble.

The way it came about was this. Henry had decided that England needed legal reform. He had this wild idea that instead of deciding trials on the basis of the defendant's degree of buoyancy in water, as in the current system, they should do wacky things like listen to evidence and organise twelve-man juries. He also had the even crazier notion that this system should be applied not only to common criminals but also to slightly less common criminals, like priests. This, however, brought him into conflict with the Archbishop of Canterbury, his erstwhile best friend Thomas

Becket. Thomas argued that as men of the cloth, priests were only answerable to God for their sins, and the last thing they wanted to do was draw His attention to them by holding a public trial. Instead they should do as they had always done and let the Vatican cover things up.

Henry, however, was not to be dissuaded. When Thomas began dismissing all the bishops who had taken the king's side, Henry lost his temper. 'Will no one rid me of this troublesome priest?' he raged. 'Metaphorically speaking, of course.' Four knights took him at his word. On 29 December 1170, they stormed Becket's cathedral at Canterbury and, before a group of horrified monks, stabbed him to death at the altar.

The murder caused an outcry. The Pope immediately declared Becket a saint, and Henry was forced to do penance. He walked to Canterbury barefoot, wearing only a sackcloth, then had himself flogged naked at the door of the cathedral. His humility won him the forgiveness of the Pope who was just sorry he hadn't been there to watch, and restored his reputation with the public. His wife Eleanor, meanwhile, wondered if this was the start of something fun.

Richard the Lionheart and the Crusades

Despite stoically refraining from murdering any more clergymen for the rest of his reign, Henry's last decade in power was a troubled one. Aided and abetted by Eleanor, his four surviving sons, Henry, Richard, Geoffrey and John, kept playing the classic filial trick of trying to claim their inheritance before their father had actually died. Eleanor spent much of the period imprisoned by her husband, and things might have got very ugly much sooner had Henry and Geoffrey not both died from illness and accident before things got too out of hand.

To make matters more complicated, in 1187 Pope Gregory VIII suddenly ordered a crusade to the Holy Land. The aim of the crusade was to kick Muslim Turks out of the Holy Land so that it could be given back to the rightful historical inhabitants of the region, French knights. It was actually the third one of its kind. The first crusade of 1095 had succeeded in not only killing all the Muslims in Jerusalem but, as an added bonus, most of the Jews as well, leaving plenty of room for the famed order of French knights known as the Knights Templar to move in. It had been followed, however, by a gradual return to the area by the Turks, who bred a lot quicker than the celibate knights. A second crusade had done little to cull their numbers, and in 1187 a new Turkish leader by the name of Saladin had united their disparate tribes and retaken Jerusalem.

Frederick Barbarossa of the Holy Roman Empire, Philip II of France, and Henry II of England heeded the Pope's call. Henry intended to take his son Richard with him, but just before they were due to leave in 1189 Henry died, giving Richard the throne he craved so badly. The people of England were delighted with their virile new king, who was renowned for his bravery, strength and extensive knowledge of France. As they placed the crown on his head, they chatted excitedly about the years of peace and prosperity they could now look forward to.

"Okay, bye then," said Richard, and disappeared to the Holy Land.

Although Richard had had to tax the daylights out of his new kingdom in order to pay for his army, his nobles forgave him because they knew it was all in a good cause. At first, all went well for the crusaders, with Richard proving himself to be a fearless leader. At the siege of Acre, he continued to fight even when his mouth was rotting with scurvy, inspiring his men to throw themselves repeatedly against the walls in a desperate bid to get upwind of his breath. But gradually things began to fall apart. Frederick Barbarossa drowned in a river while bathing, and then Philip II decided that rather than liberate the Holy Land from the Muslims, he would rather go back home and liberate most of France from Richard.

Richard, however, battled on, determined to do everything he could to avoid going back to England. But eventually sheer lack of friends forced him to seek peace. In 1192, he negotiated a truce in which Saladin's only concession was to grant Christian pilgrims access to Jerusalem. England would have their king back at last, and not a moment too soon since Richard's ugly brother John had been busy plotting to steal his throne. But on the way back from the Holy Land, Richard was captured and imprisoned by his enemy Duke Leopold of Austria, who demanded a ransom of 100,000 pounds of silver. It was a huge sum, almost three times the annual income of England, but given a choice between being taxed a quarter of their property and having John continue as king, the barons' reaction was: "Only a quarter?"

In 1194, Richard finally returned to the tumultuous cheers of all the people of England, who could scarcely wait for his reign of justice and glory to begin.

"Okay, bye then," said Richard, and went to France.

He never came back. His war with Philip went well, but in 1199 he was shot in the shoulder by a young crossbowman as he besieged a castle. Gangrenous once more, Richard had the boy brought to him, but instead of having him executed he showed his generousity by letting him go with 100 shillings. His nobles considered this a fine gesture, until they remembered where Richard had got all his money from. When the king died a few days later, they tracked the boy down and flayed him alive. And thus the tone was set for the reign of King John.

King John and the Magna Carta

Having left no children, the only rivals for succession to Richard's huge Angevin empire were his brother John and his twelve year-old nephew Arthur. Dangerously for John, many nobles in France were known to favour Arthur. But with typical cunning the wily king managed to subtlely outmanoevre his young opponent by beating him to death and dumping his body in a moat. This tactic proved very successful and it was one John never forgot.

Once he was secure on the throne, John set about applying himself to his life's work: losing every scrap of land Richard had left to him. It began when John was asked to mediate in a dispute between two powerful French families, the Lusignan and the Angoulame, who were due to marry into one another. John's solution to the problem was typically ingenious: he married the eleven year-old Angoulame heiress himself. The Lusignans, however, were far from happy and appealed to Philip II, who proceeded to kick John out of almost all his French possessions. So humiliating was this defeat that from then on John began to be known as John Softsword, though unfortunately not by his eleven year-old wife.

The loss of Normandy posed a serious problem for King John, because it now meant he would have to spend his reign in England. For the next twelve years the English received more attention from their ruler than at any time since the Norman invasion, which would have been fine if that ruler had been anyone but John. It wasn't that John was a lazy king or even an incompetent one. In fact, he was an active, hard-working, and efficient administrator, as kings often were when they needed the money. The problem was that, unlike his arch-enemy Robin Hood, John didn't use his administrative gifts to steal from the rich and give to the poor; he stole from both the rich and the poor and gave to himself.

He also got in trouble with the Church, which was never a good thing for your legacy when monks wrote all the history books. A dispute with the Pope over who should be Archbishop of Canterbury ended with the whole of England being placed under a papal interdiction. For six years, there were no church services, christenings or weddings, placing the soul of every English person in jeopardy.

"Well, at least you get a lie-in on Sundays," argued John.

But it didn't wash. Matthew Paris, the medieval chronicler, was typical in his verdict: 'Hell is too good for a horrible person like him.'

In 1214, John made another pathetic attempt at getting his lands in France back, but when that failed the barons had had enough and rebelled. With no other alternative to the throne, other than Arthur's gently rotting corpse, the barons were forced to devise a new focus for their revolt. Out of desperation, they came up with the Magna Carta. Fundamentally it was a list of everything they hated about John's rule, and it was a wonder they managed to whittle it down to just 63 clauses. A mix of the very specific ('All fish-weirs shall be removed from the Thames, the Medway, and throughout the whole of England, except on the sea coast') to the rather more abstract, its most significant clauses concerned the rule of law:

To no one will we sell, to no one deny or delay right or justice.

No free man shall be seized or imprisoned except by the lawful judgement of his peers or by the law of the land.

In future no official shall place a man on trial upon his own unsupported statement, without producing credible witnesses to the truth of it.

If this all seemed a bit too modern and progressive, the barons made sure to include a few other clauses just to remind people they were still in the Middle Ages:

No one shall be arrested or imprisoned on the appeal of a woman for the death of any person except her husband.

Heirs may be given in marriage but not to someone of lower social standing.

In order to ensure the articles were observed, the barons stipulated that 25 of their number should be elected to a Council to keep an eye on things. Having drawn up the charter, something of a rush job if the truth be told, they met a humiliated John in a meadow by the Thames at Runnymede and forced him to sign. Pledging not to go back on his word at any cost, the king returned to his castle at Windsor where he held a competition with his advisers about how quickly he could go back on his word. A year later, he was at war with the barons again. The highlight of this conflict was when John managed to lose the Crown Jewels when the cart they were being carried on sank in an incoming tide in the Wash. By this time, however, the king was already sick and a few days later, mercifully for all concerned, he died of dysentry. His body was carried south by a group of mercenaries and buried in Worcester Cathedral. The Crown Jewels, meanwhile, still lie somewhere in the Wash.

5. THE LATE MIDDLE AGES (1216 – 1485)

The far-sighted and just provisions of the Magna Carta gave medieval English kings a renewed purpose for their reigns: ignoring the far-sighted and just provisions of the Magna Carta. But having smelled the sweet nectar of power, albeit mixed with the pungent odour of dysentery, the barons were not going to give in easily. By hook or by crook or, failing that, by very hot poker, they were going to have their parliament and once they did, by God, they were going to start claiming expenses. In the end, the only way a king could hold off his magnates was by making war on France, where for the promise of glory, honour and riches there was a better than even chance the uppity sods might get themselves killed. When the war with France ended in premature defeat after a mere 116 years, the only option was to have another war, this time at home. The War of the Roses between the Houses of Lancaster and York did not end properly until 1485 when Richard III generously traded in his kingdom for a horse, thereby ushering in the rule of the sexy but unscrupulous Tudors.

Henry III: Don't Mess with De Montfort

Never in the field of human endeavour was so little achieved in so long than during the 56-year reign of John's son Henry. Given a similar amount of time, other kings called Henry would have been able to conquer half of France or slice off the heads of half the wives of Europe. The only thing that Henry III achieved was, in the words of contemporary chroniclers, 'to have smooth skin'. His role-model was Edward the Confessor, which is a bit like a pop star modelling himself on Andrew Ridgeley, and it was said that attending mass took up so much of his time each day that Louis IX of France once banned priests from travelling on his route.

The reason why Louis IX had the power to do such an ungodly

thing was that, after years of war, diplomacy and hard praying, Henry had been forced to give up his right to the French lands of his forefathers. Under the Treaty of Paris of 1259, he formally renounced his claim to Normandy and Anjou and did homage to Louis for Gascony. Even that was somewhat generous on Louis's part, but he liked seeing English kings on their knees.

What this meant was that England was now the major territory of the Plantagenet kings and they were pretty much forced to live there full-time. At the same time, the old Norman barons were also beginning to consider themselves English, even though they spoke French, dressed French, ate French, and were rude to people for no apparent reason like the French. Thus it was no surprise that, as true Englishmen, they spent most of Henry's reign complaining.

Their beef with the king was with his choice of advisors, who were, predictably enough, French. They came from the family of his wife, Eleanor of Provence, who, though not nearly as formidable as her namesake from Aquitaine, still had a knack of always getting her way. After years of tension, things eventually boiled over when Henry made a deal with the pope that the barons felt was, on balance and with all due respect to His Holiness, completely crackers. The deal was for Henry's son Edmund to become King of Sicily in return for Henry paying off all of the pope's considerable debts and then... er... conquering Sicily, then under the control of the Holy Roman Emperor. Refusing to pay the taxes for raising the expedition, the barons decided that the Magna Carta should surely have said something about prohibiting stupid French advisors and rose up in rebellion.

In 1264, under their leader Simon de Montfort, the Earl of Leicester, they defeated Henry in battle and demanded that all foreigners, that is Frenchmen, be expelled from affairs of state, together with papal emissaries and foreign bankers. Under the so-called Provisions of Oxford, they placed the government in the hands of the Great Council of Barons with de Montfort under overall control. Naturally, Henry refu`sed to go quietly.

"Simon *de* Montfort?" he protested as he was led into house arrest. "Isn't that, like, a *French* name?"

"Fermez la bouche," replied Simon.

Simon de Montfort was indeed French. He was also, as it turned out, dangerously open to new ideas, which was even worse. Knowing that he lacked support in the kingdom as a whole, the free-thinking Simon decided to expand the Great Council of Barons to include commoners. Instructed to hold elections open to all forty-shilling freeholders, each shire and free town sent two representatives to the Parliament of 1265, where, as befitting such a historic occasion, they held a long and constructive debate about who was going to pay for their accommodation while they were in London.

In the end, however, they didn't get to stay long, because later that year Henry's son Edward escaped from captivity and led an army against the usurpers. De Montfort's baronial allies, having been forced to spend several weeks in close proximity with people they normally used to wipe their horses' shoes on, deserted him in droves, leaving him to be killed and dismembered at the Battle of Evesham. It was a messy end for the revolutionary de Montfort. He left, however, a powerful and lasting legacy that would not soon be forgotten, and he is now the only major historical figure to have a bridge named after him on the north east stretch of the A47 near Evesham.

Edward I: Massive Shanks

When Henry died of illness in 1272, he was succeeded by his manly and imposing son Edward. At six foot two inches, Edward towered over his contemporaries and was awarded the nickname Longshanks. Just how long Edward's shanks were has been lost to history, but his wife, Eleanor of Castile, was apparently satisfied because she bore him no fewer than fourteen children. As king, Edward was an irascible and intimidating figure, so frightening that when the Dean of St Paul's went to him to complain about the high level of taxation, he dropped dead the moment he was brought into the king's presence.

Edward spent the first years of his reign rearranging the royal administration, and after doing that decided it might be even more fun to rearrange the Scottish and Welsh administrations as well. In 1282, the Welsh rose up in rebellion led by Llywelyn ap Gruffudd and his brothers Dafydd and Gruffydd ap Gwenwynwyn of Powys, who were worried that Edward's plans to impose a new administration on them might also include vowels. Edward responded with a full-scale invasion that ended with Wales being made into a principality of the crown, with all the associated English institutions of counties, sheriffs, law courts, and mild year-round grumpiness.

After that he turned his attention to Scotland. For the past hundred years, relations between the two nations had been relatively tranquil. But when Alexander III of Scotland died without leaving an heir, the Scottish nobles were forced to ask Edward to arbitrate on the succession.

"Sure! Anything to help out one of my vassal states," replied Edward generously.

"Eh?" said the Scots. "But we're not one of your vassal... oh damn."

Edward did choose a king for the Scots, and then demanded that he provide troops for his new war with France. When the new Scottish king refused, Edward marched up north, placed him in irons, and then made off with the Scottish coronation stone, the Stone of Scone[*].

"Let's see you crown someone now!" he giggled as he legged it back to London.

---

[*] The Stone of Scone remained at Westminster for the next 700 years, until Prime Minister John Major agreed to give it back to the Scots in 1996 in return for three pieces of shortbread and some highland toffee.

But what Edward failed to realise was that Scotland was full of scones that were as hard as stones, and soon a new enemy had emerged in the form of the strategically gifted, if unconvincingly accented, William "Braveheart" Wallace played by Mel Gibson. Braveheart routed an English army at Stirling Bridge and then began to ravage the northern countryside, creating panic with his ruthless hit-and-run tactics and drunken anti-Semitic ranting. Fortunately, even the Scots eventually began to tire of him and Braveheart was betrayed to Edward, who had him executed as a warning to other actors intent on making stupidly inaccurate films about British history. It didn't work, however, and in 1306 Robert the Bruce declared himself King of Scotland, leaving Edward so furious he quite literally poo-ed himself to death.

Although Edward's reign ended with an awkward smell in the air, he had been a hugely popular king. His reign saw the permanent establishment of a House of Commons, which became the forum through which medieval kings sought acceptance for new taxes. The parliament established in Edward's reign became known as the Model Parliament as it set a precedent as an occasion in which, in return for taxation, the people's representatives could air their grievances against the royal administration. In summoning the Parliament of 1295, Edward had proclaimed, 'What touches all should be approved of by all, and it is also clear that common dangers should be met by measures agreed upon in common.' What he meant of course was, 'Shut up and give me your money so I can go kick Scottish and French butt.' But the principle of parliamentary consent for new taxation became well-established, setting the scene for hundreds of years of wrangling and debate.

Edward II: Just Rubbish

With a rambunctious parliament and a seething war with Scotland, it was important that England had a strong, manly king to unite the magnates behind him. So when Edward II decided to celebrate his coronation with an evening of fancy dress, poetry recital and embroidery, it is fair to say there was a touch of consternation. By 1311, it had become clear that the only person Edward wanted united behind him was his young French lover Piers Gaveston, leading the barons to drop a subtle hint to the feckless king by stabbing his favourite to death. The murder sent Edward into such a depression that he kept Piers's corpse beside him for the next month.

In Scotland, meanwhile, Robert the Bruce was gaining inspiration from a spider, which gives you a clue as to the quality of his other advisers. The spider was attempting to swing from one part of a cave to another, and as the Bruce watched it try again and again until it succeeded, he learned a valuable lesson about not believing apocryphal tales with zero historical basis. In 1314, he besieged the English garrison at Stirling Castle, forcing the distinctly unwarlike English king to march north with an army of around 17,000 men. The two sides met at Bannockburn outside the town, the English outnumbering their enemy by more than two to one. Unusually for a medieval battle which were normally done and dusted in a few mad hours, the fighting carried on for two days. On the morning of the second day, the Scots paused in their advance to kneel in prayer. 'They pray for mercy!' remarked Edward excitedly. 'For mercy, yes. But from God not you,' one of his attendants retorted. 'These men will conquer or die.'

As it turned out, it was much more the former than the latter. As the rampant Scots pushed the English forces back, the king's bodyguards realised that retreat was the only option. They dragged Edward away on his horse, fleeing to Dunbar Castle and from there by ship to Berwick. The remaining English forces were routed and only a single group of foot soldiers made it back to the English border.

Humiliated and with few friends left at court, Edward decided he needed some new people to unite behind him. Since Piers Gaveston was looking a bit worse for wear by this time, he chose the next best thing, Piers's brother-in-law Hugh Despenser the

Younger. Unfortunately, Hugh and his father proved to be unscrupulous and greedy, which would normally have been fine of course, except they did it at the expense of Edward's other nobility. The crunch came when Edward gave them permission to seize the property of the de Clare family in Wales. In 1321, the barons revolted again under the leadership of the powerful Earl of Lancaster and the Marcher lord Roger Mortimer. A year later they met forces loyal to Edward at Boroughbridge near York, where, by some fluke that he never managed to replicate, Edward's army somehow won[*].

Finally, here was a chance for Edward to clear the air with his barons and make a fresh start, which he did by having thirty of them hung, drawn and quartered. This, however, only made the surviving ones even more desperate to hold themselves together. In 1325, the king made yet another – and this time fatal – mistake. After a dispute erupted with the King of France over some rubbish or other again, Edward sent over his French wife Isabella to hammer out a deal. Known as Isabella the Fair, she was said to be the most beautiful woman in Europe. The problem was that after twenty years of watching her husband fornicate openly with nubile young Frenchmen, without letting her touch any of them, she was understandably frustrated. The only person she ended up hammering anything out with was Roger Mortimer, who had managed escape from the Tower of London after Boroughbridge and flee to France. When Edward made the further error of allowing his young son to follow Isabella to France, the three of them returned with an army to depose Edward and take the throne themselves.

Isabella vented her hatred for Hugh Despenser by having him dragged by horses to the execution ground, where he was hung, castrated, disembowelled, and cut into four pieces.

"Still think he's better looking than me?" said Isabella to her

---

[*] The fluke being that Edward wasn't actually there.

husband.

Edward himself was imprisoned in Berkeley Castle, where on the night of 11 October 1327 terrible screams were heard coming from his cell. Some claimed he had been murdered by having a red-hot poker thrust up his bottom, while others maintained it was just Edward organising a final evening of poetry recital.

Edward III: Longbows and Glory

Edward III was only fourteen when his father's end met its fiery end, but by the age of seventeen he had got tired of watching Mortimer fiddle with his mother and had him murdered at Nottingham Castle. He ruled for the next 47 years, becoming one of England's most successful monarchs of all time, assuming that success was measured in the number of dead Frenchmen you left behind, which in medieval times, of course, it was.

Trouble began in 1337 when Philip VI confiscated the duchy of Gascony. The standard operating procedure in such a scenario was to travel to France and do homage for it. But the young Edward III decided to try a different diplomatic tack instead. He declared that he was the rightful king of France.

"On what grounds?" demanded a startled Philip VI.

"On the grounds that we've all been having incestual sex for so long that my mother is now your sister."

With the kings refusing to back down, the two nations braced themselves for a long and painful conflict. So dire were the prospects that when people began calling it the Hundred Years' War, Edward and Philip berated them for a lack of ambition.

After a slow start, Edward crossed the Channel in 1346 with 15,000 men and bumped into a massive French army at Crecy. Heavily outnumbered, Edward was fortunate that many of his archers had mastered the use of a relatively new kind of bow. Six feet in length, the English longbow required such strength to draw that it actually deformed the user's skeleton. A skilled archer could fire ten arrows a minute compared to the crossbow's two and pierce armour at 200 yards.

The longbow became the foundation for a famous victory[*] as the English archers repulsed a series of desperate French cavalry charges, dropping arrows 'with such force and quickness that it seemed as if it snowed', according to the French chronicler Froissart. So crucial did the longbow become to English military strength that Edward soon made archery the only activity that could be practised on village greens, though some of the archers complained about no longer having maypole dancers to aim at.

A year after Crecy, Edward lay siege to Calais, giving the English a stronghold from which they could raid the surrounding countryside and defend their valuable wool trade. Calais was to remain in English hands for the next 200 years. After a ten-year interlude caused by the Black Death, the English relaunched their campaign at Poitiers, defeating another vastly superior French force thanks to the valiant leadership of Edward's son, the Black Prince. The desperate French were not quick enough to flee the battlefield, which was odd as that was normally something they excelled at, and their new king John II was captured.

Unfortunately, that was as good as it got for Edward III. When the French king died in captivity, having failed to convince his nobles it was worth paying a ransom for a monarch called John, he was succeeded by the much more reliably-named Charles V. At the same time, Edward himself was slipping into dotage and began to spend his days mumbling vaguely about how he used to be a war hero while a bed nurse smiled indulgently and washed his flaccid longbow. By the end of his reign, the English were left with just the coastal towns of Calais, Bordeaux and Bayonne. In 1377, the king died one year later than his son the Black Prince, who passed away from illness aged 45. He was succeeded by Richard II, his ten year-old grandson.

---

[*] famous in England that is; less so in France

The Black Death

Despite the bumbling end, Edward III had been a strong and popular ruler, whose reign had seen his nation rise politically, prosper economically and diversify culturally. There was very little bad you could say about a king like Edward. But if you really had to find something to criticise, really tried to nitpick, you might just point to his less than stellar record on health and safety.

In 1348, the bubonic plague had already been raging on the continent for a year. It had been brought over on Italian merchant ships returning from Turkey, perhaps not the greatest trade deal the Italians had ever made. In June 1348 a ship from Gascony docked at Weymouth Harbour in Dorset, carrying its usual cargo of exquisite wines, expensive cheeses and the finest French rats. One of the sailors who emerged from the hold was found to be deformed with unsightly purple swellings on his body. Naturally the good people of Dorset, not known for their diluted bloodlines, saw nothing strange in this until they noticed that he also appeared to be dead. Within two months the disease he carried had spread to London and within a year covered the entire country. Up to half of England's six million people were killed and a quarter of Scotland's one million.

On the continent, the plague had brought chaos and collapse, with people descending into religious extremism and wholesale massacres of Jews. In Britain, however, people took the events relatively calmly, perhaps helped by the fact Edward I had expelled all the Jews from England back in 1290. Economically, however, there were serious repercussions. The sudden labour shortage drove up wages, but since medieval economists did not understand the economy any better than modern economists do, there was widespread confusion as to why. The landowners knew they didn't like it, however, and taking advantage of the English people's innate horror of inflation, Edward III passed the Ordinance of Labourers, which fixed wages at pre-plague levels. It was enforced ruthlessly and became one of the grievances that sparked the Peasants' Revolt in 1381.

Still, the changes wrought by the plague were irreversible. As feudal lords noticed that not as many peasants were turning up for farming duty anymore, serfdom gradually declined. By 1400 it had been replaced by a form of tenancy, in which peasants still had to spend every day in back-breaking labour on a tiny plot of land but now had to pay rent for it too.

Richard II: Not Quite a Lionheart

Richard II was the last member of his lineage, the House of Plantagenet, which, frankly, is never a good sign. Despite the series of crises that punctuated his reign, however, he had all the attributes of a good king: tall, handsome, intelligent and only mildly insane.

Richard faced his first crisis in 1381 when he was only fourteen years-old. But then his mother explained to him that it was quite normal to grow hairs down there, allowing the young king to concentrate on his next crisis, the Peasants' Revolt. The long-term causes of the revolt lay in the peasants' frustration at their leaders' failure to grasp even the most basic principles of supply and demand. The immediate cause, however, was the levying of a series of poll taxes, a charge of one shilling per person irrespective of income. Richard could not understand the peasants' grievance, as the tax had been *very* popular with his nobility, but he soon discovered the depth of their anger when a spontaneous uprising sprang up throughout the south-east. Under their leaders Wat Tyler, John Ball and Jack Straw, the disparate group of rebels stormed London where they murdered the Lord Chancellor and High Treasurer. Ball's famous rhyming couplet summed up the radical nature of their endeavour: 'When Adam delved and Eve span, who was then the gentleman?'

After two days of anarchy in London, the young king agreed to meet the rebels at Smithfield, riding out bravely to speak with Wat Tyler:

Richard: Hello, revolting peasant. What's your name?

Tyler: Yes it is, sire. How did you know?

Richard: How did I know what?

Tyler: Exactly, sire!

Richard: What?

Tyler: Sire?

Realising that this could quite easily go on all day, the Mayor of London pulled Tyler off his horse and ran him through. Only the king's calm leadership prevented the situation turning ugly. He assured the mob that he did indeed have every intention of honouring their demands that his ministers be dismissed, the poll tax abolished, serfdom ended and the entire edifice of feudalism systematically dismantled, in fact he had been intending to do that anyway, no really he had! So the peasants went home, whereupon Richard sent an army after them and had all the ringleaders put to death. 'Rustics you were and rustics you are still. For as long as we live we will strive to suppress you,' the king told them. It was a good feudal motto.

It was a brilliant start to his reign. Despite his tender age, Richard's resolute actions at Smithfield had saved England from a dark future of equality and fairness, inspiring generations of leaders ever since. Unfortunately, however, this was the highlight. In 1386, he faced another revolt, this time by parliament, who objected to his choice of favourites. Richard's response was that he 'wouldn't even dismiss a scullion from his kitchen at parliament's request,' to which parliament replied apologetically that the king must have misunderstood because what they actually meant was that his favourites should be *executed*, not dismissed. This he was forced to do two years later under threat of deposition[*].

For the next eight years, Richard ruled relatively peacefully, even if inside he was seething. He satisfied his thirst for revenge by demanding a new level of adoration for the kingship that he

---

[*] because we all know what *that* meant

worked hard not to earn. He liked to sit for hours upon his throne in the great hall and any courtiers his gaze fell upon immediately would be obliged to throw themselves to the ground, causing a scene that, to be fair to Richard, must have been almost constantly hilarious. As time went on, the king became more and more unhinged. He negotiated a 28-year truce with France, but most of the money this saved he wasted on massive full-length portraits of himself.

Then in 1397, just as people were thinking he was mad in a harmless, eccentric kind of way, he suddenly had all the ringleaders of the 1386 crisis rounded up and executed, perhaps mistaking them for peasants. He also exiled to France the most powerful noble of the realm, Henry Bolingbroke of the House of Lancaster, after a minor dispute. Richard thought that his new ally the King of France would stop Henry from ever returning to take revenge. But he had forgotten that the French liked to change rulers almost as often as they did mistresses. When the French king fell from power, Bolingbroke returned to his seat of power in the north. With most of Richard's troops away quelling a revolt in Ireland and nobody much minded to take their place, the 32 year-old king had no choice but to surrender. He was imprisoned in Pontefract Castle, where, having promised he wouldn't execute the former king, Henry let him starve to death instead. By this time the upstart noble had already taken the throne himself.

Henry IV: Better than Catherine Zeta-Jones

Henry IV had a tough time of things in his fourteen year reign. Having stolen Richard's crown, he now found it fit uneasily on his head, not only because he was a usurper with no real claim to the throne but also because he had a disfiguring skin disease that left his skin and scalp covered in itchy red pustules. As a result of both these misfortunes, he spent most of his time fighting off repeated insurrections and infections.

His first act, after starving his predecessor to death, was to display the dead king's emaciated body in public. But this did not stop persistent rumours that Richard had, in fact, survived the rebellion and taken refuge in Scotland. Richard's supporters were never a serious threat to Henry's throne, owing to the fact there weren't very many of them, but they were one of many thorns that pricked Henry's side throughout his reign.

Another prickly thorn was a Welsh landowner named Owain Glendwr, recently voted the second greatest hero in Welsh history, one place above Tom Jones and eleven places higher than Catherine Zeta-Jones[*]. Owain had served in the army of Richard II, but when Henry failed to hear his grievance about an aggravating English neighbour, the Welshman organised a massive rebellion that soon spread throughout Wales. Henry mustered an army in response. But this did not scare the brave rebels who, determined to kick the English out of their lands for good, fled to the hills and refused to fight. Periodically they would come down and burn a few English people for warmth, but they would be gone again before anyone had time to fight back. Owain himself was never captured and after 1410 was not seen out of the hills again, leaving some optimistic Welshmen to speculate that, like a Japanese soldier still fighting World War II in the jungle, he might still be there.

The most dangerous point in Owain's rebellion came when he allied himself to an out-of-favour English noble named Henry 'Hotspur' Percy. Percy actually got as far as fighting a battle with Henry and his son Harry at Shrewsbury, the first battle in which English longbow archers found out what it was like to be shot at by English longbow archers. The battle ended in dramatic fashion when Percy was shot in the face having lifted his visor. His supporters, mistaking him for Henry, shouted joyously that the king was dead, whereupon Henry jumped up and shouted, 'No, I'm not. Percy is!' Percy's attempt to reassure everyone that it was

---

[*] really

another case of mistaken identity was made much less convincing by the arrow sticking out of his head.[*]

Other than that, not a lot happened in Henry's troubled reign. He died in 1413 from his skin disease and had himself buried in Canterbury Cathedral next to Thomas Becket, who was making a bit of a comeback at this time. Despite his face being covered in constantly erupting mounds of pus, he managed to father six healthy children, leading many historians to argue that the biggest hero of Henry's reign was actually his wife Mary.

Henry V: Live Fast, Die Young

Much of Henry V's modern reputation rests upon the plays of William Shakespeare, which people like to pretend they have read. In *Henry IV Parts I and II*, he is portrayed as a dissolute waster who spends his time drinking with layabouts like John Falstaff. Then in *Henry V*, he miraculously transforms into a strong, serious king, coldly repudiating his old friend the moment he is crowned.

In real life, however, Henry was just as boring in his youth as he was as king. The kernel of truth in Shakespeare's otherwise shoddy web of lies is that as a prince Henry had some ties with the Lollards, a group of religious heretics who translated the Bible into English, a valuable service that generally led to them being burned alive. One of these Lollards was a man named John Oldcastle, which was the name Shakespeare originally gave to the character Falstaff. On becoming king, Henry quickly came to his senses and began burning the Lollards too, including his old friend Oldcastle. Since this was a tricky special effect to achieve on stage, Shakespeare missed it out.

As king, the 26 year-old Henry decided to renew the Hundred Years' War with France, gaining the necessary taxation from a parliament eager for some real excitement. Pressing his claim to

---

[*] Percy lent his nickname to Tottenham football club, who, in memory of their brave and tragic hero, never win anything either.

the throne of France on the grounds that his father had starved to death the only person who might possibly have had a genuine claim, he invaded with around 10,000 men and quickly found himself facing a French army five times the size at Agincourt. With defeat certain, Harry stood before his men and roused them with his great St Crispin's Day speech immortalised by the Bard: 'God's peace! I would not lose so great an honour, As one man more methinks would share from me, For the best hope I have!' to which his soldiers shouted back in a single triumphant voice: "Sorry, what?"

Fortunately, their bemusement didn't matter because in order to make the best use of their huge numbers of heavy armoured knights, the French had chosen a narrow, sodden piece of ground where horses couldn't manoeuvre. Forced to plod forward on foot, most of the knights were picked off at will by Henry's archers, while the rest were hacked to death as they sank into the mud. 'For hearing this I must perforce compound, With mistful eyes or they will issue too!' shouted Henry to widespread confusion.

The victory at Agincourt set up a series of further campaigns that climaxed in 1419 with the English army reaching the walls of Paris itself. Inside, the mentally unstable French king Charles the Mad was powerless to prevent his court recognising Henry as the heir to his throne on the grounds that they might as well seeing as he was so close by. He married the king's daughter Catherine to seal the deal, at which high point Shakespeare wisely elected to end his play.

Happy to find that he was suddenly able to say things people could understand at last, Henry continued to make war on his soon-to-be subjects. Eventually, however, the constant grind of siege and soliloquy took its toll on his health and in 1422 he succumbed to dysentery, in keeping with his character crapping upon the kingdom of France right to the very end. He was 35 years-old and had missed the death of Charles VI by just two months. His baby son Henry was named King of France with his brother John as regent. Catherine took Henry's body back to England where he was buried at Westminster Abbey next to the body of Edward the Confessor who was, for some strange reason, Henry's hero.

England Loses 100 Years' War to a Girl

When Henry V died in 1422, England's power was on the rise. The English language had replaced French as the language of English government and the English king had replaced the French king as the biggest baby in Christendom. The fact that Henry VI was only one year-old should not have presented any long-term problems, so long as he grew into the kind of man his father was. It was slightly unfortunate, then, that one turned out to be the age at which he pretty much reached his peak. Pious and simple-minded on his good days and catatonically insane on his bad ones, Henry's rule led to anarchy, civil war, and the loss of England's entire territory in France to a teenage girl, Joan of Arc. Apart from that, though, he was almost as successful as his father.

To be fair to Henry, he was only six years-old when Joan of Arc came on the scene. A simple peasant girl, she had received visions from God telling her to take charge of the French army and drive the English from France. Travelling to the siege of Orleans, she somehow managed to secure an audience with the Dauphin, Charles, the rival to Henry for the French throne.

"Now, you're absolutely sure God told you to take charge of the army?" asked Charles, a naturally cautious man. "The *entire* army."

"Absolutely."

"Your experience in military command being...?"

"The fact I dress like a man."

"Right."

Whatever his private reservations, Charles allowed Joan to join his troops whom she rallied them into a frenzied God-fuelled attack, which forced the English to lift the siege. For the next two years Joan continued to inspire her countrymen, until eventually she was captured by the Burgundians. The Burgundians, who had allied themselves to the English during Henry V's years of triumph, sold her to the English, who realised the brave young woman must either be a heretic or a saint. They tried to ransom her back to the French, but it seemed Charles had had enough of teenage girls stealing his thunder and refused to pay. The English burned her at the stake.

Joan's unfortunate end did not stop the French advance, however. As the war continued, the English longbow gradually began to lose ground to gunpowder, which had been just one of the many things crusaders had brought back from the Holy Land[*]. A few cannons powered by gunpowder backed up by primitive handguns for the infantry could destroy the massed ranks of archers, leaving the opposing army open to the traditional cavalry charge attack. Thus deprived of their main battlefield advantage, the English had to rely on superior tactics instead, which unfortunately they had used the last of back at Agincourt. When Bordeaux fell in 1453, Calais was left as their sole remaining possession in France. Thousands of disaffected, unpaid soldiers trudged their way back home, marking the official end of the Hundred Years' War.

Throughout all this, Henry VI had stayed at home, concentrating on the important work of babbling incoherently and dribbling into his food. His only achievement was the founding of Eton College, a hallowed institution where for generations to come Britain's aristocratic leadership would be carefully groomed to become incoherent, babbling lunatics too. The loss of Bordeaux in 1453 sent the king into total mental breakdown. Unable to speak or even lift his head, he became incapable of even the most rudimentary duties of kingship.

His collapse was just what the enemies of Lancaster had been waiting for. Years of weak leadership had left powerful nobles vying for supremacy at court, but the most powerful of them all,

---

[*] syphilis being the other

Richard of York, had been excluded by his political rivals. With the king incapacitated, Richard made his comeback and, with the support of Neville, the Earl of Warwick, managed to have himself appointed as Protector of the Realm. This, however, was in the face of opposition from Henry's feisty wife Margaret and other Lancastrian supporters, and so when Henry made a sudden recovery from his illness on Christmas Day in 1454 the stage was set for a rose-coloured showdown.

Lancastrians vs Yorkists

The War of the Roses takes its name from the white and red roses of Yorkshire and Lancashire, which the two sides felt symbolised their homelands more attractively than, say, urban decay and inner-city rioting. Between 1455 and 1461, the warring roses fought no fewer than nine major battles, with the last eight coming in a climactic eighteen-month stretch from 1459.

Events kicked off when Henry made his dramatic recovery from madness on Christmas Day 1454. Margaret took the opportunity to banish Richard of York from court. Richard responded by gathering a small army and making his way to St Albans in order to intercept the royal party, which had called a great council in Leicester. The two sides had a brief reluctant battle, won by the Yorkists. A vacant-looking Henry was later found singing alone in his tent having been abandoned by his advisers and servants.

For the next five years, there was a bit of a stand-off as Henry flitted in and out of madness and, as a consequence, Richard flitted in and out of power. Things got so tense that eventually the Archbishop of Canterbury attempted to negotiate a reconciliation by holding a 'love-day' procession through the streets of London, culminating in a communal mass at St Paul's. With the Lancastrian and Yorkist nobles forced to walk together hand in hand behind the king, it remains to this very day one of the weirdest events ever to have taken place in the capital. Yorkist plotting resumed just before the sermon.

In 1459, the war finally kicked off properly. Richard was again supported by his friend Warwick, who had now taken on the somewhat ominous nickname of the Kingmaker. Victory at the Battle of Northampton in July 1460, in which Henry was once again discovered singing in his tent, emboldened Richard to seek parliament's approval to take the throne. To Richard's dismay, however, parliament ruled that, however disturbing and annoying, karaoke was not sufficient grounds for deposition. If Richard wanted the throne, he would have to wait until Henry was dead.

In retrospect, this was probably not the best way to bring about an end to the war. But in the next big battle at Wakefield, it was Richard not Henry who ended up dead, giving the triumphant Lancastrians the perfect opportunity to come up with the mnemonic Richard Of York Gave Battle In Vain to help them remember the colours of the rainbow. In their excitement, however, they had forgotten that Richard had an eighteen year-old son called Edward, who gathered a huge army with Warwick and met the king's forces at Towton in Yorkshire.

It proved to be the largest battle of the war. An estimated 50,000 men took part and more than 20,000 were killed, the greatest recorded loss of life on English soil in history. Edward and his forces gained a decisive victory, and most of the Lancastrian leaders were either killed or executed. Henry and Margaret, who had somehow contrived to miss the battle, fled north to Scotland, with Henry singing happily all the way. Only the strongest sense of marital duty prevented Margaret from killing him herself.

Edward IV and the Kingmaker

Six foot four inches tall, strong as an ox, a brilliant general, a skilled administrator, and the father of ten children, it was as though Edward IV had been put on earth just to show how superior Yorkshiremen were to their cousins across the hills[*]. Crowned to

---

[*] literally their cousins in many cases

rapturous applause in 1461, he ruled in two phases: from 1461 to 1470 and from 1471 to 1483. The unusual gap year in the middle came about after the following conversation with his friend Warwick the Kingmaker:

Edward: Hey, Kingmaker, thanks again for making me king.
Warwick: My pleasure, sire. Enjoy it while you can.
Edward: Sorry? What do you mean by that?
Warwick: Well, I'm Warwick the Kingmaker. Did you think I was just going to retire?
Edward: Damn.

Warwick's second round of kingmaking was caused by his anger at the young Edward's refusal to be as imbecilic and easy to control as his predecessor. Unfortunately, when he managed to re-install Henry VI on the throne, he found that people had rather got used to having a monarch who was six foot four and could do strong, manly things like feed himself. He lasted only six months before Edward returned from exile in Burgundy and entered London unopposed. Warwick's only real ally, Edward's brother the Duke of Clarence, switched sides and Edward defeated his erstwhile benefactor at the Battle of Barnet, clearly the last time anybody bothered fighting over that particular territory. Henry was imprisoned in the Tower, where a few days later he died of 'melancholy', not as mysterious as it sounded since most people would be pretty melancholic if they were being strangled to death.

The rest of Edward's reign was peaceful, as the king devoted himself to maintaining law and order, reforming the royal finances, investing in the City of London, and drinking and gorging himself into an early grave. The only notable event was the interesting death of his traitorous brother the Duke of Clarence, whom Edward finally got round to executing in 1478. According to legend, the well-known drinker was 'drowned in a butt of Malmsey wine' in the dungeons of the Tower, which was probably slightly preferable to being hung, drawn and quartered. Edward himself died suddenly at the age of forty, by this time almost as slow and inactive as the man he had deposed.

Richard III: Murdering Humpbacked Monster

As with Henry V, the popular image of Richard III comes from Shakespeare, who frankly has a lot to answer for. The Bard, living in the time of Richard's enemies the Tudors, portrayed Richard as a vicious humpbacked monster who murdered his innocent young nephews in their sleep. In reality, however, the Yorkist king was a decent able-bodied nobleman of impeccable character who might just as easily have murdered his innocent young nephews when they were awake.

During the reign of his brother Edward IV, Richard had served ably as the Lord of the North, where he was regarded with much affection as someone who would do absolutely anything to get his hands on power. When Edward died in 1483, Richard was appointed Lord Protector for the king's twelve year-old successor Edward V. Richard had his nephew lodged in the Tower together with his younger brother 'for their safety', giving the princes all the comfort their status demanded.

"Help yourself to the Malmsey wine, boys," he said generously. "Go on, really get your heads in there."

But in the weeks leading up to Edward V's planned coronation, Richard was told, to his absolutely genuine premeditated shock, that Edward IV's marriage to the boys' mother, Elizabeth Woodville, had been invalid since he had apparently been betrothed to someone else, making the two boys illegitimate. Fed up of war, parliament decided to agree and Richard took the throne. The Princes in the Tower, meanwhile, continued to thrive for a few weeks more, even if the Malmsey wine was starting to taste a bit funny, until they suddenly disappeared from public view. Everyone assumed that Richard had had them murdered, and the bones of two young children dug up in 1674 by workmen in the Tower are widely believed to be those of the young princes.

Child-murderer or not, Richard did some good things in his short two-year reign. He instituted the Court of Requests, to which poor people who couldn't afford legal fees could apply for their grievances to be heard. He also introduced the concept of bail to protect suspected criminals from imprisonment before trial.

In the end, however, the dodgy manner in which he had taken the throne led to his swift downfall. The House of Lancaster had one remaining claimant to the throne, a relatively minor Welsh noble named Henry Tudor, who had spent most of the last twenty years in exile in Brittany. His first rebellion in 1483 floundered when his ships got caught in a storm, but when he tried again two years later he managed to bring Richard to battle at Bosworth Field in Leicestershire.

Initially outnumbering his enemy, Richard's army was decimated when his main ally, Sir William Stanley, switched sides at the last minute. The situation desperate, Richard led a cavalry charge aimed at killing Henry directly. 'A horse! A horse! My kingdom for a horse!' he shouted desperately until his men pointed out he was sitting on one. Despite the king's personal bravery, he was cut down by Stanley's men, the last English king to be killed in battle. Henry Tudor was crowned on the battlefield, with legend having it that he found Richard's crown hanging on a hawthorn bush. The dead king's body was stripped naked and paraded through the streets of Lancaster before being dumped unceremoniously beneath a car park in Leicester. For all intents and purposes, the War of the Roses was over and, like it or not, the Lancastrians had won.

6. THE TUDORS (1485 – 1603)

With the end of the War of the Roses, Britain officially passed out of the Middle Ages and into what the Tudors modestly liked to call the Tudor Age. As if aware of the significance of the transition, the Earth celebrated the moment by plunging Europe into a Little Ice Age. Fortunately, the canny Tudors had a plan to keep people warm during the long freezing winters. They tied them to large wooden stakes and set fire to their legs, using either Protestant or Catholic matches depending on their mood. Yes, the Tudors might have been just minor aristocracy, but this didn't mean they weren't mad. Excepting the underage Edward VI, just four monarchs ruled during the entire Tudor period, which would normally have been a good thing for the stability and well-being of the realm, only in this case it wasn't. The first half was all about the boys, and in particular Henry VIII's mad desire to have one. The second half, however, belonged to the girls with Bloody Mary, Queen Elizabeth and Mary Queen of Scots all campaigning for their equal feminist right to chop each other's heads off.

Henry VII: Show Me the Money
As a minor Welsh noble whose only claim to the throne of England was that one of his mother's ancestors had once rolled around in the hay with the Duke of Lancaster, it was probably a good thing that Henry Tudor had found Richard III's crown hanging from a hawthorn bush because wearing it was the only thing that made him king. It wasn't surprising, then, that his first act as monarch was to marry Elizabeth of York, the daughter of Edward IV, thereby uniting the two rival houses and putting an end to the War of the Roses for good. It was a bit unfortunate that nobody had thought of doing something like that before. The wedding was a fairly muted affair, owing to the fact that most of the guest list had

been either slain or executed by one or other of the happy couple's families. But Henry and Elizabeth were a good fit together and, as third cousins, shared a lot of the same DNA.

With the War of the Roses having thinned down the field so drastically, would-be rebels were forced to cast their nets widely in order to find a proper rival claimant to the throne. And, when that failed, they just made them up. The first pretender to be plucked from obscurity was Lambert Simnel, a boy who not only appeared to have two surnames but also claimed to be the son of Edward IV's brother Clarence.

"Do you mean the same son of Edward IV's brother Clarence that I have locked up in the Tower of London?" asked Henry, puzzled. "Because I'm pretty sure he's not called Lambert. It's probably Edward or Richard or something."

Lambert's supporters were soon defeated at the Battle of Stoke, which ranked with the Battle of Barnet as one of the more unlikely battlefields of British history. But rather than execute the young lad, Henry made him a servant in the royal kitchens, where he failed to invent Simnel cake because people had been eating that for 200 years already.

As if Lambert's rebellion hadn't been embarrassing enough, three years later another pretender appeared called Perkin Warbeck, who claimed to be one of the Princes in the Tower.

"But you're not *in* the Tower," said Henry, puzzled once more. "And anyway, I'm pretty sure the historical consensus is that they were murdered by their evil uncle."

Bereft of support, Perkin was quickly captured and, not being much of a cook, put to death.

The failure of the rebellions left Henry VII free to do the things he most enjoyed, which, as it happened, turned out to be only one thing: making piles and piles of dosh. All of Henry's actions were devoted to this single great pursuit. In foreign policy, he negotiated a Great Agreement with Flemish merchants to enable him to make loads of dosh from English wool. Then he negotiated the Treaty of

Etaples with France to enable him to make even more dosh from English wool. After that, he negotiated the Treaty of Perpetual Peace with Scotland, a name so optimistic it can only have been irony, which betrothed his daughter Margaret to James IV of Scotland and, almost certainly, enabled him to make loads of dosh from English wool.

Domestically, he implemented a brilliant Catch-22 scheme called Morton's Fork to trap nobles into paying more taxes. Named after his Archbishop of Canterbury – like any self-respecting clergyman, a master of extortion – it involved asking the unwary noble whether he lived modestly or extravagantly. If he answered that he lived modestly, he must be saving money and so could afford to pay more tax. If he said he lived extravagantly, he was obviously very rich and so could afford to pay more tax. If he claimed to live neither modestly nor extravagantly, then he'd obviously had the foresight to get himself a decent lawyer.

By the time of his death from tuberculosis in 1509, Henry VII had amassed more than £1.25 million in personal funds, about £648 million in today's money. He had not been a popular king, 'more feared than loved', and his two principal tax-gatherers were executed for corruption the minute he died. However, he had successfully brought an end to a century of civil war and managed to pass on a prosperous and peaceful kingdom to his son and successor, Henry.

Henry VIII: The Golden Years

Unlike his staid and sensible father, who was so dull even wool merchants found it hard to stay awake at meetings, Henry VIII packed so much action into his 38-year reign he was the first English king since William the Conqueror to be allocated more than one section in this book. For the first twenty years of his reign, things went pretty smoothly for the young king, mainly because he left all the minutiae of ruling to his adviser Cardinal Thomas Wolsey, thereby freeing himself up to concentrate on more important matters of state, like having parties. He cultivated the image of the Renaissance Man, creating a court that attracted the brightest artists, poets and scholars from all over Europe. Henry himself was an accomplished sportsman, poet, writer and musician, at least everybody told him he was, and he was fluent in Latin, French and Spanish.

Unfortunately, all this cultural achievement did not come cheap and, as Henry VII tried desperately to roll his way out of his grave, Wolsey regretfully informed his master that they had run out of money.

"It's all right!" said young Henry brightly. "I'll just sell some of my poetry!"

"Yeeees," replied Wolsey. "I was thinking more along the lines of extorting loans from people and not paying them back."

"Oh okay, you're the clergyman, I suppose."

The financial situation was exacerbated when, in league with the Spanish, Henry decided to renew the war with France in order to expand England's territories beyond Calais[*]. This in turn led to war with Scotland with whom England were, as ever, at perpetual peace. The French adventure ended pretty successfully with the French paying a subsidy to Henry to leave them alone, so to recompense Henry decided to spend more on the peace ceremony than he had on the actual fighting. On the so-called Field of the Cloth of Gold near Calais, he entertained the young French king Francis I with two weeks of feasting, drinking, hunting, jousting and vomiting, with Henry doing most of all of them. At one point during the festivities, Henry challenged Francis to a wrestling match, the French king eventually winning the bout by throwing Henry to the ground. Luckily this did not restart the war.

As for Scotland, who had invaded England while Henry was

---

[*] The war saw the first action of Henry's flagship the *Mary Rose*, which was to sink in the Solent during a later skirmish with the French in 1545. It was finally raised from the depths to much fanfare in 1982, though by then they'd signed a peace treaty.

leading his forces in France, their advance into Northumberland was halted at the Battle of Flodden, where Scottish pikemen were slaughtered in their thousands by English arrows. The Scottish king, Henry's brother-in-law James IV was killed in the battle, leaving the throne in the hands of the seventeen month-old James V.

Flush with victories against England's two oldest enemies, by 1529 Henry VIII was a hugely popular figure with everyone except the people who had lent him money. In private, however, the king himself was becoming increasingly frustrated, and for a man as virile as Henry this was a very Great Matter.

The King's Great Matter

Henry had married Catherine of Aragon, the attractive and intelligent daughter of Ferdinand and Isabella of Spain and the aunt of the Holy Roman Emperor, at the very beginning of his reign in 1509. Five years the king's senior, Catherine had been married to Henry's older brother Arthur before his death from illness in 1502. Ironically as things were to turn out, the new king had had to gain special dispensation from the pope to marry his sister-in-law on the grounds that Catherine's marriage to the fifteen year-old Arthur had not been consummated.

For the first years of their marriage, the glamorous new couple were very happy together. The only strain on the relationship was the failure of the queen, after numerous still-births, to provide Henry with a desperately-wanted male heir. By 1529, she was over forty years-old and had had only a single child called Mary, which was a very unconvincing name for a boy. By marrying his brother's widow, Henry was beginning to think his marriage was cursed.

At the same time, he had become openly infatuated with one of the queen's ladies-in-waiting, Anne Boleyn. Having already had an illegitimate child with her older sister Mary, Henry was amazed when Anne turned down his advances with the words, 'I would rather lose my life than my honesty.' Anne had not yet realised, of course, that by marrying Henry it was possible to lose both. Her demurral, however, only served to make the frustrated king's great matter all the greater.

Henry quietly suggested to Catherine that she should retire to a nunnery for the greater good of England, as he liked to call his penis. Catherine, however, was not a woman to be trifled with. Even her enemy Thomas Cromwell said of her, 'If not for her sex, she could have defied all the heroes of history,' to which Henry may have muttered darkly, "I think you mean *the* sex." When she flatly refused his request, he was forced to appeal to the pope for an annulment. Empowering Wolsey to act on his behalf, he cited deep spiritual and philosophical differences with his wife in the sense that she was getting a bit chubby. Unfortunately for Henry, however, the pope was under the control of the Holy Roman Emperor, who was not inclined to agree to the divorce of his noble aunt.

Henry, under pressure from Anne, blamed Wolsey for the failure and had him dismissed from court[*]. His replacement was Sir Thomas More, the author of the visionary work *Utopia*, which had imagined a land in which everyone swapped houses every ten years and no-one worked more than six hours a day. He was less crazy than he sounded. More initially cooperated with Henry's cause, but as a good Catholic began to grow uneasy at the increasingly inventive swear words Henry was using to describe the pope. In 1530, Henry had Catherine banished from court and gave her rooms to Anne. Attractive and intelligent but with Protestant tendencies and a small deformity on her nail that might have kind of looked like an extra finger if you squinted hard

---

[*] Wolsey had not done himself any favours by living even more extravagantly than Henry himself, his magnificent palace at Hampton Court rivalling any in England. After his dismissal, Wolsey was recalled to London to face treason charges, but died on the journey from illness. It saved cleaning the axe.

enough, Anne was obviously a witch. When the Archbishop of Canterbury died in 1532, she used black magic to have her reformist family chaplain Thomas Cranmer appointed in his place. With cold winds of anti-papal ideas blowing over the court, coupled with thunderclaps of regal frustration and looming clouds of royal divorce, all the ingredients were set for a perfect political storm.

The English Sort-Of Reformation

The English Sort-Of Reformation had its origins in 1517 when a German monk named Martin Luther nailed his 'Ninety-five Theses' about the Catholic Church to a church door in Wittenberg. Luther had become disenchanted with what he saw as abuses within the Church, primarily the sale of 'indulgences' by which sinners could have their allotted time in Purgatory reduced by donating money to good causes (often conveniently involving Church officials). Luther taught that charity and good works were an unnecessary distraction from the true path to salvation, which was faith and faith alone. He also took issue with the primacy of the pope, who was far too rich for Luther's liking[*], and the special status given to bishops and priests. Naturally, this didn't go down all that well with bishops, priests or the pope, who quickly had the renegade monk excommunicated.

Thanks to the introduction of the printing press to Europe by Johannes Gutenberg in 1439, however, Luther's Ninety-five Theses spread quickly around the continent. Many German princes adopted Luther's teachings, always happy to do something to annoy the pope, and it wasn't long before copies of the Theses had reached England. With his canny sense of irony, considering the events to come, Henry VIII actually made a spirited defence of the Church's teachings in a treatise called the Defence of the Seven Sacraments, penned with his friend Thomas More in 1521. Pope

---

[*] and rather too fond of young boys, according to rumours

Leo X awarded him the title of Defender of the Faith for his efforts, a proud appellation that, somewhat bizarrely, still adorns English coins. Within England, however, there were plenty of influential people who thought Luther had got things spot on. Two of these were Archbishop Cranmer, who had spent time in Lutheran circles in Germany, and a young lawyer named Thomas Cromwell, a canny and capable adviser to Cardinal Wolsey.

Despite Henry's support for the teachings of the Church, he got as annoyed as anyone with what he saw as the pope's frequent meddling in English affairs – particularly, of course, the English affair he was enjoying with Anne Boleyn. In January 1533, he finally married Anne and had Archbishop Cranmer declare his marriage to Catherine null and void. Pope Clement immediately excommunicated him, and so with the help of his new chief minister Thomas Cromwell, Henry had parliament pass a series of acts removing papal authority over England so that God realised excommunication didn't really matter anymore. In 1534, the Act of Supremacy declared Henry to be supreme head of the Church of England, giving him the power to decide doctrine and appoint bishops, and making it treasonable to criticise Henry or his leadership of the Church. For Thomas More, this was an act too far and Henry had him executed for refusing to pledge his support.

The Dissolution of the Monasteries

The following year, with the support of Thomas Cromwell, the king began the dissolution of the monasteries. It is hard to exaggerate just how large an institution the religious houses were in Henry's kingdom. There were almost 900 monasteries, priories, friaries and convents in England, with more in Wales and Ireland. According to some estimates, as many as one in fifty adult males were in religious orders. Henry's official motivation for putting them all out of work was, of course, anger at the way in which these supposedly celibate monks and nuns engaged in shamefully wild orgies and deviant sexual acts, which, in their arrogance, they wouldn't let Henry join in. There was also the small bonus of being able to take all of their money and land, handy with the poetry market still being in the doldrums.

The first step in getting rid of them was Thomas Cromwell's infamous visitation of the monasteries in 1534 and 1535. Sending out commissioners to tour the country and report, in a completely unbiased way, exactly what they thought Cromwell wanted to hear, the king's chief minister compiled a lurid catalogue of monastic misdeeds, some of which Henry hadn't had chance to try yet. The next year, the dissolution began in earnest. Not all the monateries were targeted at first, and many monks left more or less voluntarily, taking advantage of a cash payment or pension in return for going quietly.

In the north of England, however, where alms-giving monasteries often provided the only support for people who weren't talented enough to move down south, the dissolution provoked rebellion. Led by a charismatic barrister from London named Robert Aske, the Pilgrimage of Grace attracted more than 30,000 rebels, posing a genuine threat to Henry's authority. Henry sent the Duke of Norfolk to deal with them, but seeing the strength of their numbers, the duke promised a general pardon and restitution of their grievances. Aske believed him and, trusting the good judgement of a king who had just overturned centuries of religious tradition for the sake of his sex life, dismissed his followers. Henry promptly had him executed along with 200 of his followers, snuffing the rebellion out. The dissolution proceeded with more alacrity from then on, eventually netting the Crown at least £1 million, almost enough to get Henry through an entire meal.

Despite this straightforward victory, the English Reformation brought chaos and confusion as different religious practices spread. Henry, who remained fundamentally Catholic in his faith, tried to put a stop to it in 1539 with the publication of the Six Articles, which reaffirmed established traditions such as transubstantiation, confession and clerical celibacy. Thomas Cromwell was executed a year later in part for his failure to enforce the Six Articles effectively. Cromwell protested that, while he had been able to persuade people to accept transubstantiation and confession again, on the part about clerical celibacy it was all a bit too late.

The Less Than Merry Wives of Windsor

As all this was going on, Henry in his indefatigable way was still finding time to divorce or behead most of the women in his court. His marriage to Anne Boleyn did not work out well, with Anne's stubborn insistence on having opinions, thoughts etc. quickly grating on Henry's limited patience. It didn't help that the only child she had been able to carry to birth was another girl, Elizabeth. Anne's fate was finally sealed in 1536 when her shock at a serious accident suffered by Henry while jousting led her to miscarry her child. As she lay in bed recovering painfully, Henry comforted her with the thought that it would have been very hard for her to look after a new baby anyway without her head. He gave her palace rooms to his latest mistress, Jane Seymour, while he moved Anne to slightly less spacious new quarters in the Tower of London. Declaring that his marriage had been the product of witchcraft, he had her executed along with five men with whom Anne had somehow found the time to commit adultery, incest and high treason.

The jousting accident had severe repercussions for the rest of Henry's reign. The leg wound he suffered became infected and ulcerated, and Henry was never able to exercise again. Never a small man to begin with, he became increasingly obese and eventually had to be moved about in mechanical contraptions, including a stairlift. His final suit of armour was measured at 52 inches at the waist, meaning the 6 foot 1 inch king was well on the way to becoming as wide as he was tall. Scientists believe the infection may even have affected Henry's brain, causing the violent mood swings that marked the king's descent into near-madness.

A year after Anne's death, Jane Seymour bore Henry a boy at last, Edward. But the birth was a difficult one, as Edward met his voluminous father for the first time and promptly tried to climb back in. Jane died a few days later, leaving Henry to mourn his only 'true wife'. In 1540, he decided to marry again. Understandably, there was not a rush of volunteers from the women of England, and so Cromwell looked overseas, hoping to find a good Protestant girl who could advance the reformation in England. He came up with Anne of Cleves, a German princess so plain in appearance Cromwell had to send the best artist in the land, Hans Holbein the Younger, to paint her portrait.

"Whatever you do, don't paint her next to a horse," warned Cromwell.

Holbein did his best, but when Henry finally met his bride he was not impressed. Calling her a 'Flanders Mare', he refused to ride her, divorcing her a few months later and executing Cromwell for good measure. Anne was happy to admit the marriage had not been consummated, with some sharp-eared witnesses hearing her joyful neighs from as far away as Portsmouth.

Henry's next bride was the young and beautiful Catherine Howard, one of Anne's ladies-in-waiting. But Catherine was not altogether enamoured with marriage to a man who had to be lowered on top of her by crane, choosing instead to have an affair with the dashing courtier Thomas Culpeper. Henry had her executed in February 1542.

The years were running out for the increasingly unwell king. But he found time for one last marriage, this time to the older and wiser Catherine Parr. Catherine reconciled Henry to his two daughters, putting them back in line to the throne after Edward. She remained, whole and fully necked, at Henry's bedside when he died four years later in 1547. Henry bequeathed to his three children a bankrupt, divided and tyrannical realm. According to legend, his last words were 'Monks! Monks! Monks!', a reference, perhaps, to the only people in England left in a more desperate state than Henry himself.

Edward VI: Precocious and Dead

Edward's short reign was notable for it being the first time a genuinely Protestant ruler had sat upon the throne of England. Brought up under the influence of Archbishop Cranmer, Edward was just nine years-old when he ascended the throne and just fifteen years-old when he descended it after a fatal bout of tuberculosis. A precocious child, by the age of eleven he had already penned a treatise on 'the pope as antichrist', impressing his tutors who had just asked him to write about his summer holidays. Dominated first by the Duke of Somerset and then the Duke of Northumberland, the Regency Council that ruled in his stead followed his Protestant lead, repudiating transubstantiation, abolishing clerical celibacy and forcing all services to be conducted in English. Wall paintings in churches were whitewashed and images of saints taken down and destroyed. Archbishop Cranmer's Book of Common Prayer became the cornerstone of the new religion, proving that you didn't need to speak Latin in order to bore people to sleep.

The changes brought upheaval and unrest to several parts of the country. People in Devon and Cornwall rose up against the imposition of English services in the the so-called Prayer Book Rebellion of 1549, protesting that things had been much simpler when they didn't understand what the priest was going on about. The rebels were also angry about rapidly rising food prices, brought on in part by the Council's debasing of the currency to help pay for another war with France and Scotland. Inevitably, the rebellion was suppressed, with the loss of at least 5,500 lives. But no sooner had the Prayer Book Rebellion ended when another uprising kicked off in Norfolk over the issue of enclosure, the practice by which landlords blocked off land that had once been common grazing ground. So convinced were the rebels of the justness of their cause that they assumed the ruling lords would be on their side, right up to the moment the ruling lords actually *were* on their side, armed with swords.

In early 1553, Edward began suffering from high fevers, vomiting and bleeding, which left the prospect of a stable succession in tatters. The next in line to the throne was his half-sister Mary, but since she had been brought up as a Catholic under the influence of her mother Catherine of Aragon, the Protestant leader of the Council, the Duke of Northumberland, was determined to find a more suitable candidate. Fortunately, he had just the girl: Edward's sixteen year-old cousin Lady Jane Grey, who happened to be, by an incredible coincidence that Northumberland swore he had not even thought of, his daughter-in-law. The stage was set for religious chaos.

Mary I and the Counter-Reformation

The only product of Henry VIII's marriage to Catherine of Aragon, other than a lot of very unhappy monks, Mary was another precocious child. When she was just four, she drew great excitement from a visiting French delegation with a virtuoso performance on the virginals[*]. She could read and write Latin by the age of nine and by the age of twelve was already staging her own mock-burnings of Protestant clergy.

When Edward VI died of tuberculosis, Northumberland duly had Lady Jane Grey proclaimed as queen. But on the very same day, a letter arrived from Mary ordering the Privy Council to proclaim her as queen instead. As people suddenly began to realise why Henry had been so keen to have a son, Mary gathered up an army at Framlingham Castle in Suffolk and prepared to march on London. Northumberland's support fell away, and on 19 July, just nine days after Lady Jane had been made queen, Mary entered London unopposed and took the throne. Jane and her father-in-law

---

[*] a kind of harpsichord before you say anything

were beheaded, lending a somewhat sombre atmosphere to the next family Christmas.

The execution pretty much set the tone for Mary's five-year reign, except that instead of beheading, the queen found she could stay a lot warmer if she burned people instead. In this she may have been influenced by her husband, the future Philip II of Spain, who re-started the Spanish Inquisition to stamp out heresy and common sense. Under the Heresy Acts, Mary reaffirmed the Six Articles of her father's reign, once more reversing the policy on clerical celibacy to the great confusion of the clergy and their new wives. In February 1555, the burnings began with Bishops Ridley and Latimer and went on to claim 283 victims in total, including Archbishop Cranmer himself.

The burnings were not popular, and in fact Mary's short reign was a disaster in more ways than one. It rained almost constantly for some reason, leading to economic misery and widespread famine. Her marriage to Philip, which she had arranged herself, was unpopular too, with the king speaking no English and the queen little Spanish. Worse still, Philip persuaded Mary to join his war against France which led to the loss of Calais, England's final remaining continental possession. Mary said on her deathbed that they would find the word Calais engraved on her heart, presumably because the words 'murderous mad cow' wouldn't fit.

The only plus-side was that Philip spent so little time in England with his wife that she failed to produce an heir, despite an embarrassing false pregnancy that ended in nothing but hot air. Thus the throne of England was able to pass safely away from Spanish hands and into the safe mitts of Elizabeth I, who resisted Philip's inquisitive entreaties far more effectively than her older half-sister. Mary's death from cancer in 1558 was greeted with an outpouring of polemic against her reign from Protestant sympathisers. It began with John Knox's classic tome *The First Blast of the Trumpet Against the Monstrous Regimen of Women*, which described the fairer sex as 'sick and impotent', only one of which we can assume was an accurate description of John Knox himself. By the 17th century, the soubriquet Bloody Mary had been applied to the dead queen, drowning memories of her murderous reign in a swift succession of high-strength vodka cocktails.

Elizabeth I: The Virgin Queen

Taking the throne at the age of 25, Elizabeth I, aka the Virgin Queen or Good Queen Bess, ruled for 44 years until her death in 1603, making her the sixth-longest reigning monarch in English history. As Queen of England and Ireland, she provided much-needed stability for her realm, and, at least until the last fifteen years of her reign, ruled strongly and wisely with the help of trusted advisors like Sir William Cecil.

Her greatest triumph in those years was to calm people's fears over religion by reassuring them that, whatever their private beliefs, she wasn't going to force them to marry her. Although Protestantism again became the official religion, with the Book of Common Prayer sending congregations into rapturous excitement the moment they woke up, the penalties for non-conformance were light. '*Video et taceo*,' the Queen said. 'I see and keep silent.'[*]

The only major religious problem she faced was with her cousin Mary Stuart, Queen of Scots, a Catholic brought up in France who had succeeded to the throne of Presbyterian Scotland. Like all the best Catholic girls, Mary had appalling taste in men, her first husband being the King of France and her next two both proven Scottish murderers. After King Francis's death from an ear infection, Mary, the only surviving child of James V of Scotland, returned to her father's kingdom to take up the throne. There she fell in love with the dashing but arrogant Lord Darnley, who proceeded to stab to death Mary's private secretary in front of her eyes while she was seven months' pregnant. After the birth of her

---

[*] not to be confused with *video et tacos*, Elizabeth's favourite Friday night in

child, Mary fell for another Scottish noble called Lord Bothwell, who murdered Darnley by either strangulation or gunpowder or possibly both. When Mary agreed to marry Bothwell anyway, she found herself implicated in the crime and, for the first and last time in history, both Catholic and Protestant lords were united in their opposition. Mary was forced to abdicate the throne in favour of her one year-old son, James, while she herself fled to England on a fishing boat before beaching up on the Cumberland coast.

Elizabeth welcomed her beloved cousin with nineteen years of house arrest. Mary had a claim to the throne of England, as almost everybody did by now, and soon became the focus of Catholic plots against Elizabeth. Eventually, the Babington Plot of 1586 implicated her directly, after coded letters were intercepted and deciphered by spies placed in her castle by Elizabeth's clever spymaster Sir Francis Walsingham. The following year, Mary was beheaded at Fotheringhay Castle in Northamptonshire. Even then, however, the drama was not over, for when the executioner picked up her severed head to show the crowd, it proceeded to fall to the floor leaving the shocked axeman with a wig in his hand. Poor Mary never lived the humiliation down.

The other major issue faced by Elizabeth in these years was, of course, the marriage question. She had no shortage of suitors in the early years, mainly foreign kings and noblemen who were attracted by the youthful queen's radiant tax-collecting system. Elizabeth's excuse for turning them down was that she had already married herself to all her subjects, which required a quite colossal amount of bed-work as it was. Her other excuse was that she didn't want to endanger the independence of England by marrying a foreigner, forgetting that by not leaving an heir she was putting the nation in very real danger of being ruled by a Scot.

Historians have offered other possible reasons too. One is that as a fourteen year-old she was subject to improper advances from her forty year-old protector Edward Seymour, who was spotted tickling her and slapping her on the buttocks, and that this put her off intimacy for life[*]. Another is that she was always in love with her childhood friend Robert Dudley, the Earl of Leicester, who was considered too unscrupulous and unreliable to be an appropriate husband for a queen. Although Dudley went as far as pushing his wife down the stairs to free himself up for Elizabeth, the match was opposed by all the queen's advisors on the Privy Council, who figured he was more the kind of man that Mary Queen of Scots would go for.

The Spanish Armada

As the only Protestant country with a decent navy, England was at the fulcrum of foreign affairs during Elizabeth's reign, even if the queen herself was a bit half-hearted about the whole thing. From 1585 to 1604, the nation was embroiled in war with Spain, the European top-dogs at the time due to their conquest and colonisation of the New World following the voyages of Christopher Columbus. To celebrate this clearly temporary state of affairs, Philip II was busy torturing the Protestant nations of Europe in order to convert them back to Catholicism. When England aided the Protestant Dutch rebellion against the Spaniards, the furious king responded by launching a huge armada with which he aimed to invade England and throw Good Queen Bess on her back.

When the flotilla of 130 Spanish ships was spotted off the south coast in July 1588, legend has it that the English vice-admiral Sir Francis Drake was playing bowls on Plymouth Hoe. Drake refused to act until the game was over, because there was nothing more exciting in Tudor England than bowls. As it turned out, however, Drake and his fleet didn't need to do a great deal of fighting, as, in keeping with their national character, it was almost inevitable the Spanish would find a way to defeat themselves. Accordingly,

---

[*] Seymour was eventually executed on suspicion of trying to marry her, a verdict that probably put off the more casual suitor from then on.

having arranged to rendezvous with the Duke of Parma's invasion army on the coast of Flanders, there was no surprise when the duke didn't make it, having been blockaded by Dutch flyships. The Spanish fleet was forced to cluster together in a shallow port, giving Drake the opportunity to send in eight fireships, which scattered the armada in panic.

After a brief battle, the smaller but more manoeverable English ships pursued the Spanish up the east coast of England. On the mainland, however, the nation still feared invasion, prompting Elizabeth to ride in armour to a small force gathered at Tilbury in Essex. There, she gave a rousing speech to her men: 'I know I have the body of a weak, feeble woman, but I have the heart and stomach of a king, and of a king of England too.' Her horse could only be grateful it wasn't the stomach of her father. The Spanish knew when they were beaten. Having rounded Scotland on an intended retreat back to Spain, they were hit by a huge Protestant storm that destroyed more than a third of their ships, many of them landing in pieces on the coast of Ireland. Stories still abound of Spanish descendents living in Ireland to this day, recognisable only by their vain attempts to teach the locals how to play football properly.

The Elizabethan Golden Age

With England safe from the terrors of pointy beards and round-the-clock flamenco dancing, there was time for the nation to enjoy a brief Golden Age. The first aspect of the Golden Age was the heroic exploits of English privateers like Francis Drake and John Hawkins who, with the blessing of the crown, would sail out to the New World and, regardless of the personal dangers to themselves and their crews, get quite spectacularly drunk. They also captured Spanish merchant ships full of gold and silver, earning the brave 'Sea Dogs' great fame and fortune that they would then fritter away hopelessly on gold earrings.

Drake was the epitome of the great adventurers of Elizabethan

England. Not content with his exploits in the New World, he became the second man to circumnavigate the globe on his vessel the Golden Hind, even now regarded as one of the most ridiculously-named ship in history. Unlike Magellan, Drake managed to both survive the trip and burn a lot of Spanish colonies on the way, claiming what is now California for the English crown. His most famous attack was on the Spanish port of Cadiz in 1587, where he 'singed the beard of the King of Spain' by destroying 37 Spanish ships. The attack delayed the Armada by over a year. Slightly less to be celebrated was Drake's involvement in the African slave trade, where he joined his cousin John Hawkins on some of England's first slave voyages to west Africa. The old sea dog eventually died at the age of 56, contracting dysentry while anchored off the coast of Panama. His lead-lined coffin was dropped into the sea where divers have been searching for it ever since.

Drake's major rival in the adventuring stakes was Sir Walter Raleigh, another of Elizabeth's favourites, who founded England's first attempt at a permanent settlement in North America at Roanoke. He called the colony Virginia to celebrate the queen's unbroken hymen, but the settlers were wiped out in mysterious circumstances three years later, giving rise to the nickname The Lost Colony. Raleigh did succeed, however, in bringing back tobacco and potatoes to England, and people soon found that filling their lungs with toxic smoke was an excellent way of masking the taste of the potatoes.

The second aspect of the Golden Age was, of course, the arts. Born around six years after Elizabeth assumed the throne, William Shakespeare wrote around 154 sonnets and 38 plays, his troupe building their own theatre, the Globe, on the south bank of the Thames. His work was patronised and enjoyed by the queen herself, and, though little is known of his private life, it made Shakespeare wealthy enough to buy the second-largest house in Stratford, where he died in 1616. His contemporary Christopher

Marlowe, whom Shakespeare greatly admired, was even more revered in his lifetime. As well as writing plays like *Doctor Faustus* and *The Jew of Malta*, Marlowe was also a magician, spy, homosexual and heretic, occasionally all at the same time. He died in 1593 in tragic circumstances, stabbed to death in a bar shortly after his arrest for blasphemy. Rumours persist that Marlowe may have been responsible for some of Shakespeare's plays, because without those rumours desperate English professors would have no reason to get paid.

With trade, exploration and the arts flourishing, Elizabethan England was as economically and culturally vibrant as at any time in her history. It had a strong centralised state, thanks to reforms instituted by Henry VII and Henry VIII, and was far more stable than its rivals on the continent, who were constantly embroiled in religious wars. But as the queen grew older, her grip on the country grew weaker and England's golden age slowly came to an end.

The Decline of Elizabeth

The victory over the Spanish Armada proved to be the highpoint of the remaining years of Elizabeth's reign. Age had caught up to the once attractive queen, a bout of smallpox in 1562 having already left her skin mottled and scarred. Half-bald and with black rotting teeth, she announced her determination to remain a virgin to her death, and, for once, the Privy Council agreed that this was probably the best thing. Events at home and abroad mirrored the queen's decline. Despite her increasingly powerful navy, England's war with Spain dragged on in stalemate, draining the Treasury of resources desperately needed for Elizabeth's make-up. As taxes and resentment grew, the queen became increasingly intolerant of Catholics agitating in the realm. This led to the infamous era of 'priest holes', where Jesuit priests were able to evade state prosecution by hiding away in secret rooms within the houses of sympathetic aristocrats.

By the turn of the century, Elizabeth's health was beginning to fail, and her councillors turned their attention toward who would succeed her. Fearful of an uprising, Elizabeth refused to name an heir, leaving the Privy Council with little choice but to look up north, where 36 year-old James VI of Scotland, son of Mary Stuart, was busy burning witches. He seemed to be just the kind of man England needed, and behind the scenes the Council worked hard to make it happen. In 1603 Elizabeth died at the age of 69. James took a high-speed coach down to London and was crowned a few months later to surprisingly enthusiastic applause.

7. THE STUARTS AND THE CROMWELLS (1603 - 1714)

The 118-year rule of the Tudors had seen Britain transformed from being a rigid feudal society into a thriving, upwardly-mobile nation-state, where, with enough energy and determination, anybody of any rank or gender could get themselves burned at the stake for believing the wrong thing. But all that was set to change under the stewardship of the Stuart dynasty. For the Stuarts were convinced that the solution to Britain's problems was not executing their enemies for religious reasons; it was getting *themselves* executed for being really stupid. It took many years of furious money-wasting and seven years of civil war, but eventually Charles I realised his lifetime's ambition of ending his reign as the shortest monarch in British history. Although Oliver Cromwell and his Roundhead friends failed to turn Britain into a permanent republic, they provided the impetus for the rise of parliament and the decline of the monarchy, leading inexorably toward the quiet reign of Queen Anne, whose major contribution to British political history was having furniture named after her.

James I and the Gunpowder Plot

Having already been King of Scotland since the age of one, James I took the throne of England in 1603, determined to prove that experience didn't count for much. His upbringing in Scotland had been dire, as most upbringings in Scotland tend to be. His father had been murdered, with his mother an accessory; his mother herself had been executed and four of his regents had died violently. His boyhood tutor was a sadist, forcing him to curse his mother as he was beaten. When James reached adulthood, he became convinced that Scotland was full of witches who were plotting to take his life. He had more than 4000 burned at the stake, the vast majority of them women.

He was also almost pathologically unhygienic. A keen hunter, he refused to dismount to relieve himself but defecated in the saddle, leaving himself soiled and filthy. When he made a kill, he would rip open the animal's belly and all but climb inside. Despite the state this left him in, he rarely changed clothes and bathed just once a year, believing it to be unhealthy. A hater of women and openly homosexual, he would kiss and fondle his male courtiers in public, while continuing to insist that sodomy was an unpardonable sin. Although scholarly and intellectual, penning treatises on theology, witchcraft and monarchy, he was also a garrulous talker, a habit made even more annoying to his English companions by his thick Scottish accent and an over-large tongue that caused him to stutter. Court life was an absolute joy.

The Gunpowder Plot came just a year into his reign. A group of twelve Catholic gentlemen led by Robert Catesby had hatched a plot to murder the king and all his nobles at the State Opening of Parliament. Having killed the king, the plotters aimed to kidnap his young daughter Elizabeth and place her on the throne under their control. The problem with the plan, however, was twofold. First, the State Opening of Parliament kept getting delayed due to plague, which rotted the gunpowder as fast as the plotters could row it in. Second, some of the plotters began to realise that by blowing up parliament, there was a pretty good chance they would kill quite a few fellow Catholics at the same time, something that under the strict rules of Catholicism you weren't allowed to do on feast days.

Eventually, as the fifth of November finally approached, an anonymous letter was sent to Lord Monteagle, the brother-in-law of one of the plotters, warning him to stay away from the Houses of Parliament just in case they, I don't know, happened to explode for some reason. Monteagle passed the note to the virulently anti-Catholic Lord Salisbury, who informed the king. On the night of November 4, a search was made of the croft beneath the House, where an ex-soldier named Guy Fawkes was discovered with a pocket watch, several matches and 36 barrels of gunpowder.

"I'm... er... here about the fireworks display?" Guy offered.

But that particular tradition hadn't started yet, and over the next few days on the rack Guy told his interrogators everything they needed to know in increasingly bad handwriting. Catesby and the other ringleaders fled to the countryside where, as they prepared to make a last stand, they finally managed to get the gunpowder lit, detonating themselves in the process. Fawkes and the other survivors were hung, drawn and quartered, and from then on it became an annual tradition to commemorate the occasion with bonfires and fireworks. Rough effigies of Guy Fawkes were made, and by the 19th century the word 'guy' had come to mean a 'badly-dressed person'. Since this pretty much included every man in Britain, eventually guy took on the more general meaning used today.

The Puritan Movement

The Puritan movement had its origins with a French theologian named John Calvin, who had decided that Martin Luther's strict insistence upon prayer, piety and fasting sounded a bit too much like good fun. Calvin believed that not only was faith more important than good works, but that God had in fact already decided who was going to heaven on Judgement Day and there was pretty much nothing you could do about it. But just in case you weren't sure whether you had been 'elected' or not, you could increase your chances of salvation by listening to dreary sermons, wearing incredibly drab clothing, and beating your children to a pulp, just as Jesus had taught.

The most radical of the English Puritans were known as Separatists. They felt their beliefs were incompatible with the Church of England, since the head of the Church of England was the king and the Separatists didn't believe the king should have a head. Persecuted under Elizabeth for their refusal to attend church, they had had hopes that her successor James might be more sympathetic to their cause, seeing that he enjoyed burning witches and never took a bath. This, however, turned out not to be the case, and the only concession the king made to their demands was to authorise an English translation of the Bible, the Authorised King James Version, a classic as far as authorised versions of the Bible go.

Eventually, the Separatists realised that the only place for them to go was America, where religious extremists could not only worship as they pleased but also earn good money as hosts on talk radio. And so it was that in 1620 around a hundred Pilgrims boarded the Mayflower at Plymouth and sailed away to the east coast of America. Upon reaching the promised land, they founded a new settlement, which, displaying the kind of imagination Puritans were renowned for, they decided to call Plymouth.

As it happened, they had actually been aiming for a different place on the east coast called Jamestown, where a group of English settlers had been successfully starving to death since 1607. The Jamestown settlers had eventually been rescued by a local Indian girl named Pocahontas, who married one of their leaders, John Rolfe, and thus initiated a period of peaceful coexistence between settler and native that lasted a period of almost three whole days. It was John Rolfe who discovered the miracle of tobacco growing, which ensured the survival of the colonists. By 1619 the Jamestown colonists had also discovered the miracle of dark-skinned African slaves, who, with a bit of encouragement[*], had agreed to grow the tobacco completely free of charge. Suddenly there were heaps of filthy lucre to be made in America and simple God-fearing Puritans were not going to miss out. By the end of James's reign, some 80,000 had made the journey, changing the landscape of the great continent for good.

Charles I and the Puritans

---

[*] whipping

The foiling of the Gunpowder Plot was the highlight of James I's reign, which was unfortunate seeing that he still had twenty years to go. While James was not a bad king on the whole, except in terms of the smell, he had a consistently rocky relationship with the parliament he had helped to save and soon began to wonder whether those Catholic plotters might have had a point after all. He was a believer in the divine right of kings, declaring that anyone who opposed the monarch was 'spitting in the face of God.' Needless to say, the parliamentarians were not so sure, particularly since with his over-grown tongue it was generally James doing most of the spitting.

Tiring of their constant demands, James refused to summon parliament for seven years, relying on sources of revenue that did not require the approval of the Commons. Business loans were one major source; another was cash for honours. By the end of his reign, knighthoods could be got for a mere £220 while baronetcies, a title James had simply conjured up out of thin air, went for £1,095. When the king eventually died in 1625 of arthritis, gout, kidney stones and heaven knows what else, he left a peaceful but uneasy realm to his son Charles, who purposefully set about making the situation a whole lot worse.

Charles's problem was that he had inherited his father's belief in absolute monarchy and his shortness of stature, but not his determination to end his reign at the same height he began it, if you catch my drift. He had problems with parliament right from the start when he insisted on relying on the incompetent counsel of George Villiers, the Duke of Buckingham, the favourite and alleged lover of his father. It was Buckingham who coaxed Charles into pursuing a war with Spain after a personal quarrel with the Spanish chief minister, and it was the expense of that war that brought the first stirrings of discontent from parliament.

Things became worse when, again with Buckingham's support, Charles married Princess Henrietta Maria of France against parliament's wishes. Henrietta was a good match in every way except for the fact she was Catholic. The combination of the king's marriage and his friendship with a prominent supporter of Arminianism, a milder version of Calvinism, named Richard Montagu persuaded the MPs that Charles was secretly planning to return the nation to Catholicism. The result was that every time Charles called parliament to raise taxation to pay for his war with Spain and to buy himself new shoes, shirts, palaces etc., they insisted on reading out endless resolutions against Arminianism, popery, and, rather more justifiably, the Duke of Buckingham.

When Buckingham led a failed naval expedition against Spain in 1626, parliament tried to impeach him, only for Charles to have two of their members arrested. Only the assassination of Buckingham in 1628 by a disgruntled army officer saved things from getting entirely out of hand, but that only served to exacerbate the rift between king and country as Charles spent two days grieving in bed while the rest of the nation held street parties.

The following year, when the MPs objected to the king's demands for yet more money, Charles angrily dissolved parliament after a single day, barely enough time for the MPs to even pronounce Arminianism let alone explain what it really meant. Arresting eight of their leaders, one of whom was to die in prison, the king proceeded to rule for the next eleven years without recalling parliament. Known as the Personal Rule or the Eleven Years' Tyranny, depending on whether your name was Charles or not, the years were marked by the king's increasingly high-handed methods of rule. Even after he was forced to make peace with Spain through lack of funds, the inability to raise taxation through normal means drove Charles to take increasingly desperate measures. He took forced loans from merchants and gentry and imprisoned anyone who refused to pay. He then revived obsolete feudal war taxes like ship money, which he levied on every town in return for royal protection against marauding... Vikings or something.

As if this was not bad enough, he continued to fuel the fears of the Puritans by appointing the Arminian sympathiser William Laud as his Archbishop of Canterbury. Together, he and Laud initiated a series of reforms to reduce Calvinist influence in the church, closing Puritan social clubs (which were almost as much fun as they sounded) and insisting on the use of the Anglican Book of Common Prayer. Opponents were tried in the Court of the Star Chamber, where torture was routinely used to gain confessions. The Star Chamber could inflict any sentence except death and became notorious for the cruel punishments it imposed, including whipping, branding, ear-cropping and, in extreme cases, the Book of Common Prayer. Another 30,000 Puritans fled to America in search of the freedom to whip, brand and mutilate people themselves.

The Scottish and Irish Rebellions

Unfortunately for Charles, that still left quite a lot of Puritans in Britain. Many of them were in Scotland where they formed the dominant Presbyterian church, the only thing in Scotland greyer than the weather. Charles had rather forgotten about his northern kingdom since his birth there in 1600, and when he and Laud ordered the use of the Book of Common Prayer without consulting either the Scottish parliament or the Kirk, he was shocked when they got rather upset. The first service to use the new liturgy in 1637 ended in a riot after a member of congregation threw her stool* at the minister's head, and soon the Scots signed a National Covenant rejecting any religious reforms that threatened to make their churchgoing less dreary.

Charles interpreted the unrest as a rebellion against his royal authority. Having a fair idea about what the English parliament might say about paying for a war against Puritans, Charles raised an army without their consent. He marched to the Scottish border with his commander the Earl of Stafford, only to get cold feet

---

* the type for sitting on

when he realised the Scots would likely fight back. By 1640 the Scottish Covenanters were confident enough to cross the border themselves and they routed Strafford's army at the Battle of Newburn, occupying much of Northumberland and Durham. In November, Charles was finally forced to reconvene parliament who, having not sat for eleven years, were in no hurry to stand up again. It became known as the Long Parliament.

The Scottish rebellion didn't worry parliament unduly, some of whose leaders, like John Pym, were rumoured to be in secret league with their Presbyterian brethren. But there was trouble in Ireland as well that escalated tensions further. Ireland was divided on religious lines between, on the one hand, the Gaelic Irish and Old English, who were predominantly Catholic; and on the other, the New English settlers who were Protestant. As Lord Deputy of Ireland, Strafford had been confiscating land from the Catholics to give to the New English settlers while at the same time imposing Laudian Anglicanism on the settlers and building up a Catholic army to support the king. As a result, he had become the only man in history to successfully unite the Irish – against himself.

The Long Parliament, meanwhile, had begun impeachment proceedings against Strafford on the grounds that he planned to use the Irish army against them (though, given Strafford's track record, the 350 unarmed Puritan MPs would probably have won). Charles was forced to disband the army through lack of funds, whereupon the Catholic and Protestant Irish reverted to type and began killing each other over the land confiscation. Stories of English settlers being massacred by Gaelic Irish fuelled anti-Catholic sentiment in England while the general breakdown of the king's authority spread to London, where mobs harangued anyone opposing Pym and his parliamentary party.

The Road to Civil War
Under this atmosphere, the Long Parliament continued to press their demands. When Strafford's impeachment trial collapsed due

to lack of evidence, Pym had the Commons declare him guilty anyway with only 59 of the 493 MPs opposing. The House of Lords acquiesced, thanks to 79 of the 124 peers suddenly remembering they couldn't make it to the vote on account of their lawn needing mowing. Charles was too nervous to veto and Strafford was duly beheaded three days later.

Pym and his supporters were not at the stage where they would start to demand the head of the king himself, which was still utterly unthinkable, but such was Charles's anger and distress there was a very real danger his head might fall off on its own accord. After the execution of Strafford, parliament continued to force him into more humiliating concessions. Ship money and other irregular forms of taxation were abolished, as was the infamous Star Chamber. Parliament was required to be summoned at least once every three years and could not be dissolved without its own consent.

The king had little choice but to agree to the demands in order to get funds for the army in Ireland. The Commons, however, distrusted his motivation, still fearing he might use the troops against them. Pym had them pass a Militia Ordinance that would wrest control of the army away from the king. For many this was a step too far, but whatever support Charles might have had vanished with his next move. Under pressure from his wife Henrietta Maria, who warned him 'to pull these rogues out by the ears or never see my face again', Charles demanded the arrest of five MPs, including Pym, on suspicion of collusion with the invading Scots. When parliament refused to hand them over, he marched into the Commons with 400 soldiers to arrest them himself.

It was an unprecedented and shocking act, the first and last time an English monarch, or in fact any sane person, would ever volunteer to go into the House of Commons. It was also fruitless as the five men had had prior word and slipped out by boat as Charles burst in. On his knees, the Speaker of the House refused to tell the king where they had gone, leaving Charles to lament: 'All my birds have flown.'

His move had destroyed his one monarchical trump-card, that he was a bulwark against radicalism and disorder. Parliamentary supporters seized London and Charles was forced to flee north.

The First Civil War

As Charles travelled north, the vast majority of people were praying the dispute would blow over so that the country could go back to being the mild, religiously-confused dysfunctional tyranny they knew and loved. But on August 20, the king raised his standard at Nottingham, an official declaration of war, and both sides began to arm. Parliament had control of London, East Anglia and the south-east, giving them access to England's trade routes, credit supply and navy; while Charles had northern England, Wales and Cornwall, giving him access to a powerful array of seaside views and meat pasties. Frankly, when Charles's royal standard blew over during the first night, it seemed like a pretty clear omen.

Financially, the parliamentarians had a clear long-term advantage, but militarily the two sides were evenly matched. The first pitched battle at Edgehill in October 1642 ended in a draw, and Charles withdrew for the winter to Oxford, which became his base for the rest of the war. Now recruitment began in earnest. The parliamentary army, under the Earl of Essex, became known as the Roundheads, actually a term of abuse alluding to the close-cropped haircuts favoured by fashion-conscious Puritans. The long-haired Royalists, commanded by Charles's dashing nephew Rupert, were called Cavaliers for their fondness for riding horses, generally over the newly-sown crops of peasants.

In the years 1643 to 1645 more than one in ten adult males was in arms and skirmishes were occurring all over the country. The opposing forces were divided into 'associations' whose job was to keep their area clear of enemy troops. Some parts of the country, such as East Anglia and the south coast, saw little fighting; while others, like the Midlands and the Thames valley, were constant war zones. Alliances shifted as commanders switched sides according to circumstance, playing absolute havoc with their soldiers' hair styles, and ordinary folk wailed as occupying forces imposed increasingly heavy taxes on the areas under their control[*].

Large battles were less frequent and often indecisive. By 1644, the Roundheads had realised that neither side had a clear advantage and so, as proper God-fearing Christians, decided they'd better cheat. They negotiated an alliance with the Scots, asking for 20,000 troops in return for £31,000 a month and a promise to abolish bishops in England. The chance to kill lots of English people *and* get paid for it was hardly one the Scots would turn down, and at Marston Moor in July 1644 their help proved decisive. In one of the largest battles ever fought on British soil, 4000 royalists were killed and all their armaments seized, leaving northern England in parliamentary hands.

One man in particular proved his worth in the battle, a certain Cambridge MP by the name of Oliver Cromwell. His 'Ironsides' cavalry regiment smashed into Rupert's men, opening up the battlefield for victory. The thickset Cromwell had had no prior military experience. But he did have a nose like a potato and an uncanny ability to sniff out weaknesses in the enemy's lines. After Marston Moor, he became a key figure in the war. When a subsequent battle ended in stalemate due to a mistake by one of the Roundheads' aristocratic generals, Cromwell fumed about incompetent noble commanders and demanded the creation of a New Model Army composed of around 22,000 professional soldiers.

Over the next winter, the Model Army was glued together with Cromwell as second-in-command and the experienced Lord Thomas Fairfax as commander-in-chief. In June 1645, they

---

[*] One tax was known as the 'scot' and those who dodged it successfully were said to get off 'scot-free'. So there.

destroyed the cavalier army at Naseby, a battle so frantic even Charles himself threatened to get his sword out. After that, the unpaid royal armies began to dissolve into the countryside, leaving Cromwell's paid professionals to clean up one town after another. In June 1646 Oxford itself was captured. Charles travelled in disguise to seek sanctuary at the Scottish camp at Newark, but the Scots' deep-seated loyalty to the parliamentary ideals of giving them loads of money persuaded them to hand him over to the Roundheads. Cromwell's army intercepted him on the journey south and imprisoned him at Hampton Court.

The Second Civil War

With the country exhausted and broken by civil war, it was obviously in everybody's interests to have another one straightaway. In November 1647, Charles escaped from Hampton Court by boat and made it to Carisbrooke Castle on the Isle of Wight. When he began to receive reports of an upsurge in his popularity, probably due to the fact he wasn't doing any actual ruling now, he negotiated an alliance with the Scots for a second civil war, one that this time he was determined to lose a lot quicker. For the promise of, just for a change, the abolition of bishops and big dollops of cash, the Scots invaded once more.

In August 1648, Cromwell's army crushed the invasion at Preston before disposing of smaller royal uprisings around the country. Charles was brought to London where parliament sat down to decide what to do with him. Most MPs would have been content with the king agreeing to constitutional restrictions on his authority, but there was a sizeable radical contingent who argued that one of these constitutional restrictions ought to be not having a head. Cromwell himself was a reluctant supporter of execution, calling it a 'cruel necessity'. In December 1648, the Long Parliament was purged of 370 moderates and royalists, leaving only a 'rump' of 154 radicals chosen by the army.

Charles's trial lasted seven days before he was found guilty of 'treason, blood and mischief'. On 20 January 1649, he was executed outside the Banqueting House in Whitehall. He wore two shirts to prevent himself shivering in the cold lest it be mistaken for cowardice. As Charles's head was severed with a single stroke of the axe, a large groan went up from the crowd, who, frankly, had been hoping for a bit more gory hacking. Cromwell allowed his head to be sewn back on to his body afterwards, but if Charles appreciated the gesture he didn't show it. The Rump Parliament struck the monarch's image from the official seal, abolished the House of Lords and declared a republic. 140 years before the French, the English had had their revolution.

The Commonwealth
After seven years of civil war, England was now under the control of a single, obdurate and fanatically religious leader surrounded by a council of obsequious yes-men. But apart from that things were different from before. For a start, Cromwell had a proper army. His first act as leader was to take his troops to Ireland, where after eight years of religious warring Catholic royalists had gradually taken control. Fuelled by memories of the anti-Protestant massacres of the early 1640s, Cromwell unleashed terror on the emerald isle. Some 80,000 Irish were killed or sent into slavery in the Americas while many more succumbed to famine or plague. Most brutal of all was the siege of the town of Drogheda whose defenders were slaughtered wholesale even after surrendering. The Drogheda commander was beaten to death with his own wooden leg, leaving him with a permanent limp. It is estimated that during the three-year repression the Irish population dropped by as much as 25 percent, and they still haven't forgiven Cromwell to this day.

Meanwhile, across England's northern border the Scots had got confused again and crowned Charles's eighteen year-old son as Charles II. In 1651, they invaded England once more, this time for the cause of royal restoration. Cromwell defeated them promptly at Worcester, where young Charles hid for the night in the branches of an oak tree before fleeing to France disguised as a servant. Thousands of English pubs were later renamed the Royal Oak in honour of the event.

Having put Scotland and Ireland back in their places, Cromwell could now finally turn his attentions to England. Worried that his homeland might be getting nostalgic for the hardships of civil war, Cromwell decided to ensure that peacetime was even worse. Pubs and brothels were closed; sports, games and stage-plays were outlawed; bright clothing and make-up were banned; swearing was criminalised; and adultery was made a capital offence. People grumbled that next they'd be abolishing Christmas, and so Cromwell did that too. It was not popular, and soldiers had to be sent to the streets to sniff out cooking turkeys or geese.

The ideal of parliamentary democracy never quite materialised either. The Rump Parliament was split between rival radical factions, such as the Levellers, the Diggers, the Seekers and the Ranters, who squabbled endlessly over who had the silliest nicknames. The Levellers wanted social equality and the Diggers agrarian communism, while the Ranters wanted nothing at all but were very adept at shouting[*]. There were even Muggletonians who disputed the existence of reason. By 1653, Cromwell had had enough. With the sympathy of every English king in history, except perhaps Charles I, he strode into the Commons and sent the MPs packing, calling them 'mercenary wretches', 'sordid prostitutes' and 'venal slaves'. The MPs were outraged, because no-one had ever accused them of being slaves before, but had little choice but to obey.

Unfortunately, the new parliaments proved no less fractious, and in December 1653 Cromwell agreed to be appointed as Lord Protector with all the powers of a monarch. He divided the country into eleven provinces, each with a major general tasked with enforcing the Puritan laws. For all intents and purposes, England

---

[*] needless to say, the Ranters made the best MPs

became a military state. But it did not stop the spread of political and religious radicalism. New constitutions were drawn up almost daily, and there were even proposals for Cromwell to be made king. The Lord Protector refused the title, but humbly agreed to be addressed as Your Highness and to sit on the throne of Edward the Confessor.

The ancient king, however, soon had his revenge. In 1658, Cromwell died of illness, probably a recurrence of malaria he had contracted on campaign in Ireland. He named his eldest son as successor, forgetting for a second that he was pretending not to be a king. Richard Cromwell, however, did not have the experience, charisma or the gigantic nose to hold together the Protectorate. Within nine months, Cromwell's governor in Scotland had marched south to gain control. Rather than seize power himself, however, he accepted the popular mood that it was time to have a proper incompetent king again. There was only one available, Charles II, who happily signed an agreement to accept the supremacy of parliament and pardon those who had helped to kill his father. He returned from exile in Europe to great rejoicing, accompanied by the old leader of the Roundhead army, Thomas Fairfax.

Charles II: the Merrie Monarch

If England had wanted to find a leader any more different to Oliver Cromwell than Charles II, it would have had to look quite far. Perhaps even as far as France. Debonair, charming and extrovert, the thirty year-old had spent the early part of his exile in the court of Louis XIV, and clearly there was something about the Sun King's lifestyle that had rubbed off. While Cromwell had disapproved of sex and outlawed adultery, Charles seemed determined to take care of the pent-up frustrations of the nation's ladies personally. He had at least seventeen mistresses and fathered fifteen illegitimate children, awarding most of them land and peerages. His most famous mistress, the actress Nell Gwynne, was still in his thoughts on his deathbed, where his last words were a plea to his brother to 'Let not poor Nelly starve.'

His own wife, Catherine of Braganza, was infertile, leaving him without any legitimate heirs, a problem that would haunt the latter part of his reign. But for now, all was fun. Bars, theatres and brothels thrived once more and the 'merrie monarch' wandered the capital's parks with his spaniels, chatting with his people and determined to do anything but actual real work. He had an interest in science, patronising the new Royal Society with its sexy line-up of scholars like Christopher Wren, Isaac Newton, Robert Hooke and Robert Boyle. He even had his own laboratory created, though naturally his main scientific objective was to find a way to stop himself getting syphilis. Popular lore has it that Charles's personal physician, a certain Earl of Condom, offered the most practical solution, consisting of an oiled sheath made from sheep intestine[*].

Even parliament was on the king's side. The strongly-monarchist Commons had the bodies of the regicides, including Cromwell, dug up and hanged to make sure they never banned brothels again. Then they purged the Church of its Puritan clerics, imprisoned nonconformists and restored the Book of Common Prayer, which suddenly seemed as racy as the Kama Sutra. This time, stools remained firmly under bottoms where they belonged. To cap it all, a Stuart king finally won a meaningful battle when England's trade war with Holland, begun under Cromwell, led to the capture of the Dutch colony of New Amsterdam. Charles renamed it New York, after his brother James Duke of York, and Londoners rejoiced that there was finally a place in the world where people even ruder than themselves could live. It was 1665 and everything was swell.

Plague, Fire and Whigs

---

[*] Charles's ancestors in Scotland, of course, already had something similar, except they called it haggis.

Picture the scene. Sewage running in open drains down the streets. Cobbles slimy with dung, slops and garbage. People walking with handkerchiefs pressed to their faces to shield out the stench. Rats, flies and thieves everywhere.

Sadly, however, London was no better 350 years ago. Plague was a fact of life in the unsanitary city with periodic outbreaks throughout the 17th century. But the outbreak in 1665, ultimately Britain's last, dwarfed them all. While the rich fled the city, the poor remained behind, and within a year 100,000 people had died, one in five of the population. Authorities suspected animals might be involved in spreading the disease and ordered cats and dogs to be culled. The rats looked on, trying not to smirk.

By March 1666, the worst was over and people returned to their homes, confident that nothing this bad could possibly happen to the city again. Six months later, it burned down. The cause was a fire in a baker's shop in Pudding Lane near London Bridge, which was quickly spread by strong winds. The Mayor of London dithered in plans to create firebreaks by demolishing adjacent buildings, and after three days almost all the structures within the city walls had been destroyed. The diarist Samuel Pepys called it 'the saddest sight of desolation I ever saw', and this from a man who had his penis cut open to remove gallstones. Amazingly, only six people were said to have died in the fire, though many Catholic French immigrants were attacked as rumours of arson spread. Eventually, they pinned the blame on a simple-minded French watchmaker named Robert Hubert, who claimed to have started the fire under instructions of the pope, a well-known expert on the layout of Pudding Lane bakeries.

Six years into his reign and suddenly the king's life of pleasure and debauchery didn't seem quite so appropriate, even if it helped somewhat to repopulate the capital. When the Dutch sailed up the Thames and brazenly towed away the navy's flagship, Charles's extravagant lifestyle took the blame. A year later, when peace was finally made with Holland, Charles undermined it personally by negotiating a secret deal with his friend Louis XIV to fight the Protestant Dutch in return for French subsidies. This meant the king was siding with Catholics over Protestants, and if there was anything more guaranteed to rile up parliament than that it had not yet been discovered.

From then on, things went rapidly downhill. In 1673, parliament passed the Test Act to bar any Catholic from holding public office. Unfortunately, this included James Duke of York, the next-in-line for the throne, who had converted to Catholicism on the continent in the 1660s. James refused to abjure his faith and made matters worse by marrying the Catholic Mary of Modena after the death of his first wife. If they had a son, England could be returned to Catholicism for good. Appalled by the prospect, parliament went for broke and tried to pass an act preventing the marriage from being consummated, clearly having not yet heard about Charles's novel use for sheep intestines.

Soon, things got so heated that political parties began to emerge. As if already aware of the fundamental principle of democratic politics, even the names of the parties were insults. The MPs who wanted James barred from the throne were branded Whigs after radical Scottish Presbyterians, while their opponents were dubbed Tories after Catholic Irish bandits.

In the turmoil, Charles struggled to remain jovial and, if possible, in bed. A Catholic in his heart, he kept his beliefs to himself and it was this prudence, along with the king's general good-natured tolerance, that helped to prevent the situation spilling into violence. Nevertheless, the winters of 1678 and 1679 saw effigies of the pope being burned in the streets, while the atmosphere in parliament became so whiggishly toxic that Charles decided to rule without it, relying on funds supplied by Louis XIV. In 1683, he and his brother survived an assassination attempt on the way back from racing at Newmarket, where they had been putting Louis's money to good use. But two years later the king died of a stroke at the age of 54. The throne passed to James, but

Charles had long doubted his brother had the political skills to sit on it very long.

James II: Catholics and Bed Pans

In many ways, James should have made a much better king than his brother. Serious-minded if ill-tempered, he was a distinguished soldier and a hard worker, even, unusually for a Stuart, outside the bedroom. The problem was that he was unashamedly Catholic and so was his wife, and James had neither the flexibility nor the nous to see that for a country that now burned effigies of the pope to keep warm at night, this might lead to trouble.

Things went badly from the start. After an armed rebellion by the Protestant Duke of Monmouth was put down, the 'bloody assize' under Judge Jeffreys executed 300 of his supporters and sentenced hundreds more to whipping or transportation. The extremity of the punishments shocked even royalist Tories. But James responded by appointing Catholics to the military, judiciary and privy council to ensure the same kind of treatment for Protestants next time. Parliament's objections to this were heightened by events in France, where Louis XIV had begun a persecution of Protestant Huguenots. The Protestant refugees fled to England in their tens of thousands, telling tales of Catholic atrocities in alluring French accents that you couldn't help but listen to.

James's answer was to issue a Declaration of Indulgence, which promised to tolerate all faiths, Anglican, Catholic and nonconformist alike. The Declaration could have been viewed either as a far-sighted appeal for broad religious freedom or as an excuse to repeal the Test Act and place the country in the clutches of bloodthirsty Catholic tyrants – one's interpretation largely depending on whether you were a modern revisionist historian or a 17th century English person. Unfortunately for James, in 17th century England the latter considerably outnumbered the former. When seven bishops refused to read the indulgence in church,

James had them imprisoned in the Tower, not exactly allaying suspicions.

The only hope for the country was that James and his wife remained childless. If that were the case, the throne would go to James's daughter Mary from his first marriage who, just in case things weren't confusing enough, was not only firmly Protestant but married to one of the great Protestant heroes of Europe, William of Orange. William had spent his entire adult life fighting the Catholic French in his Dutch homeland, promising 'to die in the last ditch' rather than give up the cause. Considering that Holland was basically one big ditch, this was no mean boast. It was Charles II that had persuaded a reluctant James to marry his daughter to William, and now the couple held the hopes of a nation in their union.

Unfortunately, James was still hard at work and in 1688 his efforts finally bore fruit in the form of a baby boy, James Stuart. Under normal circumstances, the birth of a royal child would be, like now, a cause of national celebration, generally to the point of stomach-churning nausea. But the headlines in 1688 were that little Jimmy must have been smuggled into the royal chamber in a warming-pan, a cunning papist plot to take over England by stealth. The whole nation was devastated.

Seven English peers, without the approval of parliament and certainly not of the king, sent a letter to William's court in The Hague, requesting military intervention. Sensing the chance to pull himself out of the ditch at last, William frantically readied preparations for an invasion. He amassed a fleet of 463 ships and 40,000 men, a force three times the size of the Spanish Armada. In November 1688 they set sail across the Channel.

The Bloodless Revolution

James II, determined not to go down without a fight, gathered an army of around 19,000 men on Salisbury Plain and immediately got a very nasty nosebleed. "Bloodless revolution indeed!" he muttered and decided to go back home. In truth, though, nobody argued with his decision. England's towns and navy had already declared for William and James's chief commanders had switched allegiances. Even his own nose was not on his side. He fled Whitehall Palace in the dead of night, dropping the Great Seal into the Thames, as if believing this would somehow shut down the entire government of England. After unfortunate recapture by fishermen off the south coast, he was quietly allowed to escape to France by William, who felt this was easier than executing him or waiting for him to bleed to death from his nostrils.

William entered London to great crowds of people waving orange ribbons, which nicely matched the orange sashes worn by the thousands of Dutch soldiers who marched alongside. If their Protestant saviour was a bit shorter than people had imagined, and a bit more hunched, and surprisingly wheezy and asthmatic, and rather bad-tempered and tetchy, and frankly rubbish at English, that didn't matter. At least he wasn't Catholic, which meant MPs could finally start getting angry about something else for a change. Like the fact they had just allowed their nation to be successfully invaded by a foreign power for the first time since 1066, the same foreign power that England had been at war with three times since the civil war. Or perhaps it was just James II that was angry about that.

Glorious revolution or inglorious invasion, it made no difference. In April 1689, the new royal couple were crowned as William III and Mary II and the nation rejoiced. Parliament moved quickly to ensure that the mood of optimism would be used to usher in a new era of tolerance for people of any belief and creed, just as long as that belief and creed didn't include anything about clerical celibacy, transubstantiation, purgatory etc., which were obviously just satanic. They enshrined these freedoms in a Bill of Rights, which guaranteed the independence of judges and gave parliament the sole right to levy taxes, raise armies and wage wars. Above all, no monarch was permitted to be or to marry a Catholic, a far-sighted decree that to this very day continues to prevent Tony Blair from becoming king.

James II did try to make a brief comeback, landing in Ireland with a force of French troops who were eager to start another vastly amusing English civil war. Irish Catholics joined his cause, and in 1690 James faced William for a final showdown at the Battle of the Boyne. The Dutchman was wounded by a cannonball early in the fight, but eventually his troops won the day. James fled back to France and never returned. William became King Billy, the hero of Irish Orangemen ever since, while James was nicknamed *Seamus an Chaca* by the Irish Catholics he deserted, 'James the Shit'. He died in exile eleven years later, still dreaming of the English throne.

Less Than Bloodless War in Europe

The throne securely in his hands, William could now mold England into being the pure, utopian Protestant paradise he had always dreamed of: that is to say, a giant base for his war with France. He spent as little time in London as possible, whose dirty air aggravated his asthma. Parliament paid for the war begrudgingly until a Scottish banker named William Paterson and an aristocratic statesman Charles Montagu devised a brilliant new method for raising public funds. They called it the Bank of England. The basis of the scheme was that the Bank, a private profit-making corporation, would lend money to the government in return for the right to issue bonds and print money. Investors were sought for the new venture, though many of them understandably cautious about such a novel style of business:

"I'm sorry, did you just say we could *print money*?"

In twelve days the government raised the £1.2 million pounds necessary for the war, and a wondrous new phenomenon came into being: the National Debt.

King William's War ended in stalemate in 1697. Parliament ordered the army to be drastically reduced in size and 80,000 soldiers were demobilised in one turn. Many of them found profitable new careers as highwaymen, who became so common in London that William ordered the first streets to be lit with oil lamps*. Apart from that, however, there wasn't a lot for the king to do except pretend to listen to the Whigs and Tories squabble about whatever it was they liked to squabble about nowadays. His beloved wife Mary, by far the more popular of the royal couple, had died of smallpox in 1694 and everybody was pretty much waiting for the asthmatic Dutch bugger to pass away too. The thick smoke from the new oil lamps would help with a bit of luck.

In 1701, parliament passed the Act of Settlement to prepare for his demise. With Mary having borne no children, the throne would pass to her sister Anne. If Anne died without heirs, and after eighteen miscarriages and infant deaths, that seemed rather likely, it would go to the only Protestant candidates available, the House of Hanover, distantly related through marriage to James I's daughter Anne.

In 1702, the king did indeed meet his demise. In the end it was not the oil lamps that did for William but a mole-hill in Richmond Park that tripped up his horse. The king broke his collar bone which led to a fatal bout of pneumonia. He was buried in Westminster Abbey next to his wife, finally achieving his lifetime's ambition of ending his days in a ditch.

Queen Anne: Less Charismatic than Furniture

Anne was 37 years-old when she inherited the kingdom, and it was fair to say she had seen better days. Plagued by ill-health and afflicted by gout, she had become so obese she literally had to carried into meetings. The main problem with her sitting on the throne of England was that there was a very good chance she might

---

* Actually just one street, which happened to be the one he used a lot between St James's Palace and Kensington Palace.

break it. It was not fair to say that she disliked the responsibilities of being queen. But, if given the choice, she would have preferred to just drink tea; or brandy when nobody was looking. Supportive of the Tories and disdainful of the Whigs, she generally left the business of government to moderates like John Churchill, the Earl of Marlborough. She herself spent much of her time with her formidable best friend Sarah, the Earl's wife.

Two major events dominated Anne's reign. One of them was a senseless act of cruelty that brought untold misery to millions of innocent people for centuries to come, while the other *wasn't* union with Scotland. The formal joining in holy matrimony of the nations of England and Scotland was ratified in 1707, the culmination of several years of hard negotiations enthusiastically supported by everyone except the English and the Scots. Daniel Defoe, of *Robinson Crusoe* fame, estimated that for every Scot in favour of the union there were 99 against, though it's conceivable the one Scot in favour was already planning to maroon himself on a desert island. Anne, however, was fervently supportive, possibly because she was running out of people willing to carry her, and eventually bribery and threats succeeded in persuading the Scottish parliament to vote itself out of existence. 45 Scottish MPs were invited to sit in the parliament of the Kingdom of Great Britain, free to make their voices heard, if not very clearly understood, in the new nation.

The second event of Anne's reign was a massive eleven-year war with France, an extremely important and necessary conflict in the sense that Britain won. The cause, as if one was necessary, was the issue of the Spanish succession. The Spanish king had died without an heir and, having not had a war for almost an entire week, the Bourbon king Louis XIV had decided to claim the throne for his grandson Philip. The thought of having Bourbons in charge of both France and Spain, creating a kind of Catholic super-biscuit covering the entire continent, was more than the Protestant nations could bear. For once Anne was in full agreement with the Whigs that Britain had to lead the charge, and in a scene that must have resembled Jabba the Hutt assembling his bounty hunters, she gathered her generals together and sent them off to war.

They were led by her favourite John Churchill, fortunately the most skillful military commander of his day. In 1704 he defeated the French at Blenheim on the Danube, earning himself a dukedom and enough land to build Blenheim Palace, the birthplace of his descendent Winston. Then in 1709 he defeated them again at Malplaquet near Mons. Unfortunately, by then the nation was getting tired of war, even one they were winning, and the 20,000 allied casualties suffered at Malplaquet turned public opinion toward peace. In the 1710 election, the Whigs were trounced by the anti-war Tories and Churchill lost his place. By 1713 peace had finally been negotiated. Britain gained French territories in the Americas and a small strategically-placed rock called Gibraltar populated mainly by monkeys. Crucially, it marked the end of French power, at least until Napoleon, and the beginning of British dominance in Europe. And that, of course, was the most glorious revolution of all.

8. REVOLUTIONS (1714 - 1815)

The end of the Stuart dynasty and the coming of the nondescript Hanovers marked the end of Britain's obsession with kings and queens. From now on, monarchs kept their heads but used them very little. This, of course, created a major problem for historians, who suddenly had to come up with much more imaginative titles for their books. For the period from 1714 to 1815, most went for *Revolution* because this seemed certain to sell the most copies. There were agrarian revolutions, scientific revolutions, financial revolutions, industrial revolutions and political revolutions, sometimes all at the same time. Instead of monarchs like Henry VIII and Elizabeth I, there were people like Robert Walpole, William Pitt, Robert Clive, James Watt and Adam Smith, who together helped to turn Britain into the modern democratic corporate elitist nightmare we know today. We owe each and every one of them.

George I and the Hanovers

There were as many as 55 other people with a stronger claim to the English throne than George I, but unfortunately they all happened to be at mass when the Whigs popped round to ask them. The single Protestant candidate, 54 year-old Prince George of Hanover, spoke no English and openly disliked England. He had distinguished himself in his life so far by keeping his wife imprisoned in a German castle for having had an affair with a courtier. The courtier himself, meanwhile, was rumoured to be buried somewhere beneath the palace floorboards, having been quietly murdered and dismembered. As for George himself, he openly kept two mistresses, one fat and one thin who were nicknamed the Elephant and the Maypole. All in all, then, the Whigs were perfectly satisfied with their choice.

There was only one thing the Hanovers hated more than England, and that was their own family, understandably perhaps. George I quarrelled endlessly with his son the future George II, who in turn hated his son so much he literally couldn't stand to be in the same room as him. The only Hanover who didn't turn out to hate his children was George III, but this was because he was mad. Now these bad-tempered aristocrats, accompanied by a court full of Germans with 'names like a bad cough', were the kings of England. The Stuart kings had caused trouble by claiming they ruled through divine right; the Hanovers couldn't even be bothered to make the pretence.

When George I arrived on English shores, the kingdom was still not as secure as it appeared. In 1715, the Old Pretender James Stuart inspired a revolt from Scotland, determined not to let bedpans be the only thing he was remembered for. He got as far as Dundee before he remembered how cold it was in Scotland and fled back to France, ill with fever. The insurgents who had fought on his behalf were defeated by a government army and that was that. Most of the rebels were eventually granted pardons, the notable exception being the famous Scottish outlaw Rob Roy MacGregor who escaped to his highland home in Inverlochlarig Beag on the Braes of Balquihidder, which the English could not even pronounce let alone find.

The Agrarian Revolution

As the political revolutions of the last century began to die away, a revolution of another kind had been quietly taking place in the British countryside. Since the end of the previous century, new agricultural techniques had begun to significantly increase the productivity of the land. Chief among them was the discovery that, instead of leaving one third of the land fallow each year to regain its fertility – the medieval system of three field crop rotation – the same effect could be achieved by planting turnips on the unused land instead. Britain's Secretary of State, nicknamed Turnip

Townsend, encouraged the introduction of the new four crop rotation across the land.

Britain led the way in the agrarian revolution, being one of the only countries in Europe that considered turnips to be actual edible food. In 1701, Jethro Tull invented a horse-drawn seed drill that planted seeds evenly and straight, allowing farmers to finally achieve their long-held dreams of working while drunk. Meanwhile, people whose names didn't get used for progressive rock bands developed manouverable ploughs that could be pulled by fewer horses than before. This created a social revolution of sorts as well. As fewer hands were required to work the land, women gradually ceased to labour in the fields alongside the men, moving into more domestic roles inside the home.

Further economic progress was brought about when parliament passed the first Turnpike Act in 1706. The Turnpike Act permitted the introduction of a toll on a section of the main road between London and Chester (the old Watling Street). It was followed by a series of further turnpike applications from businessmen around the country, which turned roads that had once been free into profitable money-making ventures. Despite the widespread unpopularity of the tolls, the money was used both to improve old roads and construct new ones, vastly improving travel times to and from London, at least for those who could afford it. Stagecoach companies established regular routes with timetables, giving dashing highwaymen like Dick Turpin a proper amount of planning time for arranging an ambush[*]. Just as importantly, the roads also facilitated the transport of surplus foods around the country, creating a national market that allowed people even in remote towns to enjoy the delights of British food whenever they wanted.

---

[*] The Dick Turpin legend did not become famous until a novel written 100 years after his death. In real life he was rubbish, executed by hanging just four years after he got started.

The South Sea Bubble

With a booming agricultural economy, a stable political order and a king who spent as much time as possible out of the country, Britain was in very real danger of becoming a half-decent place to live. Clearly somebody needed to step in before it was too late. Fortunately, help was at hand from a group of people who could be trusted to single-handedly turn any positive situation into a national catastrophe. These people were, of course, bankers.

The problem the bankers aimed to exploit was the national debt which, thanks to the War of the Spanish Succession, had ballooned to over £50 million. The Bank of England, despite enterprising schemes like the first national lottery, had not been servicing this debt effectively enough, leaving the cash-strapped government with two possible solutions. They could either engage in careful fiscal restructuring aimed at eliminating waste and curtailing rampant government corruption, or they could....

"What was that you said? Rampant government corruption? Yes, let's do that!"

The scheme was this. Create a new company called the South Sea Company and grant it a monopoly on some future but as yet non-existent trade to South America. Force all holders of government debt to surrender it to the new company in return for shares. Buy shares yourself and convince everyone that the company is bound to make massive profits just as soon as Spain agrees to give up all its trading posts in South America and hand them to Britain, which it definitely will do, honestly, because the Spanish are really charitable like that, being Catholics and everything. Bribe any politician who might notice you're lying out of your bottom. Quickly sell your shares before everybody else realises you're lying out of your bottom too.

For eight months it was wildly successful. From January to August 1720, the share price of the South Sea Company skyrocketed from £100 to £1000. Everybody who was anybody and quite a few people who were nobody bought into it, up to and including the Elephant and the Maypole. Other investment opportunities sprung up in its wake – for square cannon balls, for wheels of perpetual motion and, most enticing of all, 'for carrying on an undertaking of great advantage, but nobody to know what it is'. All found willing investors.

Then in September the bubble burst and the shares became worthless. Thousands were ruined overnight and the nation was shell-shocked. The postmaster general committed suicide, the chancellor of the exchequer was thrown into prison and the leader of the House of Lords had a stroke. It was proposed that the bankers who had profited from the scheme be tied up in sacks filled with snakes, until people decided it would be cruel to the snakes. Everybody was extremely contrite and sorry about the whole affair and swore that in the unlikely event of anything like this ever happening again, they would definitely find someone else to blame next time.

The Rise of Robert Walpole

Robert Walpole, an earthy Norfolk landowner, had been a prominent Whig politician since 1701. He had managed to escape being tainted by the South Sea Bubble scandal, despite being friends with most of its prominent backers and selling his own shares for 1000% profit. In fact, the only thing that definitively connected Walpole to a bubble was that he looked like one. A hard drinker and a proficient eater, he was a rotund twenty stone with jowls bigger than most countries' national debts. In 1721, with most of his senior colleagues either in disgrace or in prison, he became First Lord of the Treasury, soon acquiring the title 'prime minister' and a house in Downing Street with a black door just large enough to fit his belly through.

Walpole's political motto was 'Let sleeping dogs lie', and if that failed he just bought the dogs off with money from the Civil List. He trod a moderate path between the more extreme Whigs and Tories, a 'Third Way' if you like, seizing the electoral 'Middle Ground'. Unlike later Third Way prime ministers, however, Walpole thought it preferable to avoid wars rather than start them. In 1734 he boasted, 'There are 50,000 men slain this year in Europe, and not one of them British.' With George I speaking no English and Walpole speaking no German, the prime minister communicated with his king in Latin, a good way of ensuring the monarch didn't pry too closely into the nation's affairs.

Free from war, the national debt was gradually brought under control and Britain felt relaxed enough to have another mini-golden age, its first since Good Queen Bess. Instead of Shakespeare and Marlowe, there was the wit of Swift, Johnson and Pope. Jonathan Swift, an Anglo-Irish satirist and pamphleteer, published works such as *Gulliver's Travels*, and, even better, *A Modest Proposal for Preventing the Children of Poor People in Ireland Being a Burden on Their Parents or Country*, in which he recommended that impoverished Irish parents sell their children to the rich as food. Samuel Johnson, meanwhile, laboured for nine years over his Dictionary of the English Language, at least two of which he wasted trying to think up a witty definition for the word 'lexicographer'[*]. Finally, Alexander Pope, certainly not the greatest name to have as a Roman Catholic in Britain, gained fame and riches as a poet and satirist despite his religion, celebrated for his translation of Homer and his own works like *The Rape of the Lock*.

The esoteric wit of London's intellectual elite would have gone over the heads of the majority of the city's poor, working-class inhabitants. Fortunately, however, the illiterate masses of this period were the perfect comedy audience in that they were, more or less permanently, smashed out of their heads. The reason was the proliferation of cheap domestic gin. In the 1720s, there was one

---

[*] He came up with 'A writer of dictionaries, a harmless drudge', which was okay but not great.

gin shop for every eleven houses and you could quite easily drink yourself to death on a few hours' wages. Women fell prey as much as men, leading gin to become known as Mother's Ruin. In 1736, parliament finally got around to forcing up prices through tax and licenses. But though consumption was curbed, that did not stop enterprising bootleggers swapping juniper berries for cheaper ingredients like turpentine and sulphuric acid. It wasn't too bad if you added enough lime.

The Fall of Robert Walpole

Robert Walpole remained in power throughout the 1730s, even as people gradually began to sober up and realise that most of the nation's surplus food production had ended up around the prime minister's waistline. He survived the death of George I in 1727 and, after initial tension, persuaded his successor George II to reappoint him. The new king ruled much like his father. Later in his reign, he boasted that he had never exceeded his constitutional limits as monarch; but since he spent half of his time in Hanover and the rest of the time in bed with his mistresses, this was not as impressive as it sounded.

By 1741, Walpole had been in power for twenty years, destined to be the longest-serving prime minister in history. His time, however, was about to run out. The cause was war with Spain. It was precisely the kind of foolhardiness that Walpole had spent his entire career trying to avoid, knowing it could lead only to national catastrophes, like him losing power. In the 1730s, British shipping had been plagued by Spanish pirates, an intolerable affront to international trade now that the best 18th century British pirates, like Blackbeard and Anne Bonny, were dead. The final straw was reached when a sea captain named Robert Jenkins had his ear cut off by a Spanish patrol officer, who had accused him of smuggling. The severed organ was passed around parliament as proof of the dastardly deed. When a brilliant young orator named William Pitt made an impassioned speech calling for war, it was the kind of moment every MP had dreamed of: " *'ear 'ear!*" For the horrified Walpole, the only consolation could have been that at least Jenkins hadn't been castrated instead.

The War of Jenkins' Ear drew Britain into a protracted naval conflict with Spain and France. The new-found patriotic fervour gave rise to the anthem *Rule Britannia*, which was more a prediction for the future than a fact of the time. Walpole found the whole thing distasteful and it was no surprise when he lost a no-confidence vote in 1742. He retired to his manor house in Norfolk to spend more time with his magnificent collection of art, accumulated, of course, without any recourse to political bribery or corruption.

Bonnie Prince Charlie

As the war in Europe widened into the messy War of the Austrian Succession triggered by an invasion of Silesia by Prussia, France saw an opportunity to remind people that while British ships might be ruling the waves, Hadrian's Wall had seen much better days. In 1745, they sponsored James Stuart's son Charles, aka the Young Pretender or Bonnie Prince Charlie, to land in Scotland in order to retake the English throne. The Scottish highlanders, still somehow convinced that effete Stuart princes born and raised in France also drank Irn-Bru for breakfast, rallied to his cause. Most English troops were busy fighting a proper war in Europe and the Jacobite army was able to march south unopposed. They were heartened by cheering in Carlisle and Manchester until they suddenly realised that all the hurrahs were being shouted in thick Scottish accents by men in tartan skirts. The English locals, frankly, were a bit perplexed by the whole thing.

By the time they reached Derby, with no sign of the French reinforcements that had been promised, the rebels were beginning to fear that eventually somebody in London might notice them. And indeed, in a bit of a panic, the government finally raised an army under George II's third son the Duke of Cumberland. Now, at last, Charles was able to show the benefit of his French upbringing because, although he had not been much good at invading, he was extremely skilled at running away. The rebels made it all the way back to Inverness before Cumberland caught up with them at Culloden, the last battle ever fought on British soil. Charles fled the battlefield in fear, reaching France via the Isle of Skye, while his highland supporters fought like madmen, the only way they knew how.

Cumberland was ruthless in the aftermath. Over a hundred rebels were executed and many more were transported to the Americas; the highlanders, meanwhile, were stripped of their feudal clan rights, forbidden from carrying ceremonial swords or wearing traditional tartan. Cumberland was nicknamed the Butcher, but the truth was that most people in both England and Scotland were relieved the whole Jacobite affair was over. In fact, the only thing they really came to regret about Cumberland's reprisals was that he didn't ban bagpipes as well.

The Seven Years' War and the Expansion of British Power

With Bonnie Prince Charlie back in the safety of his wine cellar, Britain returned to the European free-for-all sparked by the ambitions of Frederick the Great of Prussia. Britain allied herself with Prussia against the coalition of France, Spain and Russia, but her strategy was to leave the land war to the Prussians while she used her navy to attack the coalition's colonial possessions in North America, Africa and India. This gave rise to the first truly global conflict, the Seven Years' War from 1756-63.

The British strategy was directed by the new prime minister William Pitt the Elder. Pitt was a Whig like Walpole, but there the similarities ended. Walpole had been an Establishment man, a careful and conservative administrator of the public purse. Pitt, however, was a man of the people, aggressive and brilliant in foreign policy but so ill-suited to domestic affairs he didn't even take bribes. He was carried to power by pro-war sentiment after the

French seizure of Minorca in 1756, because there was nothing more glorious than a good foreign war that was nice and faraway.

The conquest of India was propagated less by the British government than by the East India Company, which had decided that trade would be a lot more profitable if they could get their hands on everything for free. Since the 16th century, India had been dominated by the Mogul empire, enlightened Mongols who had dropped the letter 'n' along with other traditional Mongol practices like eye-gouging. The decline of Mogul power in the 18th century, however, had seen them cede more and more territory to the British and French trading companies.

The rival companies, backed up by government armies, regularly came to blows over which of them had the right to exploit the Indians the most. In 1756, the French encouraged the Nawab of Bengal to seize the British trading post in Calcutta. This dastardly act was made even more dastardly when as many as 123 civilians and soldiers suffocated in a basement where they were being held prisoner overnight. The 'black hole of Calcutta' aroused fury back home, but revenge was soon at hand through a certain Robert Clive, aka Clive of India.

A young tearaway from Shropshire, Clive had joined the East India Company to seek adventure, realising that Clive of Market Drayton would never have the same historical ring to it. He began as a humble clerk but soon found he was more suited to conquering than counting. By 1756 he had reached the rank of lieutenant-colonel and was given charge of a small force of 3,200 troops to re-take Calcutta. He was faced by the Nawab's far greater army of 40,000 at Plessey, but thanks to the innate superiority of the white man, in the sense that his cannons worked and the Nawab's malfunctioned, he won the battle with minimal casualties. Clive went on to lead the company to victories throughout India until by 1759 Calcutta, Madras and Bombay were all in British hands.

Meanwhile, on the American continent, things were also going quite well for Britain. Skirmishes had been continuing since 1754 when a certain young officer in the British army named George Washington had been gaining valuable experience in the business of overthrowing major colonial powers by launching assaults on French forts in Ohio. Pitt expanded the conflict with attacks on French positions from Canada to Mississippi. By 1759, Britain had taken control of virtually the entire American continent. War continued in less frantic fashion until 1763. In that year, the Treaty of Paris was signed, confirming many of Britain's wartime gains and making her officially the top dog of Europe. By this time Pitt had lost his position, disliked by the new king George III. He returned to power briefly in 1766 as the king's abortive attempt to take more personal control of Britain's affairs led to political chaos. But the great populist was gout-ridden and depressed and refused to even leave his room to speak to people, not an ideal quality for a prime minister unless you're Theresa May. He resigned in 1768, eventually finding a comfortable home in the House of Lords where being gout-ridden and decrepit was the primary qualification.

Trouble in the Colonies

At the end of the Seven Years' War, Britain expected the thirteen colonies to be grateful. After all, her redcoat soldiers had just driven the French out of the continent, freeing the British settlers from potentially centuries of French ridicule about their food and dress sense. As it turned out, however, the French had never been the colonists' chief concern. That was the American Indians who still maintained a fanciful idea that they had a right to live in their own country. Thus, in 1765 when the British demanded that the colonies help pay the mother country's war debts in the form of a direct Stamp Tax, the Americans refused, arguing there should be 'no tax without representation'.

Reluctantly, the British repealed the Stamp Tax and replaced it with duties on imported corn, paper and tea, which were not unlike the custom duties the settlers had been paying for decades. But by now the Americans had decided that, on the whole, they'd rather not pay any British taxes at all, thank you very much. When the redcoats put on a show of force in the most troublesome province of Massachusetts in 1770, riots broke out in Boston and five settlers were killed. The colonists, having long ago lost the British art of understatement, called it the Boston Massacre.

As tensions rose further, the British repealed all the duties except the one on tea, because cheap caffeine was clearly the last thing the settlers needed right now. The East India Company, however, was exempted from the tax, leading rival American tea merchants to dress up as Indians* and throw the tea into Boston harbour. Now the British government was outraged and they hit back with the Coercive Acts which closed Boston harbour and increased the powers of the royal governor.

In 1774, the colonists called together a congress in Philadelphia to discuss the matter in the kind of calm and dignified manner Americans are renowned for. They demanded a repeal of all duties and issued a Declaration of Rights and Grievances, asserting the right to decide their own taxes. When the British rejected their demands, the more radical delegates, who called themselves Patriots, set up local militia known as minutemen who would be ready to take up arms at a minute's notice. It was an accident waiting to happen.

The War of Independence

In April 1775, the Massachusetts governor made an attempt to capture militia bases at Lexington and Concord. The minutemen, however, were warned of the redcoats' approach by the midnight ride of Paul Revere, a silversmith who bore an uncanny resemblance to the actor Jack Black*. Both sides were wary of commencing hostilities, but when an unknown soldier fired the 'shot heard round the world' the conflict began. The Philadelphia

---

* because why the hell not?
* really

delegates gathered again, in more belligerent mood this time, and on 4 July 1776 Thomas Jefferson published the Declaration of Independence in which he declared that all men were endowed with the inalienable right to pursue life, liberty and happiness – unless of course they happened to be his own plantation slaves in which case they mainly pursued tobacco plants.

In Britain, there were mixed opinions. Finding his voice once more, William Pitt the Extremely Elderly denounced the futility of a war that could not be won. But George III and his ineffectual Tory prime minister Lord North refused to countenance the idea of losing the colonies. The king was the first of the Hanovers to consider himself fully British, but in his periodic bouts of mental illness that caused him to foam at the mouth and shout incomprehensibly you could have sworn he was still German.

The British army was better trained and better equipped than the American militias. But they were stretched thin across the globe and had to rely on mercenaries from Germany as well as Loyalists from within the colonies. The Patriots, meanwhile, had more men and after 1777 the support of the French navy, who, in declaring war on Britain, were pursuing happiness again for the first time since 1763. For five years the war was fought up and down the east coast with the Americans gradually gaining the upper hand. In 1781, a combined French and American army attacked the major British fortress at Yorktown, Virginia. With the French navy cutting off retreat by the sea, the British general, Charles Cornwallis, was forced to surrender his army to the American commander George Washington.

Back home, the news was greeted with despair. The king and his prime minister vowed to continue the war, but after further reverses in 1782 it was clear the game was up. The following year, a treaty was signed in Paris granting the Americans full independence. Lord North lost a no-confidence vote in the Commons and the Whigs returned to power.

Pitt the Younger and the French Revolution

George III, his bouts of mental illness growing more frequent, looked around for a politician he didn't completely despise to be his new prime minister. The obvious candidate was the hard-drinking, hard-living Charles James Fox, a huge political figure[*] who championed far-sighted causes like civil rights, Catholic emancipation and the abolition of slavery. Naturally George III hated him most of all and so he was left with William Pitt the Younger, the 24 year-old son of, well, his father, who had already displayed great leadership ability in his school's nativity play.

Pitt was ridiculed for his youth and, like a war with Germany, people predicted his administration would be over by Christmas. But he was to remain in power for the next seventeen years, a brilliant administrator and skillful politician who regarded himself as both Whig and Tory – a Whory if you like, willing to go to bed with either. He was not always the most popular figure amongst the common people, a man of little charisma who exuded an air of superiority. Never marrying but with no known male lovers, he seems to have been asexual, like a very politically ambitious amoeba. But he proved to be exactly what the nation needed over the next tumultuous years, becoming what Lord Minto called 'the Atlas of our reeling globe' and one of Britain's greatest ever prime ministers.

Pitt's first major challenge, other than avoiding a steady stream of awkward marriage proposals, was the French Revolution. By 1789, decades of foreign wars had coupled with crippling food prices and massive expenditure on powdered wigs to leave France broke, starving and thoroughly discontent. Louis XVI's attempts to solve the crisis only made things worse, and on 14 July massive riots broke out in Paris. Angry crowds seized the Bastille in search of weapons, and the military hero General Lafayette, who had once fought alongside George Washington, seized control. Suddenly

---

[*] in the Walpolian sense of the term

France had a revolution on its hands.

In Britain, the reaction to events across the Channel was a mixture of shock and barely disguised glee. At last their Gallic neighbours were curbing the powers of the hated, war-mongering Bourbons and waking up to the kind of democracy that Britain had enjoyed for so long, a democracy in which any free-thinking aristocratic male landowner had the absolute freedom to vote any other aristocratic male landowner into power. Pitt forecast fifteen years of peace in Europe.

In 1793, however, things began to change colour. As the revolution descended into the Terror, republicans like Robespierre began to impose mad schemes like universal male suffrage, while the last sight French aristocrats had of their precious powdered wigs was of them falling into the basket beneath the guillotine. Pitt the Younger had begun his premiership as a liberal, but now that the French idea of liberty involved freeing people from their own heads, he wanted no part of it.

To make matters worse, just one year after the prime minister's optimistic prediction of peace, French armies marched across their borders once more, vowing to dispose of every monarchy in Europe. Although it was hard to imagine that George III losing his head would make much of a difference to his decision-making, it was a war that Britain could not afford to stay out of. The Royal Navy was duly dispatched, with their star officer Horatio Nelson commanding vital battles at Corsica, Cape St Vincent and Santa Cruz de Tenerife and only losing an eye and an arm in the process.

In Britain, meanwhile, Pitt imposed a raft of oppressive measures against freedom of speech, suspending habeas corpus and outlawing public meetings. Three radical speakers were tried for treason, for which the penalty was still to be hung, drawn and quartered. Their eventual acquittal by jury brought much public rejoicing and a clamour of support for Charles Fox in his denouncement of 'Pitt's Terror'.

Irish Rebellion and the Act of Union

The French Revolution also had repercussions across the Irish Sea, inspiring a wide scale uprising against British rule. Although Ireland had its own parliament, controlled by minority Anglican Protestants who denied the majority Catholics the vote, its rulings could be vetoed by London, giving it less autonomy than the whiny American colonies before the revolution. In 1798, a rebellion was organised by the Society of United Irishmen[*], an originally Protestant movement whose twin objectives of Irish independence and Catholic emancipation had given it broad appeal across religious lines.

Fearing an alliance between the Catholic Irish and the revolutionary French, the British response was swift and brutal. Aiming to drive a wedge between the Protestants and Catholics, they enlisted the support of the extremist Orange Order, whose general view of Catholics was that they deserved to go to heaven a little sooner than they might have planned. It was hardly a fair fight. In a series of one-sided battles, the British routed the Irish rebels, killing up to 30,000 in a matter of months. At the infamous Battle of Vinegar Hill, they went on a rampage of rape and murder, burning eighty rebels alive when they set fire to a casualty station.

"Now *that*, Yankees, is a fecking massacre," the Irish might have said.

In London, Pitt sought a long-term solution. For many in the establishment, the Irish Question had already become a hot potato. The spread of that nutritional little vegetable, allied with the traditional Catholic approach to birth control, had swelled the Irish population to almost five million, over half that of England and Wales and not much less than the population today. If Wales and Scotland had been allowed into the union, why not Ireland?

"Because it's full of potato-eating papists, that's why!"

---

[*] sworn enemies, of course, of the United Society of Irishmen and the Irish United Society

thundered George III in a moment of clarity. He was strictly an English turnip man.

He was not the only opponent. In 1780, London had seen huge riots break out over proposals to ease discrimination against Catholics in Britain, so the idea of allowing millions of them into the union was anathema to many. Pitt, however, was a strong proponent and in 1800 the Act of Union was finally signed. The diagonal cross of St Patrick was added to the flag, with only the Welsh dragon left out in the cold. George III and his supporters, however, still refused to allow Irish Catholics the vote, making the reform all but meaningless. Pitt resigned in protest and the Irish settled down to hate the English ever after.

The Napoleonic Wars

Few people could have seen the coming of the humble young officer from Corsica. But then at five feet two inches tall, Napoleon Bonaparte tended to pass beneath the eye line[*]. He had distinguished himself in several daring raids during the revolutionary wars, and by 1796 had been appointed commander of the army in Italy at the age of 28. His subsequent success in Italy made him a national hero to the extent that the French foreign minister Talleyrand feared a military coup if he was allowed to return to Paris. Instead he sent the ambitious general to Egypt to attack British interests in the Mediterranean. There, however, he came up against the British hero Nelson, who showed he could beat the best the French could offer with only one eye and one arm. Nelson's victory at the Nile sent Napoleon scurrying back to Paris where, in 1799, he staged the coup Talleyrand had feared.

In 1802, after years of stalemate, a truce was signed. However, two years later Napoleon brought the pope to Paris to have himself

---

[*] Actually the truth is that Napoleon was not that short. The French inch was slightly longer than the English one; in English measurement he was more like five foot six, average for the period. But for God's sake, don't let the French know that. It'd spoil everything.

crowned Emperor of France. It was a scene captured in a famous painting by Jacques-Louis David.

"Emperor Bonaparte, stand to receive your crown," intoned Pope Pius VII gravely.

"I am standing."

Napoleon ended up crowning himself to avoid being subject to papal authority, and quickly readied an invasion force for Britain. Pitt was recalled to government and instituted an income tax, in part to pay for a series of defensive Martello towers on the south coast. But Britain's best defence was still Horatio Nelson. In October 1805, he cornered the French fleet at Cape Trafalgar near Cadiz. Slicing through the French line, he destroyed 22 of the 33 enemy ships while losing not a single one of his own. It came at the cost, however, of the admiral's life. A musket ball from a French sharpshooter hit his shoulder and went through his spine. As he lay dying on the lower decks, he sneaked in a quick kiss on the forehead from Captain Hardy before issuing his famous last words, "Thank God, I have done my duty. Now give me a bit of tongue with the next one, Hardy."

Napoleon's invasion plans were foiled. However, on land he continued to sweep all before him. Six weeks after Trafalgar, he destroyed the combined forces of Austria and Russia at the Battle of Austerlitz, giving him a free path eastwards. As Napoleon commissioned the Arc de Triomphe to celebrate in typically modest fashion, Pitt died of exhaustion and despair, sure that the battle for Europe was lost. He was just 46, but Pitt had always been a bit premature. His death left two leading Tories, George Canning and Lord Castlereagh, feuding over power. So intense did their rivalry become that it culminated in a duel on Putney Heath. Canning, who had never fired a pistol, shot wide before Castlereagh hit him in the thigh. Both men were forced to resign, leaving one of Pitt's followers Spencer Perceval to take over. Two years later, Perceval was shot to death in the House of Commons by a crazed merchant with a grudge against the government. It was another shocking development for the desperate nation, not least because the crazed merchant seemed to be the only man in Britain with decent aim.

By 1812, Napoleon was master of Europe. He had waged a vicious four-year battle with the Spanish, who had relied on new-style guerilla tactics against the superior French forces. His strategy for dealing with Britain, meanwhile, had been to impose the Continental System, a trade blockade that denied outlets for the 'nation of shopkeepers'. Britain regularly confounded the blockade through smuggling, a traditional national strength. But Napoleon's strategy really came unstuck when, suffering economically from the denial of trade, Russia announced its intention to leave the System. An angry Napoleon invaded with 680,000 troops, marching overland through Poland.

This, however, was where the great general's luck finally ended. For what Russia lacked in technology and firepower, she made up for in being really really big and cold. As the Russian armies fled east, they followed a scorched earth policy, burning everything as they went including the capital of Moscow. Supplying his vast army proved impossible and in November 1812, fearing a coup back home, Napoleon made the decision to return to France, travelling on a sleigh like a kind of evil dwarf Santa. His abandoned army succumbed to the vicious Russian winter, and as few as 22,000 soldiers ever made it out.

The little general arrived in Paris to find a welcoming party of enemy forces, except that instead of *Welcome Home, Napoleon!* the banner on the wall read *Welcome to the Obscure Island of Elba!*, accompanied by a helpful world map. Napoleon attempted suicide with a pill he had carried with him in Russia, but the truth was that the allies were being generous. Elba was an island of 12,000 inhabitants just off the Tuscan coast, and not only was Napoleon allowed to live there freely, he was even made the island's ruler[*]. He also kept the title Emperor just in case Elba ever decided to conquer the three big rocks just off its coast.

The Battle of Waterloo

Unfortunately, Emperor of Elba was never going to quite fit the great man's ego. He soon escaped, landing in the south of France with 700 men. His former army officers, having had to endure almost eleven months without starting a war, flocked to his cause and Napoleon entered Paris in triumph. Great Britain, Prussia, Austria and Russia immediately mobilised their armies and Napoleon marched into the Netherlands to cut them off. A combined British and Prussian army met the French at Waterloo, now in Belgium, on 18 June 1815.

The British troops were commanded by the Duke of Wellington, a renowned general who had one of the most successful battle records in the history of British warfare, as well as the best pair of boots. Born as plain old Arthur Wellesley in a minor Protestant Irish family, he had risen steadily through the ranks despite constant ridicule for his Irish roots. By 1813 he had been named Field Marshall and awarded a dukedom for his efforts in the war against Napoleon. His skill as a general lay primarily in his defensive tactics, which he used with great effect to defeat numerically superior forces.

At Waterloo, it was these tactics that came to the fore. Somewhat ill-equipped and comprising surprisingly few veterans, Wellington's force of 70,000 British, Irish and Dutch soldiers had to fend off repeated French attacks throughout the day, and it was only the belated arrival of 48,000 Prussian troops that finally turned the tide his way. As the French fled the battlefield, Wellington was left to reflect on what he called 'the nearest run thing you ever saw in your life'. Napoleon, opinion in France having turned against him, appealed for asylum to the British,

---

[*] prompting an immediate demand for 12,000 Russian suicide pills

somehow forgetting he'd spent the past ten years trying to starve them all to death. His appeal only earned himself exile once more, this time to the dismal island of St Helena in the Atlantic Ocean. He died cold and wet six years later, his last words recorded as 'France, army, head of the army, Josephine', a pretty accurate summation of his life.

Wellington returned to London as a hero to rival even Horatio Nelson. The tight-fitting leather boots to which he gave his name, designed personally by Wellington, became the go-to item for all fashionable dandies, while the general himself settled into a successful political career, twice serving as prime minister.

From Textiles to Railways

What was it about Britain that laid the foundations for the greatest technological advances since the invention of the wheel? Was it her stable political system that kept revolution and unrest at bay? Her growing population and burgeoning trade markets? The ready availability of finance? The determination to get annoying children out of the house and into work?

Whatever the underlying causes, the roots of the industrial revolution lay in what had been a strength of the British economy for almost a thousand years: textiles. Until the 1730s, most cloth was produced in small cottage industries, hand-woven with looms from British wool or American cotton. But between 1733 and 1785 came a series of inventions that made the business of cloth-making far more efficient, taking it out of the home and into an amazing new world of factories, mills and child exploitation. The first invention to make it on the market was John Kay's 'flying shuttle', which allowed threads to be thrown across the loom instead of being passed through by hand. Then James Hargreaves came up with the 'spinning jenny', which could spin sixteen threads at a time. Richard Arkwright took another step forward in 1769 with a water-powered spinning machine. After that, Edmund Cartwright produced the first water-powered loom and then Samuel Compton invented the 'spinning mule', a more efficient hybrid of the other inventions. It was all absolutely fascinating. When James Watt improved on previous designs to produce a working steam engine in 1781, steam began to replace water as the primary mode of power and the industrial revolution was truly on its way. By 1800, over 500 of Watt's machines were in use.

James Watt was a Scot, but most of the early inventors were hardy northern Englishmen, blessed with an innate sense of how to confuse southerners with ridiculous names for their machines. Factories sprouted in the hilly regions of the north where there were plenty of fast-flowing rivers to drive the water wheels, and cities like Manchester, Birmingham, Liverpool, Bradford and Glasgow grew exponentially as families migrated from the countryside in search of new ways to work themselves to death. The industrial machines, and the metallurgical processes developed to construct them, increased the demand for coal, mined in tunnels conveniently large enough for tiny children to crawl through.

Conditions in the mines were horrific, with accidents and gas explosions common even after the invention of the Davy safety lamp in 1816. In the factories, children as young as four were employed, their cheaper wages meaning they often outnumbered adult workers by as many as two to one. Fourteen hour days were commonplace. Mistakes earned the children beatings, particularly when impatient owners were forced to shut off the machines for a few minutes in order to fish out tiny dismembered limbs. The worst-off were the abandoned children and orphans in the workhouses, who laboured virtually as slaves in return for the charitable benefit of not quite starving to death. Epidemics swept through the overcrowded cities, the unsanitary conditions a breeding ground for tuberculosis, cholera and typhoid. Children who managed to contract all three were sometimes granted a few hours off work.

In the 18th century, the plight of workers attracted little comment. After all, life in the countryside had hardly been better with famine and turnips a constant threat. As banks rushed to invest in the new economy, progress continued apace. In 1779, the world's first iron bridge was built across the River Severn in Shropshire to facilitate the transport of coal from the mines, and in 1804 a mining engineer named Richard Trevithick produced the first steam-powered locomotive to run on rails. Some 25 years later, George Stephenson's Rocket arrived on the scene along with the world's first public steam railway. In 1829, the Rocket pulled a line of cars from Liverpool to Manchester in two hours one minute, a time modern rail companies are confident they'll beat any day now[*].

The Scientific Revolution

Back in the Middle Ages, if you were faced with some unexplained natural phenomenon, such as rainfall, earthquakes or the miracle of things falling when you dropped them, there were two possible explanations you could give: (1) It was the work of God, or (2) It was the work of Satan (and / or witches, Jews etc.) Any answer other than these was liable to get you burned at the stake for heresy. From the early 17th century, however, visionaries like Francis Bacon, Rene Descartes, Galileo Galilei and Isaac Newton began to look beyond the divine, seeking answers to their questions through rationalism and the power of scientific thought.

Francis Bacon, a favourite at the court of James I, is today regarded as the father of the scientific method, having championed the cause of scepticism and the deduction of facts from observation. Never afraid to put himself on the line, he died of pneumonia at the age of 65 while studying the effects of freezing upon meat, having seemingly mistaken himself for actual bacon. His admirer Isaac Newton, born around twenty years after Bacon's death, developed a theory of gravity after seeing an apple fall in his garden. He headed up the famed Royal Society in London and left a body of

---

[*] barring unforeseen delays

work of more than ten million words on everything from the movement of the planets to the composition of light.

By the 18th century, scientists in Britain were turning this storied scientific tradition into major advances in physics, chemistry and medicine. Joseph Priestley, Joseph Black and Henry Cavendish identified the different chemicals that make up air and water, allowing Priestley to change the world forever with the first ever fizzy drink. Humphrey Davy, inventor of the safety lamp, discovered that nitrous oxide or 'laughing gas' could be used to put patients to sleep during surgery. William Smellie developed ways to make childbirth safer, and the English physician Edward Jenner introduced the world's first vaccine to protect against smallpox. He is credited with saving more human lives than any person in history.

In other fields, the Scottish philosopher Adam Smith published *The Wealth of Nations* in which he argued that economic prosperity could best be achieved by leaving government to the 'invisible hand' of the free market. In a sign of the changing times, most of these pioneers were born to normal, middle-class families rather than to the aristocracy. Not to be outdone, however, the English nobility also made their own vital contribution to British know-how when John Montagu, the Earl of Sandwich, asked his servant to bring him slivers of meat between two slices of bread to sustain him at the gambling table.

Scientific knowledge was now a thing to be collected and nourished rather than feared and suppressed. As Samuel Johnson laboured over his dictionary, the first edition of the Encyclopedia Britannica was being compiled in Edinburgh. Meanwhile, in 1753 a doctor named Hans Sloane left his vast collection of manuscripts, natural history specimens and scientific instruments to the nation on condition that they be housed inside a public museum. The British Museum, as it became known, soon swelled with exotic plants and historical artifacts from all over the world, thanks to the tireless efforts of British travellers, like Lord Elgin, determined to safeguard the world's treasures from the people who actually owned them.

The Romantic Revolution

Not content with revolutionising the world of science and industry, the British also set about turning the poetry world on its head with the rise of idealistic young tearaways like Percy Shelley, John Keats and Lord Byron. The Romantic poets, so called because of their fierce determination to die before anyone could get bored of them, lived as freely and sensuously as they wrote, equally delighting and horrifying the strait-laced literary society of their day.

Neither Shelley nor Keats achieved fame in their lifetime. Shelley's work was rejected by most publishers due to his public advocacy of radicalism and atheism, views that had led him to be expelled from university at Oxford. A vegetarian, he spoke up for the rights of both the lower classes and animals, dying at the age of 29 in a sailing accident in Italy. His friend Keats, an even more troubled figure, died penniless at the age of 21 from tuberculosis. Tuberculosis, little understood at the time, was believed to be caused by either repressed sexual passion or excessive masturbation, but in Keats's case it was probably both. Shelley himself attributed his friend's death to the consistently terrible reviews his poetry earned. Blackwood's Magazine called one of his poems 'imperturbable drivelling idiocy', a view that sadly won't get you an A* in an English literature exam.

Of the three young men, it was Lord Byron who achieved both the most recognition for his work and the greatest degree of drunken aristocratic debauchery. Constantly in massive debt due to his licentious lifestyle, he had a penchant for both girls and boys at a time when you could be hanged for homosexuality. During his Grand Tour of Europe from 1809 to 1811, *de rigeur* for any young gentleman, he conducted an illicit affair with a fourteen year-old boy in Italy and then attempted to buy a twelve year-old girl from a family in Greece. Despite offering them £500, Byron was unable to persuade the girl's family to sell him their child, leaving him to write the poem *Maid of Athens Ere We Part* as a beautiful heartfelt tribute to his failed attempt at paedophilic slavery. When the poet returned to England, he became a hit at Regency parties in London, enjoying numerous scandalous affairs with high-born ladies, including, most scandalously of all, his own half-sister. In one particularly profitable year, he claimed to have bedded 250 women. One of his conquests, Lady Caroline Lamb, called him 'mad, bad and dangerous to know'. In 1823, tiring of a vacuous life in Italy, he joined the Greek war of independence against the Ottoman Empire. He died a year later from sepsis while being bled for a fever with unsterilised instruments.

Compared to Keats, Shelley and Byron, the other Romantic poets of the age lived longer if not necessarily any less messy lives. William Blake, a poet, painter and printer, is now considered one of Britain's greatest ever artistic figures. At the time, however, he was virtually unknown; those people who did come across his work thought him insane. More successful in commercial terms were the Lake Poets Wordsworth and Coleridge. As an idealistic young man, Wordsworth spent time in France during the Revolution, but by the end of his long life he was part of the literary establishment, serving as Poet Laureate in the seven years before his death. His great friend Samuel Taylor Coleridge had a far more troubled existence, however. A manic depressive, he was a lifelong opium addict whose professional life could be as erratic as it was brilliant. Most distressing for him personally were the regular enemas he had to receive for chronic constipation brought on by the opium. They were 'a pandemonium of shames and miseries', lending new meaning to his famous line in the *Rime of the Ancient Mariner*: 'Water water everywhere, nor any drop to drink'.

Slaves, Convicts and the Lash

Tropical diseases, poisonous snakes, venomous spiders, man-eating crocodiles: Australia had pretty much everything you could want for a successful penal colony. It had been claimed for Britain by the great navigator James Cook during his one of his three voyages to the South Pacific. In his ship the *HMS Endeavour*, Cook landed at Botany Bay in 1770, not the first European or even the first Englishman to set foot on the shores of the great continent but definitely the first to see its potential as a giant human dumping-ground. Within eight years of his discovery, the first boat-loads of prisoners were on their way. The vast majority were petty criminals, victims of the theory that criminality was passed down from generation to generation like a genetic disease or ginger hair. Among the first group was a seventy year-old woman who had stolen cheese to eat, but she soon had plenty of company as 164,000 more men and women arrived over the next sixty years. Those inmates fortunate enough to survive disease, malnutrition and flogging to serve out their sentences remained as settlers, free to pass down their criminal defects to an entire new nation.

Convicts were not the only people being transported on British ships in the 18th century. The trans-Atlantic slave trade thrived from the ports of London, Bristol and Liverpool, with at least three million Africans taken to America and the West Indies by British merchants. It was not until the 1770s that a few good-minded individuals began to think that abducting an entire continent of people, cramming them on boats and then flogging them to death might not actually be what God intended for his creation. The Quakers were the first to campaign for the abolition of slavery, followed by the Abolition Society with William Wilberforce MP as their chief advocate. Wilberforce faced a huge battle in the House of Commons, many of whose members benefitted personally from the huge profits brought by the trade. It was not until 1807 that the slave trade was finally abolished and 1833 before slavery itself was outlawed in all British colonies.

9. EMPIRE, GLORY AND BEARDS (1815 – 1900)

With Napoleon Bonaparte stranded on a windswept island in the middle of the Atlantic Ocean, no doubt feeling smaller than ever, there was only one player left on the world stage. Between the Battle of Waterloo and the First World War, Britain not only ruled the waves, she also ruled Canada, Australia, New Zealand, India, South Africa, Egypt, Nigeria, Kenya, Tanzania, Zimbabwe, Malaysia, Singapore, Hong Kong and quite a few more places besides. Her only real rival in all these years was, of all countries, Russia, which gives you some idea of the scale of the competitive slump. If Britain had only known what was coming up after 1901, she might have tried to enjoy it more. But this was the Victorian era when most people's idea of fun consisted of how much starch they could put into their shirts without snapping them. Politically, it was an era of grimly-conceded reform: electoral reform to extend the vote to people who actually had real jobs; social reform to limit how long children could work before the mine caved in on their heads; and political reform to give the Irish the right to choose whether they would prefer to die from famine or from drowning.

Stirrings of Discontent

Britain did very well out of the demise of the French empire. At the Congress of Vienna in 1815, she helped herself to a slew of fantastic holiday destinations around the world including Tobago, Ceylon, Malta, Mauritius, the Seychelles and Heligoland, which they were disappointed to find was actually in the North Sea. The head of the British delegation, Lord Castlereagh, managed to persuade the allies to pursue a policy of peace with France rather than retribution, putting the Bourbons back on the French throne, which was as much punishment as any nation deserved. The

200,000 British soldiers who had been occupying Paris trudged home.

The soldiers returned to a nation hopelessly divided by wealth and class. In the privileged circles of upper class London, the Regency period was in full swing. Named after the Prince Regent who had assumed responsibilities, in the loosest sense of the term, after his father George III had been diagnosed as mad, it was marked by ostentatious fashions and lavish parties, occasionally attended by people who hadn't slept with Lord Byron. The architect John Nash built Regent Street, Trafalgar Square, Marble Arch and an extension to Buckingham Palace, while the Regent himself, in intensive preparation for his role in *Blackadder III*, made sure the royal finances weren't frittered away on mindless extravagances like war and conquest by spending them on wine, women and card games instead.

Outside of the Prince's exalted circles, however, life was a gamble in a very different sense. In the last century, Britain's population had swelled from five million to more than nine million. By 1825, it was close to twenty million. Thanks to better nutrition and improved medical care, infant deaths were down, longevity was up and fertility rates were through the roof. The return of 200,000 sex-starved soldiers and sailors from France probably didn't help either. Nowhere was this population explosion felt more keenly than in the industrial towns of the north. While the upper classes partied in ornate Regency townhouses, the unwashed masses lived ten to a room in squalid, unsanitary shacks. Sewage ran through the streets outside and smoke from the factories made the skies so black it was hard to know if it was night or day[*].

In 1813, seventeen Luddites were hanged for smashing machines inside the factories. Named after Ned Ludd, an early proponent of the practice, the Luddites had developed into a

---

[*] The general rule of thumb being that if you weren't still at work, it was probably night.

genuine threat to the establishment; at one point more troops were fighting the Luddites in Yorkshire than were fighting Napoleon in Spain, which, again, wouldn't have made Napoleon feel any taller. They did not see themselves as enemies of progress per se, but they had seen how industrialisation had suppressed wages and stripped men of their livelihoods. After all, when you were relying on your six year-old daughter to be the family breadwinner, it had to sting a man's pride.

In London, the Luddite rebellion stoked fears of the kind of revolution that had torn apart France a generation earlier. The Luddites might hate technology, but they could probably work out how to use a guillotine. The prime minister in this difficult period was Lord Liverpool, the 'lord' part of whose title was a much closer match to his politics than the 'Liverpool' bit. He was a conservative aristocratic landowner, who had opposed the abolition of the slave trade. In 1815, he introduced the Corn Law to protect hardworking British farmers[*] by banning imports of wheat unless the price rose to eighty shillings a bushel, just about the level needed to maintain a nicely-done stately home. The law inflated the price of bread, the staple diet of the working class, bringing widespread hunger and hardship.

"Let them eat cake," Lord Liverpool might have said.

Social unrest spread around the country. In 1819, a crowd of 60,000 demonstrators at St Peter's Field in Manchester shouted for parliamentary reform, universal suffrage and cheaper bread. When a radical orator named Henry Hunt got up to speak, soldiers rushed onto the stage to arrest him, prompting scuffles in the crowd. The cavalry charged in with swords flashing, delighted to be at war again, killing eleven people and injuring 400 more. The massacre was sarcastically dubbed Peterloo after its slightly more illustrious predecessor. In response, liberals established the *Manchester Guardian* newspaper while Shelley wrote a critical poem. It was

---

[*] conservative aristocratic landowners

revolution, British-style.

As the philosopher and reformer Jeremy Bentham called for 'the greatest happiness of the greatest number', the government knew that the greatest number couldn't vote and passed the Six Acts instead, curtailing freedom of speech, publication and assembly. Just as people were beginning to think this might be a step too far, five radical republicans hatched a plot to assassinate the entire cabinet at dinner. The Cato Street Conspiracy of 1820 was foiled at the last minute by an informer, and Lord Liverpool's cabinet were able to eat their meal in peace, with extra bread.

George IV: Incredibly, Worse Than the Other Georges

During Christmas 1819, the ailing George III is said to have spoken nonsense for 58 hours straight. This would have been a British record except, of course, his dissolute son had been doing it for about 58 years. The old king died a few weeks later at the age of 81, the longest-reigning monarch so far. The Prince Regent, determined not to be one of those Henry V type figures who suddenly sober up once they're on the throne, decided to make his first act as king the public humiliation and divorce of his wife, Caroline of Brunswick. Already secretly married to Maria Fitzherbert, a two-time divorcee whose marriage to the prince had been ruled invalid due to the fact she was a Catholic, George had only agreed to wed Caroline in 1795 in return for a sizeable increase to his personal allowance. He had hated her on sight, having intercourse with her only on the first two nights of their marriage[*].

Unfortunately, despite her less than ideal marriage, Caroline was rather looking forward to being queen, being as fond of a purchase or two as her extravagant hubby. On the day of the coronation, she ignored George's order not to attend and tried to force her way past the guards into Westminster Abbey. When the

---

[*] three times in total, according to George, in case you were wondering

doors were literally slammed into her face, she ran across the road to Westminster Hall where the guests were assembling and banged on the door with her fists. It was not very seemly, and, having been previously sympathetic to her plight, the crowds jeered her as she was led back to her carriage. She died a few weeks later, possibly of cancer though rumours of poisoning never went away.

If there was any consolation for Caroline, it was that George's popularity never improved either. As the hard-drinking king slipped quickly into decline, his own personal aide confided to his diary: 'A more contemptible, cowardly, selfish, unfeeling dog does not exist.' He lasted only ten years on the throne before dying of obesity and gout at the age of 67. *The Times* obituary noted that 'there never was an individual less regretted by his fellow-creatures than this deceased king.' And, heaven knows, there had been stiff competition even within his own family.

Bobbies and Catholics

As George IV was busy drinking himself to an early grave, with the full encouragement of his personal aides, the rest of the political establishment was grappling with intractable issues like crime, punishment and Irishness. The year 1822 saw the rise to prominence of a certain Robert Peel, first as Home Secretary and then in two separate terms as Prime Minister. The son of a wealthy industrialist, Peel knew a little bit more about the working classes than your average aristocratic MP. While to most MPs, the lower classes were those creatures they occasionally saw hanging from gibbets on Westminster Bridge, Peel had realised that workers might be more useful to society if their necks were still attached to their back bones. He set about, therefore, reducing the number of crimes in Britain that carried the death penalty.

By the 19th century, the number of crimes punishable by hanging had ballooned to more than 220, ranging from theft and murder to begging without a licence, impersonating a Chelsea Pensioner, blackening one's face after dark, and being in the company of gypsies. The problem was not just the number of people who were getting executed for hanging around at fairgrounds, but also the fact that juries were becoming more and more reluctant to convict. One minute that cheeky little urchin from down the street was cheerfully begging for a bit more soup, the next he was hanging from a gibbet having his eyes plucked out by a crow. It was hard to know what to say to the parents. Under Peel's direction, the death penalty was restricted to just four crimes: murder, treason, arson in a royal dockyard and piracy with violence. Gibbeting was also abolished over time and, after campaigns led by Jeremy Bentham and Elizabeth Fry, prison conditions were gradually improved.

Peel's most famous reform came in 1829 with the establishment of the first professional police force in London, the Metropolitan Police. Though there had been a semi-professional force called the Bow Street Runners, set up in 1749 by the writer and magistrate Henry Fielding, it had consisted of only a few officers. Most criminals were still apprehended by private citizens or bounty hunters, a system that worked fine in villages where everybody knew each other but which was open to high rates of corruption in large, anonymous cities like London. Peel saw the value of a proper professional force, where the corruption could be made much more organised and official. He implemented his plan over fierce opposition, which associated police forces with the autocratic tyrannies of the continent. Peel managed to soothe fears by outfitting his officers with large ridiculous helmets that ensured they would never be able to run fast enough to actually catch anyone. People nicknamed the new policemen Bobbies and Peelers, but only because the words Filth and Pig were already reserved for describing George IV.

Along with law and order, the second burning issue of Peel's time was Irish Catholics, who, despite years of persecution, still stubbornly refused to stop breeding. The Act of Union of 1800 had brought Ireland into the United Kingdom, but Catholics, who made up 85% of the population, had been denied the vote, leading to a permanent state of simmering tension. The leader of the Irish movement was a brilliant lawyer by the name of Daniel O'Connell, who favoured non-violent agitation as a way to really get on English nerves. In 1828, he won a by-election in Clare, but as a Catholic was prevented from taking up his seat in parliament. Tension in Ireland rose to boiling-point and, faced with a possible full-scale uprising, the Tory government under Wellington and Peel reluctantly gave in to O'Connell's demands to take up his seat. O'Connell went on to become Dublin's first Catholic mayor since the reign of James II, earning the nickname The Liberator, which looked pretty good on his campaign leaflets.

The Reform Act of 1832

15 September 1830 saw the official opening of the first steam railway between Liverpool and Manchester. Crowds of admiring onlookers, including the Duke of Wellington, watched in rapturous admiration as Stephenson's Rocket hurtled down the gleaming new track and promptly ploughed into William Huskisson, the MP for Liverpool, who had forgotten to get out of the way. Even the Luddites had to stop and cheer. As it happened, Huskisson's messy demise caused more consternation than the death of the king had a few months earlier. George had been succeeded by his brother William IV, a mildly competent naval officer who had little interest in being king. Engaged in a long-standing affair with an actress named Dorothea Jordan, he left no direct heirs but fathered ten illegitimate children, one of whom was careless enough to be the direct ancestor of David Cameron[*].

The same year of 1830 saw a wave of popular uprisings against the autocracies of Europe as the rising middle classes demanded

---

[*] Meaning that if Edward and Dorothea had actually been allowed to marry, David Cameron might one day have become king, a position in which, ironically, he would probably have done less damage.

reform and representation. In Britain, the mood was hardly better. Despite the long supremacy of parliament, the electoral system it was based upon had not changed since the 15th century. The franchise was still restricted to wealthy landowners, 400,000 of them in total, while the composition of MPs was absurdly skewed in favour of rural constituencies. There were dozens of 'pocket' and 'rotten' boroughs where voters were so few in number the MP either bribed his way into office or was simply picked by the richest local. Old Sarum in Salisbury, notoriously, had two MPs representing a total of three households. Large cities like Manchester, Birmingham and Leeds, meanwhile, had no MPs at all.

The Tory aristocracy, of course, saw no reason for change. Wellington remarked that he could 'not imagine how a better system might be devised.' Their liberally-minded Whig opponents, however, were determined to bring reform. After the intransigent Wellington was forced to resign after a no-confidence vote, the Whig aristocrat Earl Grey, who had once received a present of tea flavoured with bergamot, took office. He quickly supported a bill to restructure the constituency system and extend the franchise to a grand total of 650,000 people.

The bill passed the Commons by one vote but was roundly rejected by the Lords, where 21 out of 22 bishops voted against. Riots broke out in Bristol, Nottingham and Derby, while Wellington was forced to put metal shutters over his windows. This earned him the sarcastic nickname of the Iron Duke, though Wellington tried to pretend to the ladies that it meant something else. When William IV refused Grey's plea to create enough new peers to pass the bill, the situation grew so desperate it seemed as though revolution might, finally, be at hand. Luckily, however, the Iron Duke opened his shutters before it was too late. He persuaded the king to accede to Grey's demands, and in fright the Lords quickly passed the bill. The rotten boroughs were abolished and 125 new seats created in their place. Earl Grey assured his colleagues that further reform would only come 'according to the increased intelligence of the people', which seemed to put him on pretty safe ground. However, the truth was that a vital precedent had now been set. The Reform Bill of 1832 set Britain on the road to true democracy, and the man behind it could be sure his name would forever be remembered because of it.

"Earl Grey? Oh yeah! The tea guy."

The New Parliament

Wellington's reaction to the new reformed parliament of 1833 was as politically incisive as you would expect from such an experienced figure: 'I never saw so many shocking bad hats in my life.' But it wasn't just the hats, or even the northern accents, that were hard for the old guard to understand. There were ideas as well. Soon slavery, as opposed to just the slave trade, was abolished throughout the British Empire, corrupt municipal corporations were replaced by elected borough councils, children under nine were prevented from working in factories and those under thirteen limited to eight-hour days. When six men from the village of Tolpuddle in Dorset were sentenced to transportation for organising themselves into a quasi-trade union, the government accepted a massive public campaign to pardon them and brought them back home with little more damage than a decent Australian tan. Considered all together, it was almost as if Britain's elites were starting to think of the working classes as actual real people.

It was a relief then when they came to their senses in 1834 with the introduction of a new Poor Law, designed to put the lower classes back where they belonged. A prolonged slump in agricultural wages due to a labour glut had been putting intolerable strain on the old system of poor relief, which was carried out and funded locally by individual parishes. The government proposed to bring it under central control, creating a kind of national welfare system, but with the tiny proviso that there wouldn't actually be any welfare, or much of a system.

The New Poor Law was based on the idea that the lower classes would always tend toward indolence and leisure unless they were given a proper incentive to work, rather like the aristocracy really. Since trying to improve work itself was obviously out of the question, the only option was to make indolence even worse. From now on, the law said, poor relief would only be given to families desperate enough to enter a workhouse. Workhouses themselves, of course, were made purposely horrific. Segregated from their loved-ones, inmates were forced to work all day on meaningless exhausting tasks, punished for the slightest offence and fed on almost starvation rations. With no regulations in place, they were at the mercy of wardens whose main ambition was to be sadistic enough to get their names in a Charles Dickens novel. In one institution, inmates were found gnawing on rotting flesh from bones. It was in fact Dickens who did more than anyone to raise awareness of the injustices of the system through his novel *Oliver Twist*, published in installments between 1837 and 1839.

The New Poor Law was hugely unpopular, at least with the poor, so much so that authorities dared not even impose it in most of the northern towns. Two months after the law was passed, however, the country had its revenge. In a bid to dispose of Henry I's accounting tally sticks that had been gathering dust in the basement, workmen finally achieved the ambitions of generations of Catholic revolutionaries and burned down the Houses of Parliament. So heartbroken were the people of London to see the capital's great seat of power in flames that scuffles broke out as they fought each other to get the best view. Artists like J. M. W. Turner (of Turner Prize fame) set up easels on the street and produced spectacular watercolours of the flames.

"Don't forget to paint their silly hats when they catch fire."

There were no casualties in the fire, though it was the biggest in London since 1666. It did, however, require a new premises to be built. The authorities wanted to create a building that truly represented British democracy, and so, after much discussion, they chose Charles Barry's design of a huge gothic castle with dozens of spiky parapets which would only have looked more impressive if they'd had heads impaled on them.

Queen Victoria

In the early hours of 20 June 1837, William IV passed away to the terrible grief of everyone who could actually remember he'd been king. Since he had spent his whole life frantically producing illegitimate heirs, the throne passed to his bright and attractive eighteen year-old niece Victoria.

Victoria's coronation was memorable not only for the fact that at 4 ft 11 inches tall she could barely see over the pews. It also marked the end of Britain's constitutional ties with the kingdom of Hanover since female monarchs were too sensible to be allowed on the Hanoverian throne. Thanks to Victoria, Britain would no longer suffer the humiliation of being tied to the insignificant German kingdom of Hanover. Prime Minister Lord Melbourne helped to guide Victoria through some tricky early years before steered her into marriage with her dashing cousin Prince Albert of Saxe-Coburg, thereby ensuring that from now on Britain would be tied to the insignificant German kingdom of Saxe-Coburg instead.

Falling deeply in love, Victoria married the prince in 1840, starting a new tradition by choosing a white dress for the wedding. Despite hating both pregnancy and babies, she had nine children over the next seventeen years, marrying them off one by one into the royal houses of Europe. Most of her children had inherited Victoria's haemophilia, which now spread out into the palaces of Spain, Germany and Russia, just the disease you needed when Bolshevik revolutionaries kept trying to shoot at you through the windows.

The Chartist Movement

Britain's ruling classes had hoped the 1832 Reform Act would satisfy popular demands for franchise reform. But, as Earl Grey may have foreseen in his tea leaves, the genie was now out of the bottle, and in 1839 Britain was seized by revolutionary fervour once more. The leaders of the so-called Chartist movement had looked at the popular revolutions of the continent, noted how angry crowds had used their superior numbers to capture weapon depots, storm royal palaces and overrun the government, and thought to themselves: "Yes! What we need to do is organise a really big petition...."

There were six demands on the petition: universal male suffrage*, equal electoral districts, a secret ballot, an end to property-owning qualification for MPs, payment for MPs, and annual general elections. Almost 1.3 million signatures were collected and in July 1839 the three-mile long document was presented to parliament, which quickly voted 235 – 46 not to even look at it.

"We didn't realise you could do that," said the Chartists.

There were riots across the country and one disastrous attempt at an armed uprising in, of all places, Newport. After soldiers quickly put the insurrection down, many of the Chartist leaders were arrested and sentenced to transportation. Those that remained, however, were not willing to give up easily. They realised that a new strategy was necessary, one that would really make the ruling classes sit up and take notice. A general strike to shut down the mines and factories? A blockade of public buildings and roads? An armed attack on the institutions of government and state?

"How about another petition?" suggested Feargus O'Connor, their leader.

The next petition, containing three million signatures, was presented to the House of Commons in 1842. The MPs voted not to receive it again on the grounds that the people were not exactly proving their increased intelligence.

Strikes and more riots followed before, in the midst of proper

---

* There was a brief discussion about including women too, but the Chartists wanted to make sure they were taken seriously.

revolutions across Europe, a third petition was put together in 1848. This one was said to have five million signatures, but the inclusion of joke names like Mr Punch and Queen Victoria gave the authorities the excuse to dismiss the whole thing out of hand. The movement fizzled out and poor Feargus O'Connor spent the rest of his days in a lunatic asylum, where the straitjackets made it quite hard to collect signatures.

The Chartist movement was generally regarded as a heroic failure. In the end, however, almost all of the Chartists' six points would be met. The only exception was the demand for annual general elections which, on reflection, even O'Connor might have realised was a bit barmy.

Capitalism, Corn and Potatoes

Despite the slow pace of social and political reform, the contrast between Britain with its awkward but stable democracy and the autocracies of continental Europe could hardly have been starker. While 1848 saw monarchies toppled by force in France, Austria and Italy, in Britain the only real danger to the ruling classes was tripping over the Chartists' three-mile long petition. Karl Marx, expelled from several European capitals, was free to sit in the British Library and pen a manifesto about overthrowing the capitalist state, just as long as he did it quietly without disturbing the other readers, while John Stuart Mill could warn against the 'tyranny of the majority' safe in the knowledge the majority would not bang down his door at night and disembowel him for treason.

Economically, Britain was streets ahead. Although working conditions in the factories and mines were as dreadful as ever, they still beat the cold muddy poverty of peasant farming. The 1840s saw an explosion of railway building throughout the country, helped by brilliant engineers with even more brilliant names like Isambard Kingdom Brunel. Children would flock to the tracks to watch the mighty locomotives steaming down the rails, knowing that if they were really lucky they might catch one flattening an

MP again.

In the political field, it was also a time of change. The Whigs had fallen from power in 1841, bringing Sir Robert Peel to Downing Street once more. Peel had realised that the old Tory tactic of reacting to every serious proposal for social reform by putting iron shutters on their windows no longer suited the times they were living in. His party, who had come to call themselves Conservatives under Peel's leadership, had to 'reform to survive'. Obviously this didn't mean glancing at petitions signed by a quarter of the population of Britain, but it did include grappling with something that became the burning issue of the 1840s: free trade. As the son of an industrialist, Peel understood the value of cheap imports and exports and threw his support behind a campaign to repeal the unpopular Corn Law of 1815 that had added tariffs to wheat imports, drastically inflating the price of bread.

The Anti-Corn Law League had been established by two liberal Whig MPs, but they found an unlikely ally in the Tory leader. Their nationwide campaign had been innovatively run, making use of the new penny post to raise funds and distribute literature; however, it was very much a middle-class campaign, massively unpopular with the landholding class that dominated Peel's own party. What they really needed was some hugely dramatic event that would highlight the importance of the supply and price of food.

Then in 1845 came horrific news from Ireland: a blight on the country's staple peasant food, the potato, which decimated the harvests. Ireland's food supply was devastated and the result was a crushing famine. Over a million people died in a single year and a million more were forced to emigrate to America, stuffed onto 'coffin ships' so undersupplied that thousands starved before they reached their destination.

The British government response was half-hearted, the prevailing doctrine of *laissez-faire* driving the notion that the market would take care of the problem, which it did once enough people had died. The most shocking fact was that food exports from Ireland to Britain continued without any attempt to restrict or redistribute supplies. It was enough food to have comfortably fed the entire Irish population. This more than anything else fuelled the anger of the Irish people against the British. The older generations, of course, just added it to the list.

Peel used the disaster to force through a repeal of the Corn Laws, relying on the support of Whigs and Radicals in parliament. It had little effect on the famine in Ireland, but in Britain the price of bread fell by almost half over the next thirty years. Economically it was the right move, the moment when the demands of merchants and consumers overtook the interests of the aristocracy. Politically, however, Peel's decision was suicide. Denounced by an up-and-coming young Tory named Benjamin Disraeli for 'the wilful destruction of a great party by its leader', Peel was forced to resign in 1846. He died in a riding accident a few years later. The Conservatives, hopelessly split, didn't win an election for another twenty years. It was only of slight consolation to the Irish.

Empire, Opium and Beards

The new Whig government was dominated by foreign secretary Lord Palmerston. A brilliant if controversial figure, Palmerston rarely saw the need to explain himself to his colleagues and when he did, as during a marathon five-hour speech to the House of Commons in 1848, they rather regretted asking him. A proper Victorian, when a Frenchman once complimented him by saying that if he were not a Frenchman he would wish to be an Englishman, Palmerston replied, 'If I were not an Englishman, I should *wish* to be an Englishman.'

His principle in foreign policy was one of 'liberal interventionism', which meant sending in the British navy if foreign governments so much as tugged on an Englishman's moustache. Though he kept Britain out of serious European squabbles, where she might get hurt, he was always happy to engage his 'gunboat diplomacy' in more gentle waters. In an earlier stint as foreign secretary in 1839, he had started the Opium Wars, defending the rights of British merchants to engage in the perfectly fair trade of selling harmful and addictive narcotics to the Chinese. Britain had got Hong Kong out of that little tussle, while the Chinese, of course, had just got high. In 1850, when the house of a British citizen from Gibraltar named Don Pacifico was burned down in a riot in Athens, Palmerston responded by seizing Greek shipping and blockading its ports.

These escapades made Palmerston hugely popular with the public, who loved nothing more than British ships bombarding places they'd never heard of. His colleagues, however, began to tire of his one-man show and in 1852 they shunted him over to the Home Office. Ironically enough, this allowed Palmerston to escape responsibility for Britain's biggest foreign intervention of the period, the Crimean War.

The Crimean War came about when the Russians attempted to seize ports from the Ottoman Empire in the warm waters of the Black Sea in order to have somewhere to swim during the summer. The British, who had become concerned about Russia's increasing aggression against the ailing Ottomans, joined in on the side of the Turks with, of all countries, the French in support. The result was a two-year war that was almost comical in its awfulness. The British generals, honing their incompetence for the First World War when it would really count, made decisions like supplying their troops only with light summer clothing because who knew that it got cold in Russia? At the Battle of Balaclava, the freezing troops cut eye-holes in their socks and pulled them over their heads, a fashion statement that would serve them well back home when bank robbing was the only profession available. The climax of the battle was the suicidal Charge of the Light Brigade in which 600 men were sent by mistake into the 'valley of death' straight into the full face of the Russian artillery. Tennyson's poem somehow made this sound heroic.

It says something about British military superiority that they still won the Crimean War, but the truth was that only two good things came out of it. The first was war reporting, with William Howard Russell of *The Times* becoming the first journalist to ever report directly from the front line. It was after reading one of Russell's dispatches from the Battle of Balaclava that Florence Nightingale made her decision to travel to the Crimea, the reporter's descriptions of the harsh, barren conditions the soldiers fought in convincing her that this was a place a single woman could have a seriously good time. She returned to London a hero, founding the first professional school of nursing[*].

The only other effect of the Crimean War was, if anything, even more horrifying than the Charge of the Light Brigade, and that was the spread of massive bushy beards. Until then, beards had been seen, rightly, as both unsightly and potentially criminal, but in the freezing conditions of the Crimea the soldiers had allowed their stubble to grow long for warmth. Their return to Britain prompted the great Victorian 'beard craze', reminiscent of the witch craze of 17th century Europe except this time stake-burning would have been justified. Almost all men were affected, including the great naturalist Charles Darwin, who published his groundbreaking *On the Origin of Species* in 1859. The revelation that human beings were descended from apes created a fair bit of controversy in Victorian society, particularly as it was now obvious that gorillas had less facial hair.

The Clash of the Titans

The debacle of the Crimean War led to the resignation of the Whig prime minister, Lord Aberdeen. After asking and being refused by

---

[*] She also did pioneering work in the field of statistics, becoming the first female member of the Royal Statistical Society who, until then, had had no statistical measure for counting women.

every member of the government, Queen Victoria was forced to appoint Palmerston, a figure she both distrusted and detested. Until his death in 1865, Palmerston continued his dangerous libertarian ways, joining a gathering of Whigs, Peelites and Radicals to form the new Liberal Party[*]. With a young William Gladstone as chancellor, the Liberals increased income tax and cut the number of duties from 419 to 48, lowering food prices further. On Palmerston's death, the aging Lord Russell took the premiership once more. One of the architects of the 1832 Reform Act, Russell was determined to extend the franchise further, but his bill to extend the vote to all skilled male workers with stable lodgings floundered in the Commons, leading to his resignation. The Conservatives took power again, with Disraeli their key figure in the Commons. But when protests erupted over the rejected franchise bill, the government was panicked into passing it, doubling the electorate to over two million.

If Disraeli expected the new expanded electorate to be grateful, he was forgetting that men who operated heavy machinery for a living could usually recognise a tool when they saw one. In 1868, the Tories were booted out of office and Gladstone took their place. Gladstone was a curious figure. A serious and intensely religious man, he saw his work in politics as a Christian endeavour, giving him both a prodigious work ethic and an insatiable appetite for meeting prostitutes. His entirely innocent pastime of walking the streets at night looking for fallen women to save continued throughout his adult life, as did his other major pastimes of self-flagellating and chopping down huge oak trees. None of these things were related of course. Despite being disliked by Queen Victoria, who complained that he spoke to her as if she were 'a public meeting', he went on to serve four terms as prime minister, leaving office for the final time in 1894 when he was 84 years-old.

His great rival, Benjamin Disraeli, was his polar opposite.

---

[*] just in case you were wondering where all the Whigs are nowadays

Charismatic, witty and never afraid to ditch principles in favour of votes, he climbed what he called the 'greasy pole' through oratory and charm. He was of Jewish parentage, though baptised as an Anglican himself, but he dealt with the inevitable anti-Semitic sneers with humour and grace. Queen Victoria adored him, particularly after the death of her husband Albert in 1861, which plunged her into an endless period of mourning. 'Everybody likes flattery,' Disraeli confided when asked for the secret of his relationship, 'and when you come to royalty, you should lay it on with a trowel.'

Gladstone, for his part, found his rival shamefully unrepressed. He raged that Disraeli 'bargained with diseased appetites and stimulated passions, prejudices and selfish desires.' He had to chop down two oak trees at the mere thought of the man. Disraeli, meanwhile, had no more affection for Gladstone, 'an extraordinary mixture of envy, vindictiveness, hypocrisy and superstition.' It was what the House of Commons had been built for.

Empire, Reform and Football

Gladstone called his first ministry from 1868 to 1874 'the finest instrument of government that ever were constructed', modesty, like self-flagellation, something he felt was best practised in private. The Education Act of 1870 brought the first public primary schools. Unions were legalised with the formation of the Trades Union Congress, though picketing was banned, and the civil service began to be recruited through examination rather than patronage. Women were allowed into Oxford and Cambridge for the first time and non-conformists permitted to become dons.

When Disraeli finally took office after the election of 1874, he largely continued Gladstone's domestic policies, making people wonder what the past six years of witty abuse had all been about. Now 69 years-old and so sickly he had to move to the House of Lords, he abolished the ban on picketing, made education compulsory to the age of ten and compelled new housing developments to include running water and drainage systems. Where he differed from his rival was in foreign policy. While Gladstone had been quiet abroad, Disraeli was unashamedly imperialist.

India remained the jewel in the crown of the British Empire. With the decline of France, Britain faced almost no opposition to her domination of the Indian continent, so long as you discounted the 250 million Indians themselves, which, of course, the British did. The voracious East India Company had remained in control until 1857 when a massive Indian rebellion threw the region into turmoil. The Company responded with a campaign of ruthless suppression in which at least 100,000 rebels were killed. Prisoners were executed en masse, with some tied to the barrels of cannons and blown to pieces. To clean up the resulting mess, governance of the continent had been taken away from the Company and given to the British government. Now, under Disraeli, this initially reluctant move became a point of national pride. In 1876, he passed an Act to bestow on a delighted Queen Victoria the title of Empress of India, one form of flattery where 'trowel' didn't seem to quite cover it.

As if having the world's largest ever empire was not exciting enough, the British people also gained a new thing they could temporarily be good at: sport. The first FA Cup was staged in 1871, the rules of football having been codified a decade earlier. The Rugby Association was founded in the same year, but both of these sports lagged behind cricket, which already had its first bona fide star in the form of the magnificently bearded W. G. Grace. England was world champion at all these sports, thanks to their foresight in not teaching anyone else how to play, until they foolishly agreed to play the first ever test match against Australia in 1877, which, of course, they lost horribly. It was to be more than a hundred years before the Australians finally stopped gloating.

The Scramble for Africa

Disraeli was a popular prime minister, able to invoke the passions of patriotism without, crucially, actually getting many British soldiers killed. He was the first real One Nation Tory, embracing progressive change for the masses while most of his party would have been happy with some version of enlightened serfdom. Aging and sick, he lost the 1880 election to Gladstone's Liberals, retiring to his country home and dying a year later.

At 71 years-old, Gladstone was now the Grand Old Man, or 'God's Only Mistake' as Disraeli had preferred to call him. His cabinet was similarly ancient and, though it succeeded in extending the vote to all male householders, doubling the electorate once more, it did little else domestically over the next five years. More distressing for Gladstone personally was the new mood of imperialism unleashed by his predecessor. No sooner had he managed to extricate the country from a disastrous occupation of Afghanistan, designed to stop Russian influence spreading towards India, he found himself embroiled in a mass scramble to colonise the continent of Africa.

By 1880, the British Empire was already too unwieldy, largely a by-product of the nation's insatiable appetite for trading useful products like tea and heroin. Africa didn't really offer much that the British did not already possess, except malaria, but when the government got wind of the fact that other European nations, like France, Germany, Italy and even, for heaven's sake, Belgium, were planning to get in their first, it was obvious they needed to do something. As France moved in from the west, Britain followed a policy of 'Cape to Cairo', aiming to unite her southern and northern possessions, the long-cherished dream of businessman, diamond tycoon, politician and all-round white supremacist Cecil Rhodes. Soon they had control of South Africa, Botswana, Zimbabwe, Lesotho, Swaziland, Zambia, Uganda, Kenya, Nigeria, Sudan and Egypt to which they brought all the benefits and sophistications of British civilisation, including schools, hospitals, churches and railways. Sometimes, in the spirit of Victorian philanthropy, they even let the Africans use them.

The Irish Question Fails to Get Answered Again

In 1844, Disraeli had described the problem of Ireland as follows: 'A dense population, in extreme distress, inhabit an island where there is an Established Church, which is not their Church, and a territorial aristocracy, the richest of whom live in foreign capitals. Thus you have a starving population, an absentee aristocracy, and an alien Church. That is the Irish Question.' Although, thanks to the Potato Famine, the population had become a great deal less dense, the other points still remained true. The English absentee landlords charged exorbitant rents to peasants too poor to have emigrated to America; Catholics continued to be persecuted in their own land; and in the 1870s failed harvests threatened famine once more.

The ideal solution, from a British government perspective, would have been for the island itself to emigrate to America on a particularly strong rip current. But since it stubbornly insisted on hanging around off the coast, sending over its noisy MPs to parliament and permanently on the brink of an uprising, Gladstone decided to settle matters once and for all by granting the Irish home rule. His ally in this ambitious endeavour was Charles Stewart Parnell, the eloquent and intelligent leader of the Irish Home Rule group in the Commons, who was described by Gladstone as 'the most remarkable man' he had ever met. As Gladstone entertained parliament with a three and a half hour speech on home rule, Parnell led the Land League in Ireland which ostracised the worst landlords by denying them labour for their fields and service in local shops.*

In the end, however, both their efforts proved futile. Parnell's

---

* The first of the landlords to be targeted was a certain Charles Boycott whose loud protestations to the British press gave the policy a nice catchy name.

reputation was shredded when he was discovered to have fathered three children with another man's wife, which was not something good Catholics were supposed to get found out about. Gladstone's home rule bill, meanwhile, hit a wall of opposition from Conservatives and rebelling Liberals, whose loyalties were to the Protestant Unionists in Ulster rather than the starving Catholics in the south. Ireland's long bid for home rule had never come closer, and, as the Ulster Unionists grew steadily more strident over the years, it was a missed opportunity that many would come to regret. As George V was later to lament: 'What fools we were not to pass Mr Gladstone's Bill when we had the chance!'

The Last of the Victorians
The Liberals spent six years in opposition after the failure of the Irish bill, only to squeak back into power in 1892. Gladstone was still their leader, by virtue of the fact he wasn't quite dead yet, embarking on his fourth term as prime minister half-deaf and barely able to see. Victoria was aghast at the thought of entrusting her treasured empire to the 'shaking hand of an old, wild and incomprehensible man', but considering those had been the defining traits of most of Britain's leaders since Henry V she shouldn't have been too worried. As it happened he only spent another two years in office before finally retiring at the age of 84, dying four years later.

As chancellor and prime minister Gladstone had dominated politics for almost half a century. When he was conveyed to his funeral at Westminster Abbey on the new London Underground, just managing to grab a seat when someone else got off, it was emblematic of the huge transformation Britain had gone through during his lifetime. Between 1800 and 1900, Britain's population had quadrupled to over forty million. Other than the very poor, most of her citizens had swapped mud, candles, slops and turnips for pavements, gas, sewers and fish and chips, wrapped up in newspapers as tasty as the *Guardian* or as toxic as the *Daily Mail**. Roads were surfaced with tarmac, with new-fangled cars speeding down them at speeds of up to twelve miles an hour, and trains were everywhere. Thomas Crapper had invented the flushing toilet, because his name really gave him no choice, and Joseph Lister had begun sterilising surgical tools to prevent infections. Even factories were not the dark satanic mills of yesteryear but relatively clean and organised spaces, where the danger came less from workers accidentally getting mangled in the machines than from them deliberately throwing themselves in just to break the monotony.

In politics Gladstone was succeeded by the elderly Tory aristocrat Lord Salisbury, a reminder that while some things in Britain had changed, others were just as reassuringly out of touch as ever. Salisbury believed in government with a light touch, light enough in fact that he once fell asleep in one of his own cabinet meetings. He spent a total of fourteen years in office, longer even than Gladstone, doing just enough to keep the masses satisfied but not too much to get them excited, an emotion he had never had and didn't understand. In foreign policy, it was the same. He followed a policy of 'splendid isolation', which meant 'drifting lazily downstream, occasionally putting out a boat-hook to avoid collision'. As an aristocratic landowner, he understood the value of doing nothing, declaring that it was in Britain's interests 'that as little should happen as possible.'

In this, it was hard to argue he was wrong. People who happened to find themselves around, say, the Somme in 1916 would have agreed quite heartily. Unfortunately, the rest of the world couldn't seem to grasp Britain's need for quiet. The biggest flashpoint toward the end of the century was South Africa, mainly controlled by the British but with two independent republics, the

---

* In case you're wondering, yes it was just as bad then as it was now, famous for its 'daily hate' which gave rise to the phrase Hate Mail. Also its ink rubbed off on the chips.

Transvaal and the Orange Free State, established by Dutch Afrikaners*. A gold rush in the Transvaal from the 1880s had disturbed the equilibrium, and in 1896 Cecil Rhodes backed a reckless raid to re-establish British control. The failed raid only served to whip up Boer nationalism, and after the two Boer republics signed an alliance, the British sent in the troops. It should have been a straightforward victory, but the Afrikaners, rifle-toting farmers whose aim had been carefully honed by years of shooting at fleeing black slaves, were effective horsebacked guerillas. Within a few months they were on the offensive, besieging British garrisons at Ladysmith, Kimberley and Mafeking. The commander of Mafeking, future Boy Scouts founder Robert Baden-Powell held out for 217 days, raising the morale of his starving men by awarding them with the first ever *cook-your-own-horse-and-eat-it* badge. In 1900, the British were humiliated at the Battle of Spion Kop, a hill which gave its name to several famous football stadium embankments, where regular reenactments of the battle were staged by skinheads throughout the 1980s.

Shocked by the reversals, the government sent in its most revered general Lord Kitchener, later of World War I recruitment poster fame, who somehow contrived to make the Afrikaners look like the good guys by interning their families in horrific conditions inside concentration camps. Thousands died of disease and malnutrition. Eventually, the British got the upper hand and South Africa was absorbed into the empire, though the cost to Britain's reputation and treasury hardly seemed worth it. The Afrikaners got their own guarantees of autonomy and eventually celebrated their survival by instituting apartheid. The good guys tag didn't last for very long.

The Boer War was Britain's final act of the Victorian era. In

---

* The Afrikaners, also known as Boers, had won control of the territories after their 'Great Trek' north in the 1840s, breaking free from British control when the empire outraged them by abolishing slavery.

1901, Queen Victoria finally passed away, sad to go but happy that at least she'd lasted longer than Gladstone. She had spent many of the last forty years holed up in her palaces in permanent mourning for Albert, though there were persistent rumours of an affair and possibly even a secret marriage with her Scottish manservant John Brown. Her disappearance from public view had hurt the popularity of the monarchy. However, having had the longest reign of all British kings and queens until Elizabeth II, she had given the public what they craved most in a monarch: dignity, stability and a comforting smell of cobwebs.

10. TWO WORLD WARS (1901 – 1945)

The new century began with Victoria's son Edward VII storming through the royal palaces systematically eradicating every trace of John Brown. It was an appropriate start to the 20th century, a period in which systematically eradicating every trace of other people became the primary occupation of most adult males in Europe. It had all begun so promisingly, with radical politicians like Lloyd George and Asquith tearing down the old order and Emmeline Pankhurst stunning the nation with her outlandish claim that the human race would not die out if women were given the vote. But then came the First World War, which with its misery, mud and mindless slaughter was exactly the kind of thing the Germans liked to do twice. So then we had the Second World War. After five years of bullets, bombs, blackouts and blitzes, it was a different Britain that emerged from the wreckage. An older Britain, a wiser Britain, a Britain with a surprising number of babies born with American accents.

Politics and Pensions
In 1902, Lord Salisbury decided that the chairs in the cabinet room were just not comfortable enough for sleeping on and decided to resign. His successor, everyone assumed, would be the formidable Joseph Chamberlain, the colonial secretary, and so naturally Salisbury chose someone else instead, his nephew Arthur Balfour, a man whose philosophy on life could be summed up in his own wise words: 'Nothing matters very much and few things matter at all.'[*]

Unfortunately for Balfour, there was one thing that did seem to

_____

[*] The expression 'Bob's your uncle' probably originated from the popular view that Balfour gained all his advancements from his generous relative, Robert Salisbury.

matter, at least to Chamberlain if not to people with a bit less time on their hands: tariffs. Since the repeal of the Corn Laws in 1846, Britain had generally followed a policy of free trade throughout the empire. But Chamberlain had become convinced that Britain's traditional industries were losing out to the growing economies of Germany, France and the United States and that in order to, let's say, Make Britain Great Again, the empire needed to return to protectionism.

Just as divided over the issue as they had been in the 1840s, Balfour's Tories were trounced in the election of 1906. Along with a progressive Liberal majority came 29 MPs from the new Labour Party, hard-bitten ex-miners and iron workers from the trade unions who seemed to take up a lot more space on the benches than their numbers suggested. The result was the most radical government yet formed, consisting of luminaries such as Herbert Asquith, David Lloyd George and Winston Churchill (who had defected to the Liberals over free trade). Over the next four years, Asquith and Lloyd George introduced a raft of measures to improve the lot of working families and stop the 29 ex-miners losing their tempers. There was even an old age pension of five shillings for the over seventies, though costs were mitigated by the fact nobody actually reached that age unless they were either Queen Victoria or William Gladstone.

As chancellor, the extrovert 'Welsh Wizard' Lloyd George was responsible for finding the money to pay for these policies. Failing in his attempt to reduce Britain's construction of Dreadnought battleships, he imposed a land tax and a petrol tax and increased income tax for high earners. It was a deliberately provocative act and the more the rich howled in protest, the happier the chancellor became. His favourite target for abuse were dukes: 'A fully equipped duke costs as much to keep up as two Dreadnoughts, and dukes are just as great a terror, and they last longer.'

The budget cleared the Commons easily, but in the House of Lords there was nothing more certain to wake up sleeping peers than a wisecrack about dukes. Breaking with years of tradition, they rejected the so-called People's Budget, prompting Asquith to call a general election. As Lloyd George toured the country calling the Lords 'a body of 500 men chosen at random among the unemployed', the Liberals were returned to power, albeit requiring the support of Irish MPs to reach a majority. Now the Lords had little choice but to pass the budget. But having come this far, Asquith and Lloyd George decided to deliver the punchline. In 1911, they introduced the Parliament Act which ended the constitutional right of the House of Lords to reject legislation. From then on, the Lords could discuss, delay and dribble over new bills but not get rid of them entirely. Britain would become the only two-house democracy in the world in which this restriction applied.

Emmeline Pankhurst and the Suffragettes

In our modern liberal society, it is hard to imagine how different attitudes were less than a century ago. Nowadays we have come to accept the fundamental moral principle that men should not be permitted to decide anything at all, including their own clothes. But in the 1910s, Britain had still not seriously considered giving women the vote. According to various treatises on the topic, there were several very good reasons for this:

1. They couldn't be soldiers who defended the realm.
2. They were too emotional to make sound decisions.
3. They would stop having children and the human race would die out.
4. They might start having opinions at dinner parties.

There were, of course, plenty of both men and women who saw the absurdity of the arguments. Women had in fact already been granted the vote in various types of local elections, and there were a number of suffrage movements active in Britain, notably the National Union of Women's Suffrage Societies led by Millicent Fawcett. From 1912, however, their orderly feminine campaigns were blown out of the water by the militant tactics of Emmeline Pankhurst and her suffragettes.

Emmeline Pankhurst's ire was first roused when her daughter Christabel was denied a career in law because of her sex. Founding a movement based on civil disobedience, she and her followers began chaining themselves to railings, smashing school windows, cutting telephone wires, setting fire to letter boxes, burning male-only buildings like cricket pavilions and even detonating small bombs, including at Lloyd George's weekend cottage. In 1913, Emily Davison was killed when she threw herself in front of the King's horse at the Derby, tragically causing a large number of men to lose their bets. The authorities' response was to lock the suffragettes up, around a thousand in all. When the women continued their protests inside jail by staging hunger strikes, the guards had them force-fed. These actions revolted public opinion, but instead of treating the women with more dignity, the authorities switched to releasing them and then re-arresting them the moment they'd recovered their health, the so-called 'Cat and Mouse Act'.

Whether the suffragettes helped or hindered the cause of women's suffrage is an open question. In the end, it took the decision to senselessly slaughter millions of innocent young soldiers in the mud-drenched trenches of World War I to convince people that perhaps it might be better if women had a bit more of a say in things.

The Road to War

There was not, of course, anything special about war breaking out in Europe. Warfare on the continent had been pretty much incessant ever since Julius Caesar had decided Italy was not quite big enough to keep his head inside. The only truly remarkable thing about the First World War was that, through a series of tortuous treaties and alliances, France and Britain somehow found themselves fighting on the same side. The Entente Cordiale had been signed between the two nations in 1904 in response to German alliances with Austro-Hungary and Italy. Russia joined the Entente three years later, each nation promising to aid the other in the event they were attacked. As if this were not precarious enough, there was also the issue of Belgium, which had gained independence from the Dutch in 1839. In the Treaty of London, Britain had persuaded the major powers to guarantee the neutrality of Belgium with the threat of military action if that neutrality was violated. (In the Franco-Prussian war of 1870, Bismarck had deliberately avoided invading through Belgium in order not to provoke the British into a response. It was not a German tactic that would survive the test of time.)

Tension with Germany had been building for some years as its ambitious kaiser Wilhelm II pursued a colonial policy in Africa similar to that of the British. Competition between the two nations had manifested itself in a naval race, one that had forced Lloyd George to so cruelly cut down public expenditure on dukes. That said, however, neither the tension nor the alliances guaranteed an outbreak of hostilities in Europe. Britain had, after all, avoided war on the continent for almost a century. The historian AJP Taylor famously blamed the war on 'railway timetables'[*], arguing that each European nation had a single unalterable plan for mobilising the hundreds of thousands of conscript soldiers they would need in the event of war. The most famous of these plans was Germany's Schlieffen Plan, which stipulated that if conflict erupted with the Franco-Russian alliance, they would have to strike first at Paris as quickly as possible (through Belgium, the quickest route) before turning to the behemoth of Russia, whose armies would be mobilised more slowly. It was arguably the Schlieffen Plan that turned a single incident in Bosnia into a four-year nightmare of bombs, mud and poetry.

---

[*] German ones obviously, not British; otherwise we'd still be waiting for it to start

The Sarajevo incident occurred on 28 June 1914 when the heir to the throne of the Austro-Hungarian Empire, Archduke Franz Ferdinand, was shot by a Serb nationalist called Gavrilo Princip as he was driven in an open-top car through the streets. Austria, keen for a pretext to crush Serbia, their hated rival for influence in the Balkans, sent an ultimatum to the Serbian government demanding that they virtually cede sovereignty to the Austrians as the assassination was investigated. Germany backed the hardline Austrian response, while Russia, a longtime ally of the Slavic Serbs, gave their assurances to the other side. Serbia rejected the ultimatum, which was enough to give the Austrians the excuse they needed to declare war. It was now 28 July. Russia announced they would mobilise in defence of the Serbs, prompting Germany to declare war on 1 August. Two days later the trains were already rumbling into Belgium.

It was at this point that Kaiser Wilhelm suddenly remembered the Treaty of London. His chancellor dismissed the treaty as a 'scrap of paper', but in the world of diplomacy some scraps of paper were worth a lot more than others. The British, concerned, as they had been since the days of Napoleon, about a blockade of continental ports cutting them off from Europe, demanded the Germans withdraw. When that didn't work, they activated the alliance with France and went to war. In the later words of David Lloyd George, Europe had 'stumbled and staggered' into the First World War.

All Over by Christmas
When the commander of the British forces, Field Marshall Sir John French, predicted that the war would all be over by Christmas, he was, of course, correct. It was just not Christmas 1914. Things began badly for the allies as the elite British Expeditionary Force was dispatched to Mons in Belgium, only to find themselves outnumbered three to one by the enemy. The Germans advanced to within two days' march of Paris before they were halted at the

River Marne. After fierce fighting, the allied troops managed to push the Germans back, breaking through their lines.

But just as Field Marshall French's prediction began to seem not quite so daft, the Germans decided to deploy a brilliant new defensive weapon that stopped the allies in their tracks. It was called the spade. When they saw the German trenches, the allies naturally tried to go round the outside, only for the Germans to foil their cunning ploy by digging even more trenches. To stop German counterattacks, the allies found themselves doing the same. By September there was a line of men hiding in a giant ditch from the English Channel at Flanders all the way down to the Swiss border.

For the next three years, the Western front did not move. With reams of barbed wire laid across the top and machine guns mowing down anything that moved, leaving your trench to cross the churned up mud of no-man's land was almost suicidal, certain to bring catastrophic losses to any army foolish enough to try it. So, naturally, that's what the allies did, repeatedly.

"We're going to need more men," announced the generals.

Lord Kitchener, the war minister, came to the rescue with his famous recruiting poster, declaring 'Your Country Needs You' with a moustache so fearsome it could detonate shells. As men flocked to join what was still a hugely popular war, the allies opened up fronts against Germany's ally Turkey in the east, using troops from throughout the British empire. T.E. Lawrence helped to organise Arab resistance against the Turks in Mesopotamia and Palestine, while the navy minister Churchill decided to launch an assault on the Dardanelles. In April 1915, a combined force of British, Australian and New Zealand troops landed at the beach at Gallipoli, so lacking in intelligence for the terrain ahead they were relying on Egyptian travel guides. Unfortunately, the beach proved to be not quite as nice as the brochure, and for the next nine months they remained pinned down, broiling in the summer heat as a huge pile of bodies rotted away in no-man's land. Eventually, they were forced to retreat in humiliation, leading to Churchill's resignation[*].

Back on the Western front, the war settled into a familiarly depressing pattern. On the allied side, soldiers were rotated in and out of the trenches, usually spending around a week each month in the wet, muddy hell of the front line, desperately hoping that wouldn't be the week an attack was ordered. Officers, expected to be first over the top, were killed more often than privates, 17% of them losing their lives during the course of the war compared to 12% of ordinary soldiers. As for the generals directing this horror show, they were not even competent enough to keep themselves alive, with over 200 either killed or wounded when they visited the front lines. At the end of 1915, with no sign of the stalemate being broken, Field Marshall French was removed from command and replaced by Sir Douglas Haig, like French a veteran of a very different kind of colonial warfare. The first ever conscription of able-bodied men was ordered in Britain, though Field Marshall Haig assured everybody he had a brilliant plan to make sure they wouldn't stay able-bodied for very long.

Mud, Blood and Slaughter

In Britain, the disappearance of millions of husbands to the battlefields gave the bored housewives of Britain a once-in-a-lifetime opportunity they were not going to miss out on. They went out to work. Over five million took jobs in public transport, administration, agriculture, and munitions, adding an important touch of glamour to the business of high-explosive bomb-making. It was hard to deny them the vote after that. On the whole, the British, despite the threat of bombs dropped by German Zeppelins, tolerated the war with their usual mild low-level grumbling, though there were protests in Hyde Park as food prices rose.

In Ireland, however, where the government had been too fearful to impose conscription, nationalists took advantage of the situation

---

[*] He did a bit better in the Second World War.

to rise up for independence. On Easter Monday 1916, several hundred Irish revolutionaries seized the General Post Office in Dublin and declared a republic. They had been hoping for reinforcements from Germany, but for some reason defending Irish post offices was not high on the Kaiser's current agenda. As it was, the British suppressed the insurrection with their usual sensitivity, shelling the rebels from gunboats before sending in the troops and taking control street by street. Within a week it was all over, leaving some 500 dead. Only one leader was spared, the future Irish president Eamon de Valera, by virtue of the fact he was a US citizen, a country Britain was hoping to coax into the war.

Back on the Western front, Field Marshall Haig was making preparations for a grand offensive at the Somme that he was sure would really put the word 'great' in Great War. He was convinced that the reason all previous offensives had failed was not because running directly into the face of machine guns was a flawed tactic but simply through a lack of sufficient 'weight'. If they shelled the German lines for long enough, he reasoned, their defences would be entirely wiped out, allowing the British to walk through their front lines. It was a brilliant plan with absolutely nothing that could go wrong.

On 1 July 1916 at 7:30 a.m., after a week's intense shelling, the order was given to advance. By the end of the day, 19,000 men were dead and 38,000 more wounded, cut to pieces by machine guns behind the enemy's still intact barbed wire. Instead of abandoning the offensive, Haig ordered it to continue, certain a breakthrough was imminent. By November, there were over 600,000 allied casualties, the majority of them British, with roughly the same number on the German side. They had gained a total of two miles.

Asquith was implicated in the disaster, manipulated out of office by the ever-energetic Lloyd George. Lloyd George established a leaner cabinet office as an attempt to exert some control over the generals. But as the war slipped into its third year, nothing seemed to change except the depth of the mud. The French were nearly annihilated at Verdun, their troops mutinous and their leadership in crisis. In spring 1917, Haig ordered a new offensive at Passchendaele in Flanders, assuring a highly sceptical Lloyd George that with the fine dry weather the North Sea coast was renowned for victory would be certain. Three months of incessant rain later, the soldiers were literally drowning in mud, 240,000 casualties the price for a few more miles of sodden Belgium.

From Disaster to Triumph

As 1918 dawned, somehow none of the 200 killed or wounded generals had yet managed to be Sir Douglas Haig. But then he wasn't the kind of commander to visit the front lines. By late 1917, the Russian Revolution had finally ended the war on the eastern front, allowing a million German troops to move west. Ever the gentleman, however, the Kaiser decided to even up the odds by goading the United States into joining the other side. German U-boats had been persistently targeting American shipping in the Atlantic in order to starve Britain of supplies. The strategy, which seemed reckless at best, had actually come close to working. It was only Lloyd George's decision to force a reluctant Admiralty to institute convoys for commercial vessels that had stopped Britain being starved out of the war altogether.

The American troops would eventually prove crucial, but understandably they weren't exactly in a hurry to get there. By spring 1918 the reinforcements had still not arrived. The German command, under General Ludendorff, knew they had one last chance to strike at the Western front. In March, they attacked with three million men, using spotter planes to find the weakest points in the line. The allies were pushed back as many as forty miles, Paris threatened once more. Britain frantically built more tanks, a weapon that had been in use in limited numbers since the Somme. Up till now, their biggest use had been giving the infantry something to hide behind when they broke down in the middle of no-man's land, but by June 1918 they had finally built sufficient numbers of them to count. Having halted the German advance at the Marne, the British, French and Americans counterattacked, breaking through the new German lines and suddenly finding themselves streaming through open country. As the German retreat turned into a rout, the Kaiser pleaded for an armistice to avoid invasion, having seen the kind of mess it had left in Belgium. And so on the eleventh hour of the eleventh day of the eleventh month, the guns finally fell silent.

"Just what I planned all along," said General Haig.

What, No Happily Ever After?
As millions of British soldiers trudged home from the trenches, the fruits of their sacrifice might not have been completely clear. "Hurrah! Belgium's neutrality has been restored! The Treaty of London stands!" was not a refrain you would have heard widely shouted on the streets of the capital. The mood of the country was virulently anti-German[*]. As the allies gathered at Versailles to discuss the terms of the German surrender, Lloyd George urged caution while the British press clamoured for the Kaiser to be hanged. In the end, the allies decided to let the Kaiser live but to hang the rest of the German nation instead, in a noose of reparations and occupation. The humiliated Germans took the punishment with good grace.

"Ve accept your terms. Congratulations on winning ze First World War."

"Thanks. It was a long hard fight but in the end we... hey, what do you mean the *First* World War?"

On the domestic front, Lloyd George was supreme. In the election of 1918, the vote was extended to all men for the first time

---

[*] In 1917, George V had changed the name of the royal family to Windsor, concerned that Saxe-Coburg and Gotha might sound just a teensy bit German.

and to women over the age of thirty (to prevent them being in the majority). The Welsh Wizard decided to keep together the Liberal and Conservative coalition of the war, leaving the Liberal MPs supportive of his ousted rival Asquith to join forces with Labour in opposition. The government enacted a housing act to build a land 'fit for heroes to live in' and extended compulsory schooling to the age of fourteen. But with the Tories holding the majority within the coalition, it was now Labour, not the Liberals, who were regarded as the champions of the working classes.

Unlike the Second World War, there was no post-war boom to soften the horror of a conflict that had cost the lives of over 700,000 British young men. To help prosecute the war, Britain had borrowed from the Americans and lent to the Tsar of Russia, who was less inclined to repay them now that he and his family had been murdered by the Bolsheviks. The ballooning national debt made it harder to stimulate an economy thoroughly in the doldrums. Unemployment rose alarmingly while everybody else went on strike, angry that their sacrifice had not translated into greater income and security. To make matters worse, an influenza epidemic struck the moment the guns stopped firing, claiming 228,000 lives in Britain and as many as fifty million worldwide between 1918 and 1919, a greater death toll than the Black Death[*].

Amidst all this gloom, people really needed something to keep their spirits up, to remind them that things were not nearly as bad as they could be. Luckily, for that they had Ireland. Sinn Fein won almost all the seats in the 1918 election, but instead of coming to Westminster they set up their own parliament in Dublin, the Déil with de Valera as president. The southern Irish largely accepted the authority of the new government, but with the police and army dominated by the Protestant British, there was clearly another

---

[*] Wartime censors downplayed the crisis in Europe with only the Spanish press allowed to report freely. This gave the false impression that Spain was hit hardest, hence the pandemic's nickname the Spanish Flu.

showdown on the way. Michael Collins provided the necessary glamour, leading the new Irish Republican Army into open war against the British state. Attacks by the IRA were met with vicious reprisals by undisciplined 'Black and Tan' police auxiliaries, many of them former soldiers from the trenches. The Black and Tans tortured suspects and burned villages to the ground, including the entire centre of Cork, as the country erupted into lawlessness and chaos. Finally, Lloyd George called for negotiations which led to the establishment of the Irish Free State in 1921, an arbitrary border partitioning Ireland between the Unionist north and the Republican south.

"Well, that should solve everything, shouldn't it?" said exactly no-one.

Labour Gains Power... for Five Minutes

By 1922, Lloyd George's coalition was fraying at the seams. A new recession had hit in 1920 and the Treasury was all but bankrupted by war debts and social spending. Lloyd George was approaching sixty and his boundless energy was beginning to get a bit annoying to his more staid Tory colleagues. He had been a notorious womaniser throughout his life, endowed 'like a donkey' according to an envious male aide who had seen him in the bath. The popular song *Lloyd George Knew My Father* attested to his numerous affairs and illegitimate children. But what really hurt his popularity was the more prosaic scandal of selling cash for honours to finance his large private office, which he insisted was not a euphemism for his penis. That, along with the compromise with the Irish Republicans, finally persuaded the Conservatives that they would be better off without him.

In October 1922, a group of Tory backbenchers, under the leadership of a Midlands MP named Stanley Baldwin, met at the Carlton Club in St James's and decided to withdraw support from the coalition. In the general election that followed the collapse of the coalition, the Tories won an overall majority, their jubilant backbenchers calling themselves the 1922 Committee ever after.

The exuberance of Lloyd George gave way to the conciliatory pipe-smoking Baldwin, whose gentle oratorical style was suited to the new medium of communication that was starting to sweep the nation: radio. But Baldwin's attempt to bring up the old issue of tariff reform backfired once again for his party. Calling an election to decide the issue, Baldwin's saw the Conservatives lose out to a coalition of Labour and the Liberals, with Labour as the largest party. In January 1924, George V appointed Britain's first ever Labour prime minister, Ramsay MacDonald, the son of a Scottish farm labourer.

It was never going to be an easy ride. Convinced that MacDonald's cabinet of clerks, mill-hands and engine drivers would confiscate property, murder the upper classes, and trail mud into Buckingham Palace, the mainly Tory press greeted their every move with deep suspicion. MacDonald's response was to govern with moderation, curbing the more radical elements of his own party. But this only really succeeded in alienating his own supporters. In the end, his minority government lasted just nine months, about the time it took Lloyd George to father another illegitimate child. Forced to call a general election after losing a vote of confidence, MacDonald's downfall was assured by what turned out to be a forged letter from a Soviet leader, Grigory Zinoviev, which was published in the *Daily Mail*, not, one would have assumed, the communist's original choice. The Zinoviev letter pressed for a working class uprising in Britain with the aid of Labour's more extreme members. The Tories won the election 419 seats to Labour's 151.

The General Strike

Baldwin was a largely sincere man. Earlier in his career, he had donated one-fifth of his personal fortune to the Treasury to help pay off the war debt, a noble gesture that had inspired thousands of other wealthy individuals around the country to think of reasons why they shouldn't do the same. As prime minister, he vowed to bring Britain 'tranquility and freedom from adventures at home and abroad', pleasing an electorate that had got a little tired of barbed wire and trenches. He invited the self-governing dominions of Canada, Australia, New Zealand and South Africa into the 'Commonwealth' in order to give Britain a chance at winning some medals in athletics. Unfortunately, of course, that meant none of the non-white countries could yet join because you know what Kenya is like at running.

The only real surprise of his government was the return of Churchill as chancellor of the exchequer. Determined to prove that the debacle of Gallipoli wasn't just a fluke, Churchill set about destroying the British economy in a similar fashion by fixing the pound against the gold standard at far too high a rate[*]. Her currency overvalued, Britain's coal exports were suddenly rendered uncompetitive on the global market, leading the coal companies to demand longer hours from their workers and a cut in wages. The miners' union responded with a sassy: 'Not a penny off the pay, not a minute on the day', and the TUC, feeling they ought to show solidarity, called for a General Strike. On 3 May 1926, millions of workers in all the key industries downed tools in support of the miners, bringing the entire country to a standstill.

In Moscow, communist agitators frantically penned imaginary letters calling for revolution, but in Britain that didn't seem quite appropriate in the gentle sunshine of spring. Instead the country mucked in to get things moving. Oxford students drove buses, fascinated by the novelty of working for a living, and middle-class housewives sorted the mail. Behind the scenes, Baldwin busily negotiated a settlement, managing to isolate the coal industry via a commission of inquiry. After nine days, the TUC, having become rather fearful of the movement they had unleashed, abruptly called off the strike, leaving the miners to struggle on alone and

---

[*] It's okay, nobody understood it then either.

unsuccessfully. Legislation preventing sympathy strikes soon followed, defeat for the workers almost total. The Oxford students went back to bed, exhausted but happy.

Sane, Commonsense Chaos

After the General Strike, calm returned to the nation. Though most workers still survived on meagre wages, economic progress was steady. A million cars drove on British roads by the end of the 1920s, the experience made all the more thrilling by the absence of a driving test. In fact, more people were killed in traffic accidents in the 1920s than they are today. Meanwhile, the Tory government, with Neville Chamberlain as minister for health and welfare, passed just enough social legislation to appease the working classes.

"Excellent policy is appeasement," thought Chamberlain excitedly.

The truth was, however, that in terms of economic power Britain was now dwarfed by the United States, whose tentacles and finance were everywhere. In 1929, the Tories lost the election, having extended the vote to women in their twenties, the last disenfranchised group in Britain. Under a hung parliament, Labour was put back in power under Ramsay MacDonald.

Inevitably, therefore, the United States chose this exact moment to plunge the entire world into a great depression. On 24 October, over-speculation in the bond market triggered a catastrophic crash on Wall Street. As American stockbrokers threw themselves out of their office windows, leaving the world to clean up their mess in more ways than one, European stock markets plunged. Unemployment in Britain rose from one million to a two and a half million in a single year, while the collapse of European banks brought hyperinflation in Germany. The Bank of England warned that they were on the brink of national bankruptcy, which didn't really help to calm the nerves.

The Labour cabinet proposed a programme of public works as

the economost John Maynard Keynes had advocated, but were overruled by the chancellor Philip Snowden, who was convinced austerity was the way to go[*]. When nine ministers walked out in protest, MacDonald went to the king to resign only for George V to refuse to let him. Instead, with the support of the Tories, MacDonald took Snowden's plan to the country and was rewarded with a mandate for cuts that utterly wiped out his own party. Expelled from Labour as a traitor, he continued to govern as the head of a de facto Tory government. He gradually got used to the feeling of dining alone.

On the continent, people had come to see that the solution to economic depression was to elect depraved, spit-emitting madmen like Hitler and Mussolini. The closest Britain got to fascism were the thuggish blackshirts of Oswald Mosley, a charismatic ex-Labour MP who had learned from Mussolini that by beating up Jews and Communists in London they might be able to get the trains to run on time. Instead of fascism, MacDonald and Baldwin implemented Snowden's cuts and devalued the pound by taking it off the gold standard.

The depression continued until around 1936, the year of the Jarrow Crusade when 200 unemployed walked from Tyneside to London, got a nice pat on the back and then, wisely, decided to get the train back. The same year saw the unconscionable royal scandal of the new king Edward VIII turning his back on the monarchy in order to marry Mrs Wallis Simpson, a two-time American divorcee. After being given an ultimatum by Baldwin to either give up the affair or to abdicate, Edward chose 'the woman I love'. He lived out the rest of his days with Wallis in France, buying a country house next door to Oswald Mosley, with whom he shared a love of extravagant parties and Nazi social policy.

---

[*] They were just as smart in 1931 as they were in 2010.

The Road to War - Again

After six years as chancellor, Neville Chamberlain assumed the premiership in 1937 at a time when it was becoming clear that clever adjustments to the tax system might not be the major issues of the day. Hitler had been steadily rearming Germany since his rise to power in 1933, a blatant violation of the Treaty of Versailles that the major powers had overlooked on the grounds that he was small and had a silly moustache. By 1937, however, he had invaded the Rhineland and was starting to talk about an Anschluss with Austria. Into this crisis stepped Neville Chamberlain. The son of Joseph Chamberlain, Neville was an able politician who had helped to steer Britain out of the great depression. But he was a cold and distant figure who possessed 'the mind and manner of a clothes-brush' according to a fellow MP. He was utterly out of his depth when dealing with Hitler.

In September 1938, after completing the Anschluss with Austria, Hitler declared his intention to occupy the Czech Sudetenland in order to secure living space for his ego. Chamberlain travelled to Munich to hammer out a calm and rational deal with this rabid Nazi madman. Speaking on behalf of the Czechs, whom he'd absent-mindedly forgotten to invite, Chamberlain told Hitler he could have the Sudetenland just as long as he agreed to promise not to invade anywhere else.

"I agree to promise not to invade anywhere else," replied Hitler gracefully.

If Chamberlain's Munich agreement seemed like a craven capitulation to naked German aggression, that's because it was. However, it was hugely popular at the time. Although Britain had been reluctantly arming herself since the mid-1930s, she was neither ready for war nor even remotely interested in having one. There was even a train of thought that Hitler was a useful bulwark against communist Russia, in the sense that stomach cancer is a useful bulwark against obesity. Of the major figures of the day, only Churchill spoke against appeasement, booed in the House when he described Munich as a 'total and unmitigated defeat'.

Chamberlain's triumph was short-lived. In March 1939, Hitler broke his cast-iron promise and rolled his tanks into Prague. Having signed an agreement with Stalin not to invade Russia until he was ready, he then launched a blitzkrieg on Poland. Two days later, on 3 September, Chamberlain took to the radio to announce to the nation that Hitler had rejected Britain's ultimatum to withdraw from Poland 'and that consequently this country is at war with Germany'. This time nobody said anything about Christmas.

The Not So Phony War

Britain braced itself for war. A blackout was imposed on the streets and one and a half million children evacuated into the countryside. But for the first eight months no German bombers appeared in the skies and the British Expeditionary Force in France were left cleaning their rifles. The blackout, in fact, killed more people than any actual fighting. It turned out that Hitler was too busy dividing up eastern Europe with Russia to bother with opening up a Western front, and the allies had decided it would be unwise to attack the Germans themselves until France had had a chance to properly surrender. On 4 April 1940, Chamberlain stood in front of his party and confidently declared that Hitler had 'missed the bus'.

It turned out, however, that Hitler had not been planning to come to Europe by bus. On 9 April, German ships seized Norwegian ports and installed a puppet government under the Norwegian Nazi Vidkun Quisling. They took Denmark on the same day. Humiliated, Chamberlain was forced to resign, replaced by the only man who had predicted this was how appeasement would end. In his first speech as prime minister, Winston Churchill told the Commons that his only policy was 'to wage war by land, sea and air', offering 'nothing but blood, toil, tears and sweat'. It sounded delightful.

On 10 May, Germany invaded France. As the French lines crumbled, Churchill flew to Paris to convince his allies to hold strong. He arrived to find the French government burning their papers. By 20 May, German tanks had reached the Somme and, cut off from their supplies, the BEF was forced to retreat to Dunkirk. There was nothing now to stop the German army destroying Britain's entire force. Luckily, however, the British had a secret weapon that the Nazis had not counted on: Adolf Hitler. In one of quite a few baffling orders he was to make during the next five years, Hitler commanded his army to halt, telling them to 'leave Dunkirk to the Luftwaffe'.

Nearly 340,000 allied troops, a third of them French, were trapped on the beaches of Dunkirk, the port too narrow for the big Royal Navy ships to get near. Death or capture seemed inevitable until suddenly through the fog a vast armada of 'little ships' appeared: fishing boats, river ferries, lifeboats and private yachts whose owners had risked their lives to come to the soldiers' aid. Between 27 May and 4 June, almost the entire force was evacuated, a devastating defeat turned into another plucky British triumph against adversity.

The Battle of Britain

When the retreat of your entire continental army is the most successful thing you have accomplished in the first year of the war, it's a pretty good sign that things are not going your way. In June 1940, German troops and landing crafts were massing in the ports along the North Sea in preparation for an invasion of Britain, codenamed Operation Sealion. In the face of almost certain doom, Winston Churchill provided the kind of defiant leadership that had so deserted the French: 'We shall defend our island, whatever the cost may be. We shall fight on the beaches. We shall fight on the landing grounds. We shall fight in the fields and in the streets. We shall fight in the hills. Or is it on the hills? You know what I mean.'

The Germans knew that any invasion across the Channel would leave their transports at the mercy of Britain's air force and navy, which was still floating idly in Scapa Flow in the Orkney Islands.

The destruction of the enemy's air defences by the Luftwaffe was, therefore, a crucial prerequisite to success. From July to October 1940, Hurricanes and Spitfires sparred with Messerschmitt fighters and Heinkel bombers, a daily life and death struggle just about visible to the men, women and children gazing up at the smoke trails in the sky. There was little to choose between either the skill of the pilots or the quality of their planes. What finally turned the Battle of Britain in the home nation's favour was a combination of superior British radar and, more importantly, the fuel constraints of the long-travelling German aircraft. At its height, five German planes were being shot down for each British; and thanks to her ramped-up aircraft production, Britain ended the fight with more planes than she began it with. Churchill was typically low-key in his oration: 'Never in the field of human conflict was so much owed by so many to so few.'

As far as the Germans were concerned, however, the battle was not over. Britain had been launching long-range bombing missions over Berlin for months, and it was a sense of injured pride that drove Hitler to order the same for London. For 57 consecutive nights from 7 September bombs fell on the capital, on one terrible night setting a greater area alight than the Great Fire had done in 1666. The raids soon spread further afield to Birmingham, Coventry, Swansea and the south coast ports. At night, the songs of Vera Lynn drifted down the underground stations and shelters where people huddled together. Rationing was imposed on food, clothing and fuel as German U-boats sank supply ships almost at will. The 'national loaf' of white bread was replaced by wholemeal, to the disgust of everyone then and ever since; bacon and bananas were nonexistent[*]. In a national campaign to 'make do and mend', women were told to wear ankle socks instead of stockings; their dresses had to be straight without pleats or ruffles; men's suits

---

[*] The only popular food not rationed was fish and chips after a campaign by fishermen; as a bonus, it came freely wrapped in newspaper war propaganda.

could not have turn-ups; frills were banned on knickers. It was absolute hell.

Throughout it all, the famed blitz spirit kept morale more or less intact. If they could endure yet another nighttime rendition of *The White Cliffs of Dover*, people could endure anything. The king and queen drew praise for refusing to leave London, while Churchill toured bomb-hit districts with his defiant cry that 'London can take it'. Luckily his house was in the country. The bombing began to drop in intensity from spring 1941, but the situation overseas was desperate. Hitler had driven the British garrison from Crete and Rommel had the army in Africa in retreat. Unable to land any army on the continent, Britain desperately needed the United States to enter the war, preferably a little bit earlier than they had the last time. Churchill enjoyed a good relationship with President Roosevelt and was delighted when Roosevelt won his second term in 1941.

Churchill: Congratulations again, Mr President. What were
             you campaigning on this time?
Roosevelt: Staying out of the Second World War.
Churchill: Oh.

With a Congress urging neutrality, the best Churchill could get was a Lend-Lease agreement through which the United States provided the allied powers with desperately needed supplies of food, materials and weaponry in return for a guarantee that the allies would pay them back sometime before the earth stopped circling the sun.

By itself, however, the Lend-Lease agreement was nothing more than a plaster over a gangrenous wound. To have any chance of surviving even the following year, Britain needed to bring out its secret weapon one more time.

The Beginning of the End, or the End of the Beginning, or Something

Hitler had never been fond of communists (or Jews, gypsies, gays, blacks, Poles, Slavs, priests, vagrants, Catholics, Freemasons, Jehovah's Witnesses, pacifists, drug addicts, alcoholics, disabled people or men with a full set of tackle[*]). Inside his mind, therefore, it made perfect sense to declare war on the Soviet Union in June 1941. Likewise, in the far east, where Japan was determined to make further strides in its national policy of forcing all its citizens to commit suicide, it made perfect sense to launch a surprise attack on Pearl Harbor six months later, thus bringing the United States into the war. It was just in the minds of everyone else in the world that these two acts seemed completely and utterly mental.

Operation Barbarossa took up four and a half million German soldiers, sucking in almost the entire Nazi war machine for the remainder of the conflict. Churchill had no hesitation in making an alliance with Stalin, writing later that 'if Hitler had invaded Hell I would make at least a favourable reference to the Devil in the House of Commons.' In the Devil stakes, Stalin was not far off, and at the Battle of Stalingrad in the winter of 1942 the Germans finally met their hell, albeit one where snowballs definitely did have a chance. In the east, the Japanese continued to ride roughshod over Britain's colonial empire, showing even less respect for the locals than the British had. Hong Kong fell in the weeks after Pearl Harbor, followed by the humiliating capitulation of Singapore in February 1942 when 130,000 allied troops fell prisoner. Given the brutality with which the Japanese treated POWs, very few of them made it back. But even Japan's progress could not last forever and their advance was decisively halted in June 1942 by the American naval victory at Midway.

The first notable British victory came in north Africa, still the major theatre of ground operations in the war. In August 1942, Churchill appointed General Montgomery as commander of the

---

[*] A German researcher who unearthed Hitler's long-lost medical records seemed to confirm the wartime song was true, as the flawless Aryan superman apparently had 'right-side cryptorchidism' or an undescended right testicle. Quite how the music hall performers knew is a mystery.

British Eighth Army in Egypt. Unconventional, clever and magnificently arrogant, 'Monty' transformed the flagging morale of his troops almost overnight, visiting them regularly on the front lines while bringing greater cohesion to their efforts. In October 1942, the Desert Rats dealt Rommel his first major defeat at El Alamein, capturing 30,000 of his troops and putting him on the defensive for the rest of the war. For Churchill, it was a much-needed victory and he felt confident enough to make another landmark speech: 'Now this is not the end. It is not even the beginning of the end. But it is, perhaps, the end of the beginning.' At which point his audience jumped to their feet and answered with one ecstatic voice: "Hurrah! Er... what?"

The End of the End

Churchill was right. In July 1943, the allies finally managed to get a foothold on the continent. They had been reading the enemy's Enigma codes since 1940, the number of deciphered messages rising as Bletchley Park boffins like Alan Turing increased their ability to hide the fact they were gay[*]. Now they added subterfuge of their own to the mix. Planning to land troops in Sicily, they confused the Germans by planting an invasion plan for Sardinia on a corpse dressed as a British army major. Hitler, never one to miss a chance to help the allies, duly fell for the ruse, ordering thousands of troops to be diverted to Sardinia. Sicily was taken quickly and from there it was a long hard slog up to Rome.

With thousands of British soldiers tied up in the invasion of Italy, American troops spotted their opportunity and invaded Britain. One and a half million G.I.s arrived on the island from late 1943, billeted in private homes where they were warned not to tell their British comrades how well they were being paid. 'Over-paid, over-sexed and over here' was the common refrain, though a

---

[*] Homosexuality was still illegal in Britain, and Turing committed suicide in 1954 after being convicted of indecency.

certain portion of the British population seemed perfectly happy about all three. In 1944, as General Eisenhower and General Montgomery plotted the Normandy landings, the bombing wing of the RAF under Air Marshall 'Bomber' Harris continued to pound German cities to dust on the strategic grounds that they might as well do something with all the bombs they'd made. There was little military value to the bombing and Harris was controversial even at the time, nicknamed the 'Butcher' within the RAF. Most controversial was his obliteration of the historic city of Dresden in February 1945, which killed at least 25,000 civilians. The Germans, of course, would have loved to do the same to London and had one last fling with the V1 and V2 flying bombs, over 3000 of which hit the capital in the closing years of the war.

The real action, however, was going to be in Normandy. Or would it be somewhere else? An elaborate series of diversionary tactics were implemented to confuse the Germans, including the construction of entire fields of dummy tanks. In the end, however, the landings succeeded with sheer brute force: 156,000 men on 5000 ships with a further 20,000 paratroopers dropped behind the lines. Over half were British. Churchill was determined to take part personally on HMS Belfast, but was overruled by George VI on the grounds that no battleship could possibly take his weight. On D Day itself, 6 June, nearly 4,500 men lost their lives, the worst of the fighting on the heavily-defended Omaha beach. By day's end, however, the beachheads were secured.

It took two months for the allies to liberate the city of Paris and about two weeks for the French to stop being grateful. In January 1945, the Germans made a last-ditch attempt to counterattack at the Battle of the Bulge in the Ardennes, but, just like the weight loss diets that thenceforth shamelessly played on the battle's name, their brief success only delayed the inevitable. On 28 April, Mussolini and his mistress were executed by Italian partisans, hung upside-down like a prosciutto, and on the next day Eva Braun finally married Adolf Hitler, though only on the condition they both commit suicide as soon as possible. Unfortunately for the German people, the Russians got to Berlin before the allies, having revealed the full horrors of the death camps to a revolted world. On 8 May, the German army surrendered and Britain was finally able to bring out the bunting for VE day. In one final act of defiance, Winston Churchill gave the whole country the V-sign.

11. POST-WAR BRITAIN (1945 – 1997)

Britain emerged from two world wars with her patriotism and pride at its peak. It was just everything else that was completely knackered. Alone, without any help whatsoever from the Americans or the Russians, she had defeated the Nazis and saved Europe from fascism; however, in doing so she had all but bankrupted herself. Her citizens demanded change, believing that the state owed them something after five years of wholewheat bread. The welfare state was the result: free education, old-age pensions, and a National Health Service. The NHS was a unique institution that gave all members of British society, no matter how powerless or poor, an equal right to complain about it all the time. The rest of the post-war years saw a bitter ideological battle between the political left and the political right. While Labour favoured socialism and nationalisation, with the state taking full responsibility for running vital industries into the ground, the Tories promoted free market capitalism, in which these same vital industries could be privately and responsibly managed into permanent non-existence. Margaret Thatcher won the battle as well as showing that Britain was still capable of defending its once great empire by liberating the Falklands Islands, a vital archipelago that some people in Britain could almost find on a map.

The New Order
The war with Japan was still not over when, for the first time since 1935, Britain held a general election. The Tories had wanted to keep the wartime coalition going until final victory had been achieved, but the Labour Party under Clement Attlee was tired of

choking on Churchill's cigar smoke and wanted out*. It was an acrimonious campaign, with Churchill starting what would soon become a time-honoured tradition of comparing his opponents to Nazis, saying they would need a Gestapo to impose their socialist agenda. Of course, there was no doubt the old warhorse would win. It would be an act of extraordinary ingratitude to depose the leader who had done more than any other person, apart from Adolf Hitler of course, to win Britain the war. Thus, when the votes were finally counted, no shock at all when Labour emerged with a landslide victory. Churchill was devastated, plunged into a black depression for weeks. On VE day, he had given the nation the V-sign, but he hadn't expected them to give it him back. Even the soldiers had not voted for him.

Clement Attlee assumed the premiership during the midst of the Potsdam Conference, the second of the great meetings between the Big Three of Russia, Britain and the United States to discuss the post-war international order. At Yalta and Potsdam, the two western leaders pressed Stalin on the issue of Eastern Europe, demanding that free and democratic elections be held in Russian-occupied Poland.

"Of course!" replied Stalin. "We'll call it the Democratic People's Republic of Poland or something. That sounds free."

While Stalin lied to his counterparts, President Truman, taking over after Roosevelt's death in April 1945, kept one small fact hidden at Potsdam too: he had an atomic bomb. Two in fact. In August 1945, with Japan still refusing to surrender and Russia threatening to invade Japan from the north, Truman ordered the bombings of Hiroshima and Nagasaki, vapourising two populous civilian cities in a flash of blinding fury. Japan surrendered days later. In total, Britain and her colonies had lost around 383,000

---

* It's been estimated that Churchill smoked around 200,000 Cuban cigars in his lifetime, while he drank so much brandy with his meals that guests resorted to pouring it into their shoes.

soldiers and 67,000 civilians in the war, around half the number of deaths of the First World War. By contrast, in the Soviet Union close to 27 million had died, over 13% of the population.

It was a new world in August 1945. As Britain celebrated VJ day, there was an awareness that she had lost her position as the world's preeminent power. Britain, America and Russia might call themselves the Big Three but only while the British representatives were still within earshot. There were also nuclear weapons in the equation, and it was suddenly clear that if the world powers ever decided to have a World War Three, there was a very good chance they wouldn't get to have a fourth one.

The Welfare State

The Labour Party had been very clear about what it would do if it gained power, though they were strangely tight-lipped about the Gestapo. In 1942, the coalition government had commissioned a policy report from the economist William Beveridge, who identified five 'giant evils' of disease, want, squalor, ignorance and idleness, some of which, he found, existed outside the House of Commons too. As a solution, he recommended the creation of a comprehensive welfare state with each working citizen paying a new 'national insurance' to fund it. When Labour took power in 1945, the Beveridge Report became the foundation of their domestic policy.

Clement Attlee was the perfect leader to steer Beveridge's radical proposals through. While his cabinet was packed with fiery egos like Ernest Bevin at the Foreign Office, Aneurin Bevan at health and Herbert Morrison[*] as deputy prime minister, Attlee was another quiet and modest pipe-smoker though, if Churchill was to be believed, he had 'much to be modest about'. He drove around in a small car, walked to lunch at his club and was so brief in speech that when he met the equally tongue-tied George VI for the first

---

[*] grandfather of Labour grandee Peter Mandelson, if you must know

time, neither could think of a single thing to say to each other. No great orator, he worked best behind the scenes, soothing tensions between his ministers who, as proper left-wingers, hated only one thing more than the Tories and that was each other.

Despite the laconic character of its leader, there was an early exhilaration in the slew of social reforms unveiled by the new government. The National Insurance Act of 1946 introduced child benefit, unemployment benefit, sickness benefit, maternity benefit, old-age pensions and a funeral allowance. It was a comprehensive system that aimed to protect people 'from cradle to grave', though most of the time between cradle and grave would, of course, be spent queuing for the necessary forms. Attlee's government also ensured the full implementation of the 1944 Butler Education Act, which provided free secondary education and scholarships for universities. At age eleven all children, regardless of background, were to take a national intelligence test that would allocate them to either a grammar school or a 'secondary modern', according to whether they seemed suited to a bowler hat or a flat cap.

Most revolutionary of all the social reforms was the creation of the National Health Service in 1948. Members of the medical profession fiercely resisted the plan out of fears they would lose their lucrative private patients, while the Tories had images of the working-classes stuffing their mouths with gold fillings and sweeping the shelves of chemists for free prescription drugs[*]. In fact, it was the doctors who had their 'mouths stuffed with gold', as Bevan admitted, bought off with salary increases and promises that they could keep their private practices. With the bill's passage, the NHS became the country's third biggest employer almost overnight, with 364,000 staff including 149,000 nurses and midwives. In its first year of operation, it dealt with over eight million dental patients and gave out five million pairs of thick-

---

[*] secret addiction to prescription drugs was strictly reserved for the middle-classes

rimmed prescription glasses, which only added to the British people's global reputation for style and panache.

The creation of the NHS marked the dawn of centralised state control over society. 'If a bedpan lands on the floor in the hospital in Tredegar, it should be clanging in Whitehall,' said Bevan. Key parts of the economy including the Bank of England and the coal, rail, aviation, gas, electricity and steel industries were all nationalised, covering 20% of the British economy.

End of the Party

The flurry of social and economic reform did not mask the fact that there was not a lot to cheer about in the early post-war years. Once the bunting had been taken down, Britain selected grey to be its new national colour. Grey clouds, grey fog, grey soot and grey faces. Half a million homes had been bombed out in the war and, with the end of the Lend-Lease programme, there was little money or materials to rebuild them. Thousands of people were forced to live in temporary shelters and hostels, and even sections of the London Underground. Others were allocated government 'prefab' houses constructed en masse inside aircraft factories. As a long-term solution, the government planned the construction of twenty New Towns to be built across the country, which became the beacons of British architectural excellence known as Stevenage, Runcorn, Bracknell, Telford, Hatfield and Milton Keynes. Suddenly living in the London Underground didn't seem too bad.

Naturally, the weather was atrocious as well. The winter of 1946 was the coldest on record, freezing the mines shut and forcing factories to close through lack of power. As people queued grimly for bread and coal, the government had few answers. Rationing became even stricter than during the war itself, the only option for hard-pressed housewives being black market 'spivs' who offered rare and exotic goods like salt in unconvincing Cockney accents. Weary British soldiers trudged back from the war to find that not only were they without homes, work or decent food but that all the best-looking girls had gone too, 50,000 of them escaping to the booming United States with American servicemen.

Politically, Attlee barely survived cabinet plots to oust him, the refusal of Ernest Bevin to join the rebels the only thing that kept the prime minister's pipe lit. As foreign secretary, Bevin himself was busy with the harsh realities of the post-war world. America had come to the aid of Europe once more with the massive Marshall Plan bailout, but President Truman insisted that most of the money received by Britain be spent on defence, ruining Attlee's plan to blow it all on a night out in Stevenage. As Churchill warned of an 'iron curtain' descending across the continent, Bevin took Britain into the United Nations and, soon after, the more muscular NATO alliance as a way to keep the Russians out of Western Europe. While Britain was able to play an important role in both these organisations, mainly by virtue of the fact everybody was forced to speak English all the time, she had little choice but to divest herself of a good chunk of her once mighty empire.

The most significant territory to be released was India. Thanks to the tireless efforts of Mohandas Gandhi, India had become a prominent and very audible opponent of British colonialism, less a jewel in Britain's crown and more an embarrassing boil on the side of her face. Gandhi and his supporters spent much of the Second World War in prison, but when hostilities ceased Britain finally bowed to the inevitable and granted independence. Unfortunately by then India had conflict of its own, as nationalist Hindus and Muslims suddenly found each other even easier to hate than the British. A decision was made, opposed by an aging Gandhi, to partition the country between India and Pakistan, leading to the deaths of some 500,000 people in riots as millions journeyed north and south to their new lands. Gandhi himself was assassinated by a nationalist Hindu in 1948. He had lived just long enough to see his country win a troubled independence but not quite long enough to see the looks on English faces when Indian cricketers started bowling leg spin at them.

As well as India, Britain also gave independence to Sri Lanka, Myanmar and Jordan, the latter as part of the creation of the state of Israel. War and conflict followed in those places too. Still, many parts of the empire remained under British control, including Malaysia, Singapore, Barbados, Jamaica, Malta, Cyprus, Kuwait, Qatar, Bahrain and large swathes of Africa. The impatient citizens of these nations would have to wait until the 1950s and 1960s to get their chance to hack each other's heads off.

Goodbye Labour, Hello Tories

Labour managed to squeak home in the election of February 1950 with a majority of just five seats, which would force them to call a new election just eight months later. In June 1950, the Korean War broke out and the government was forced to increase health charges to raise money to send troops. Bevan and other left-wingers resigned in protest. Having just put their feet up after defeating Japan, young conscripts found themselves lacing up their boots to fight another brutal and incomprehensible war in East Asia. Support from cradle to grave, the state had promised them, but it hadn't specified where that grave might be. The Tories stumbled back into power under Churchill.

By now Churchill was 76 years-old and his major legislative aim for his second term was to see how loudly he could snore before anyone was brave enough to wake him up. He had suffered a mild stroke in 1949 and if that hadn't slowed him enough, he had another more serious one in June 1953. The Tories had promised a 'bonfire of controls' to free the country from state power, but, apart from introducing charges for prescriptions, they kept the welfare state intact. They did succeed in increasing house construction, with Harold Macmillan the perfect appointment as a new Minister of Housing, since housing was the only thing he was less boring than. However, domestic policies were overshadowed by events in Britain's crumbling empire with armed uprisings in Kenya and Malaysia. The Mao Mao rebellion in Kenya cost the lives of as many as 20,000 natives, but it was not until 2012 that the British government finally admitted that torture had been used against the rebels, there having been some doubt as to whether slicing off ears, burning with paraffin, flogging to death and castration was really anything more than playful high jinks[*].

In 1955, Churchill finally resigned in favour of his foreign secretary, Anthony Eden. His second term could not be judged a success, though it was brightened by the coronation of Elizabeth II in 1953, the first national event to be shown on television. He eventually died in 1965 at the age of ninety after another stroke, his state funeral attracting one of the largest gatherings of world dignitaries in history.

Eden and the Suez Crisis

During his second term, Churchill had tried hard to cultivate what he called the 'special relationship' with the United States, though his refusal to wear a hearing aid in his meetings with President Eisenhower had made it a trifle difficult to share intelligence. Britain was still trying to come to terms with her loss of status in the world, but if she had any doubts that things would never be the same as they were, the Suez Crisis safely settled it once and for all.

The crisis was precipitated when the new nationalist president of Egypt, President Nasser, claimed the Suez Canal as Egyptian property on the flimsy, underhanded grounds that it was in their country. This was a blow to the British government, one of the original financiers of the canal under Disraeli, who had maintained a strong influence over the canal's operation. Anthony Eden viewed Nasser as a kind of Arab Hitler who must not be appeased.

---

[*] The victims included Barack Obama's grandfather, who, according to his widow, had pins pushed beneath his nails and his testicles crushed between two metal rods. "Yes we can," the British had said.

If he was allowed to grab the Suez, what might he go after next? The pyramids? The Sphinx? The mask of Tutankhamen? He had to be stopped. Eden conspired with the French and the Israelis to launch an attack on the upstart country. The Israelis would invade through the Sinai, and then Britain and France would use the conflict as a pretext to seize the Suez.

The military part of the plan went flawlessly. As Nasser's military retreated from the Israelis, Anglo-French planes destroyed the Egyptian air force and parachuted in an assault force. It took all of a day for them to reach the Suez before, in a small setback to their plan for world domination, they were ordered to go back home. It turned out that the US, under their strangely pacifist lifelong soldier President Eisenhower, was not really on board with a Franco-British empire, however novel it sounded, and neither in fact were many people in either Britain or France. Humiliated, Eden was forced to resign, while the special relationship with the US turned decidedly frosty.

You've Never Had It So Good

Eden was succeeded by Harold Macmillan, an elderly aristocratic tree who had lived through the Battle of the Somme. While Eden was all nervous excitement, Macmillan exuded quiet unflappable calm, a solid slab of dependable oak stood firm against the political winds. His nickname of Supermac was meant ironically, but Macmillan turned it into a compliment, his confidence in the natural order of things reinforced by the 35 Old Etonians he appointed to his government. 'Most of our people have never had it so good,' he declared in 1957, though to be fair people from Eton had always done okay.

Macmillan was a One Nation Tory of the Disraeli tradition, unafraid to use a bit of Keynesian magic to keep unemployment low and wages high. Indeed, average real pay for industrial workers rose by twenty percent in the 1950s, with further improvements to living standards helped by a Housing Act, a

Clean Air Act and a reduction in the standard working week from 48 to 42 hours. In foreign policy too, he followed a steady course, negotiating with the Soviets under Khrushchev to ease the Cold War tension while declining to join the Common Market established by six European nations through the Treaty of Rome in 1957. Where he did take risks was in accelerating Britain's nuclear weapons programme, the pressure to produce military-grade plutonium contributing to a fire at the Windscale nuclear plant in 1957. Luckily the risks were far enough away from London for the government to cover up details of the accident, which anti-nuclear groups claimed led to as many as 1000 deaths from cancer.

In 1959, Macmillan won re-election with an increased majority. Early the following year he embarked on a tour of sub-Saharan Africa, dispensing independence to a slew of British colonies as he went along. 'The wind of change is blowing through this continent,' he intoned grandly, perhaps referring to the array of psychotic African dictators who were happily lining up to take his place. Back home, people were getting used to the fact their nation didn't have colonies anymore. But they were less used to the fact that quite a few of these colonies seemed to have moved into Britain, sometimes right at the bottom of their street. Serious racial conflict began to rear its ugly head in the late 1950s, notably in the Notting Hill riots of 1958 when hundreds of white 'Teddy Boys' launched indiscriminate attacks on their West Indian neighbours.

Despite the strong economy, Macmillan's government began to lose its touch. The Beeching Report into the railways led to the axing of thousands of stations and tracks as the government realised that the key to creating an efficient modern rail network was to force people to go by car. As Macmillan's popularity faded, his government was rocked by the scandal of the Profumo affair, which managed to combine both of the nation's two favourite interests: sex and spying. In March 1963, it was revealed that the balding middle-aged Minister for War, John Profumo, had been paying for sex with a would-be model named Christine Keeler, who, it quickly transpired, had been providing a similar service for a Soviet naval attaché called Yevgeny Ivanov. In the midst of the Cold War, the nation was both fascinated and appalled by the possibility that a nineteen year-old model would be willing to sleep with John Profumo, no matter how many secrets he offered. As for the suspicion she may have passed Profumo's war secrets to her Soviet client, an investigation concluded there was no case to answer on the grounds that the whole thing was embarrassing enough as it was.

By the autumn, Macmillan was barely hanging on to his position. His friends on the cabinet urged him to resign, because that's what friends were for, and a bout of prostrate trouble in October finally convinced him they were right.

Sex, Drugs and Harold Wilson

By 1964, Britain had inadvertently found itself at the centre of an era of free love and rock 'n' roll that did absolutely nothing for Macmillan's prostrate trouble. As the first generation to be free from national service, Britain's teenagers had time to let their hair down and bring their skirts up. The Beatles had produced their first albums, leading the 'British invasion' of the United States, and Mick Jagger's lips were not far behind. While the youth of America were sticking their fingers up at the Establishment with campus sit-ins and angry protests against Vietnam, the Brits were finding emotions like anger very hard to sustain with so much marijuana in the air. In London, Mary Quant was introducing a grateful world to the miniskirt while wafer-thin supermodel Twiggy was empowering girls with the idea that they didn't need to eat in order to be happy. In 1967, the contraceptive pill was legalised and free love was suddenly still free love nine months later. With social liberalisation came the first stirrings of modern feminism, a movement towards equal pay driving a strike by 850 female workers at the Ford factory in Dagenham. They finally got what they wanted in 1970 with the passing of the Equal Pay Act.

In 1964, Labour squeaked into power under their new leader Harold Wilson. Wilson, a sharp-minded Yorkshireman who had been made an Oxford don at the age of 21, was determined to modernise Britain and his party. Capital punishment was abolished in 1965 for everything but treason and caning in borstal and prisons done away with in 1967. Homosexuality was decriminalised and the abortion and divorce laws liberalised, allowing for the equal share of household assets after separation.

Naturally, the overwhelmingly male Tory MPs opposed these liberal reforms, convinced that traditions like bare-bottom caning were an integral part of British society, particularly when they'd been a bit cheeky to matron. But after calling an early election in 1966, Wilson won himself a more comfortable majority and pressed on with reform. With a dramatic increase in education spending, Labour set about ending the selective 11-plus exam, gradually increasing the number of state-run 'comprehensives' that aimed to give pupils from all backgrounds, no matter how disadvantaged, an equal chance to beat up kids from grammar schools. New universities were opened at the same time, most radically the Open University, which provided a valuable opportunity for badly-dressed professors to appear on television.

Rivers of Blood
Despite all the fun to be had, life was not all rock 'n' roll for 1960s Britain. For one thing, there was the economy which, after a decade of partying, was beginning to look a bit worse for wear. After consistently high spending under both Tories and Labour, Britain was suffering from a huge balance of payments deficit, which the markets urged the government to improve through a devaluation of the pound. Wilson resisted for three years, but was eventually forced to cave in. 'It does not mean that the pound in your pocket has been devalued,' he told the public with about as much conviction as a Ringo Starr drum solo.

The government was dragged into numerous industrial disputes, most damagingly a six-week strike by the National Union of Seamen in 1966 which paralysed the ports. 'Beer and sandwiches at Number Ten' was the usual method of resolving conflicts; cake if you agreed to give Wilson the credit. The economy, however, was not the only headache for Wilson. There was also the perennial problem of Ireland. By 1968 the Protestant and Catholic sides had begun to arm, the IRA on one side and the Ulster Volunteer Force on the other. This marked the beginning of the Troubles, a name that was somehow meant to distinguish it from every other period of Irish history. Sectarian murders and bombings were carried out with depressing regularity, while Catholic civil rights marches invariably ended in tear gas and baton charges from the ever-enthusiastic Royal Ulster Constabulary. By 1970, the whole province was in chaos, with gun battles, rioting and arson in the major cities, particularly around Derry's infamous Bogside area, which was almost as nice to live in as it sounded. To restore order, the British government felt compelled to send in the army, a move that, of course, improved things immensely. By 1971 there were bombs on the streets of London.

As if Irish paramilitaries were not bad enough, an even greater menace to peace and stability continued to terrorise the British mainland in the 1960s. This menace was, of course, brown people. In 1968, the government decided to admit 50,000 dependants of existing Commonwealth immigrants into Britain, despite some 74% of British people saying they had preferred it when *we* invaded *their* countries. The Tory MP Enoch Powell saw where it was all going, calling the decision 'mad, literally mad' and describing a vision of British streets like 'the River Tiber foaming with much blood'. This rhetoric was a bit too much even for the Conservative Party, who expelled him from the shadow cabinet. Luckily for Powell, he soon found a new home with the Ulster Unionist Party, where frothing racist demagogues were considered normal, literally normal.

Oh Great, it's the 1970s

In 1970, the Tories returned to power under the former chief whip Edward Heath. Heath, who called himself Ted in a vain attempt to sound less dour than he was, fought the election on the promise of a new free-market approach to the economy that would deal with the sticky problems of unemployment and inflation by managing to increase both of them at the same time. He would also curb the power of the unions, bringing an end to the waves of devastating strikes that had almost crippled the previous government's supply of sandwiches. Yes, Heath told the public, it was the 1970s and everything was going to be fine.

Except it was the 1970s. The first year saw higher charges for the NHS and a squeeze on government spending. Heath had appointed a grocer's daughter named Margaret Thatcher as his education secretary, and she immediately set out her caring, sympathetic agenda by abolishing free school milk for 8- to 11-year-olds, earning herself the tabloid nickname of Milk Snatcher. To be fair, it wouldn't be the worst she ever had. Then came the stress of decimalisation, begun under the previous government. Suddenly people had to forget about twelve pennies to a shilling, two shillings to a half-crown, three half-crowns to an ounce, and twenty ounces to a foot[*] and get used to incomprehensible numbers like five, ten and one hundred. While Decimal Day itself went smoothly, old people bemoaned the loss of their beloved currency, a symbol of the befuddled, impractical randomness that had made Britain what it was. It didn't help that a year later the government ripped up the county boundaries, creating weird new entities like Merseyside and Avon and abolishing old favourites like Rutland. It was like you didn't know where you lived anymore.

Luckily, however, any confusion people felt was soon cleared up by a pair of miners' strikes in 1972 and 1974 that plunged the entire country into darkness.

---

[*] or whatever

"Yes, that's where we live," people said in relief.

Selective blackouts were imposed to save energy and a three-day working week brought in. Drivers in London would find themselves passing from areas of gleaming street lights to total darkness in a single journey. It was like the Blitz but with the British bombing themselves. An oil crisis in 1973 caused by OPEC's embargo of sales to the Israeli-friendly West sent petrol prices through the roof, causing massive queues at the pumps. Inflation rose to 20% and unemployment hit a million, the highest in thirty years.

Poor Ted Heath fancied himself as a master yachtsman but when it came to the ship of state he couldn't sail five yards without crashing into a reef. Forced to abandon any plans it had for free market reform, the government pumped money into the economy. Rolls-Royce was bailed out on the brink of bankruptcy and other 'lame duck' industries rescued out of fear of more economic shocks. The miners were finally placated with a 35% pay rise, a concession that all but guaranteed the demise of their industry in the following decade. Only one success of note was achieved by Heath: the negotiation of Britain's entry into the European Common Market in 1973, bolstered by a national referendum voting 67% in favour. When it came to Europe, referendums were clearly the way to go.

The British Disease

By the mid-1970s, Britain had lost so much confidence in herself that she was self-harming on an epic scale. While the European powers had painstakingly reconstructed their war-torn cities to their former neo-classical and baroque glories, British architects had realised that the kind of buildings people really wanted live in were huge concrete tower blocks that could catch fire at any moment. Known as brutalism, city planners were convinced this was the only style of architecture that would suit the rivers of blood they were expecting for the streets[*]. There was worse to come, as, not content with living in buildings that made you want to scratch out your own eyeballs, the self-destructive Brits decided they should dress like that too. In came platform shoes, wide psychedelic ties, massive collar shirts and bell bottom flares, fashion's equivalent of a mass suicide cult. The only consolation was that four days a week the whole country was in a blackout.

In February 1974, a desperate Heath called an early election, campaigning under the slogan 'Who governs Britain?' as if he genuinely wanted to know. Labour squeaked in under a hung parliament before gaining a majority of three seats after another election in October. Wilson and his government, however, had no answers to what the world was calling the 'British disease'. With inflation at over 20% and unemployment rising, the government increased welfare and pension spending, paid for with an increase of the top rate of income tax to 83% as well as a 98% top rate on investment income. In 1976, physically and mentally shattered, Wilson decided to retire at the age of sixty, pensions being the one thing in the 1970s that had actually got better.

James Callaghan defeated Michael Foot in a leadership contest to become Wilson's successor, having already served as home secretary, foreign secretary and chancellor. As foreign secretary he had told Wilson, 'Sometimes when I go to bed I say to myself that if I were a young man, I would emigrate.' But in 1976 he was 64 years-old and, with the endless transport strikes, it was hard to even make it to the airport. Callaghan's government was not only out of ideas, it was also out of money. Despite the first revenues from North Sea oil in 1975, chancellor Denis Healey was forced to go begging to the International Monetary Fund for a £2.3 billion bail-out, given on the condition that the government make three billion pounds in cuts to public spending. Needless to say, the cuts

---

[*] brutalism was not a nickname given by critics, you understand; it was the actual term architects chose for their own work

didn't improve the economy. However, by then it was clear that the post-war consensus of Whitehall-knows-best was dead. Full employment can no longer be guaranteed 'at the stroke of a chancellor's pen', Callaghan told his party conference glumly.

But his party wasn't listening. Boosted by a massive public sector workforce, the trade unions had swelled to a membership of thirteen million workers, growing almost as powerful and uncontrollable as Denis Healey's eyebrows. When Callaghan attempted to impose a 5% limit on public sector pay rises to curb inflation, the unions put the government to the sword once more. In the winter of 1978, naturally the coldest in sixteen years, the country was paralysed by a wave of strikes from picketing lorry drivers, train drivers, ambulance drivers, nurses, waste collectors and even gravediggers. Rubbish piled up frozen in the streets and there were disturbing reports of bodies being stored with no-one to bury them. The army was drafted in to provide a skeleton service, as it were, but January 1979 saw the country all but shut down. It was another month before an agreement with the TUC finally saw the strikes begin to die down. But by then the damage to the Labour Party was done.

In 1975, a Tory leadership election had seen Ted Heath defeated in favour of Margaret Thatcher, a leader who was, unusually for the Conservative Party, in several fundamental respects a woman. Thatcher had been merciless on Callaghan during the winter of discontent, and her campaign slogan of 'Labour Isn't Working' was handily accompanied by images of shuttered factories and piled-up garbage. She had no doubts whatsoever about the causes of Britain's prolonged economic malaise. 'No theory of government was ever given a fairer test or a more prolonged experiment,' she said of socialism. 'It was a miserable failure.' She was about to teach the country just how miserable *success* could be.

Maggie's Here

Despite the gloom of the 1970s, Britain had not remained

completely stagnant over the decade. The advent of the package holiday had seen millions of pasty-faced Brits venturing abroad for the first time, swapping fish and chip suppers in Bangor for fish and chip suppers in Majorca. Thirteen million sought the foreign sun in 1981 compared to just four million ten years earlier. Colour TV licenses had exceeded black-and-white licenses by 1977. Millions of avid viewers tuned in to shows like *Fawlty Towers*, *The Good Life* and *Blankety Blank*, while teenagers waited breathlessly for *Top of the Pops* every Thursday night, presented by all the nation's favourite sex criminals[*]. The Sex Pistols had even sworn on live television.

Into this world stepped Margaret Thatcher, Britain's first female prime minister. Declaring war on inflation, her government, with Geoffrey Howe as chancellor, increased interest rates and slashed public spending while reducing the top rate of tax to 60%. A vicious recession followed with unemployment rising to two million by autumn 1980 and three million a year later. The government's support plummeted while an open letter from 364 leading economists urged her to change course. Thatcher, with a vivid memory of Heath's painful U-turn in 1973, refused to budge: 'You turn if you want to,' she told the 1980 party conference. 'The lady's not for turning.'

The outlook, however, was increasingly bleak. Over two million manufacturing jobs were lost in the first three years of her administration, output dropping by 30%. For some reason, Employment Secretary Norman Tebbit's plan for the jobless to 'get on their bike' didn't quite succeed in turning the economy round, and by 1983 chancellor Nigel Lawson was admitting Britain was better suited to being a services economy[*]. The rock bottom came in July 1981 when the classic British summer cocktail of racial tension, inner city deprivation and heavy-handed policing

---

[*] more of *that*, later
[*] a rude and slow services economy, obviously

led to riots all over the country, including Toxteth in Liverpool, Handsworth in Birmingham and Brixton in London. Enoch Powell, still waiting for the streets to turn red, warned of a 'racial civil war'. As the clear-up began, foreign commentators were describing the once great nation as a basket case, except, of course, Britain didn't make baskets anymore.

Politically, Thatcher was fortunate to survive. The Labour Party, ever obliging, chose as its next leader the old left winger Michael Foot, who committed himself to nuclear disarmament, scruffy suits and withdrawal from the EEC. This precipitated the departure of the 'gang of four' moderates, Roy Jenkins, David Owen, Shirley Williams and Bill Rodgers, who broke away from Labour to form the centrist Social Democratic Party. At one point, the new party was leading Labour in the polls. Internally, Thatcher faced constant sniping from Heath and his 'wets', who had never forgiven her for ousting the former leader. Such was Heath's antipathy to his successor that when he described Heinrich Himmler, whom he had encountered when visiting Germany as an undergraduate, as 'the most evil man I have ever met', the emphasis was definitely on the word man.

The Falklands War

Despite the horror economy, it was not all doom and gloom in Thatcher's early years. There was the royal wedding in 1981 between Prince Charles, Lady Diana and Camilla Parker Bowles[*], which was watched globally by an estimated 500 million people who had nothing else to do that day. A year earlier there had been an even more glorious spectacle when Arab terrorists seized the Iranian embassy in London. After six days of fruitless negotiation, Thatcher ordered in the SAS who stormed the building on live television, rescuing the hostages and bringing thousands of ordinary British men and women to involuntary orgasm. Twenty

---

[*] Diana later described the marriage as 'a bit crowded'

years later, it was still being ranked as one of television's greatest ever moments, just behind the moon landing and the bit where Del Boy falls through the bar in *Only Fools and Horses*.

The Iranian siege helped to cement Thatcher's reputation as the Iron Lady, a monicker helpfully given her as an insult by the Soviet press after a belligerent speech in 1976. In truth, however, Thatcher had been relatively quiet in terms of foreign policy. Her major policy had been to slash spending on naval defence, safe in the knowledge that remote outposts of the empire like, to take an example at random, the Falkland Islands would never be attacked by anyone. Nobody paid much attention to the proposed cuts, except, unfortunately, the military junta of Argentina who had been searching for a patriotic cause to divert people from their country's disastrous economic situation. They launched an invasion of the South Atlantic islands on 2 April 1982.

The seizure of the islands came as a huge shock to the people of Britain, who hadn't realised there *were* any islands in the South Atlantic. Thatcher, however, immediately saw the need for decisive action, certain that, as a strong modern democracy, Britain required a patriotic cause to divert people from their country's disastrous economic situation. Under the advice of the Naval Chief, Admiral Henry Leach, she ordered a naval task force to take back control. With Argentina refusing diplomatic overtures to withdraw from the islands, the first British commandoes arrived on 21 April and made preparations for a full invasion. On 2 May, the Argentine cruiser the General Belgrano was sunk by a British submarine with the loss of 323 men. Though there was controversy over whether the Belgrano had been heading back to port before the sinking, the effect was to demoralise the Argentine navy which slunk back to base and never emerged again. On 21 May, Britain launched the main invasion and, despite heavy fighting in areas like Goose Green, took less than a month to retake the islands. In total, 255 British servicemen were killed with Argentina losing around three times that number.

For Thatcher, the victory was a godsend. As the Tories enjoyed a ten-point surge in the polls, Maggie revelled in her sudden global fame, becoming a world statesman almost overnight. By the end of 1982, the economy was slowly coming out of recession and policies such as giving people the right to buy their council homes were proving popular with the working classes. In the June 1983 election, the Conservatives gained a massive 144 seat majority with Labour's vote split by the SDP-Liberal alliance. Thatcher was triumphant and now the revolution could start in earnest.

Miners, Printers and Yuppies

On the early morning of 12 October 1984, Thatcher was in her suite at the Brighton Hotel writing her conference speech when a 20 lb bomb exploded in her bathroom. Planted by an IRA operative on a long-delay timer under Thatcher's bath, where even the most thorough security officer had not dared look, it ripped a hole in the hotel's facade, killing five people including one Conservative MP. Norman Tebbit's wife was left paralysed. Miraculously, the prime minister herself was unharmed. Holding an impromptu press interview, she refused to allow the conference to be delayed, insisting that she would never let terrorists get in the way of the important business of destroying the last remnants of Britain's manufacturing industry.

The first two years of Thatcher's second term were dominated by the miners' strike, a protest against the planned closure of twenty unprofitable pits and the loss of 20,000 jobs. The government had already been introducing legislation to curb the power of the unions and the miners' strike provided Thatcher with the perfect opportunity to impose her will. Preparations had already been made to counter the strike by stockpiling coal supplies to prevent disruptions to the electricity supply, and so when the National Union of Mineworkers under Arthur Scargill declared a walk-out in April 1984, the pain was felt almost exclusively by the miners themselves, particularly when the police started smashing them in the head with batons. In the end, poverty and desperation forced the miners to give in. The pits were closed and the north resigned itself to mass unemployment.

A year later, Thatcher's resolve was tested again by a strike by Fleet Street print workers after Murdoch's News International introduced new technology that would put 90% of traditional type-setters out of work. A new plant at Wapping was opened with the new technology and, despite a year of picketing and protests, the print union was utterly defeated. Rupert Murdoch was able to lay off his workers, freeing up valuable funds that his editors could put to more important use on phone hacking and police bribery. Needless to say, Murdoch became a lifelong fan of Thatcherism.

It was in the years from 1984 to 1988 that Thatcherism truly began to leave its mark. The appointment of Nigel Lawson to the Treasury sparked the sell-off of Britain's numerous nationalised industries. British Telecom, British Gas, British Aerospace, British Leyland, British Steel, British Shipbuilders, British Sugar, Britoil, Cable & Wireless, National Express, National Bus Company, National Freight, Rolls-Royce, Jaguar, Sealink, Ferranti: you could buy almost any British company in the 1980s, just as long as you didn't actually intend for it to stay British.

In October 1986 came arguably the biggest shake-up of all, the 'big bang' in Britain's hitherto protected financial industry when foreign firms were permitted to operate in the City of London for the first time. The profits from privatisation fuelled a boom in the City, helping to give Britain the highest economic growth rate in the developed world. The new breed of 'yuppies', short for young urban professional shitheads, were an advertiser's dream, shelling out unlimited supplies of cash on watches, champagne and mobile phones the size of caravans. Comedian Harry Enfield's *Loadsamoney* character parodied the new upwardly-mobile working classes, while the book *American Psycho* highlighted the growing ranks of city financiers who doubled up as serial killers.

The party ended temporarily on Black Monday in October 1987

when stock markets crashed around the world. Unlike the Wall Street Crash of 1929, however, passers-by were not treated to the spectacle of stockbrokers throwing themselves out of their office windows, no matter how long they waited around, and it wasn't long before business resumed as usual. Within a decade, London's financial industry was second only to New York's.

The Iron Lady's Fall

Thatcher won another landslide in the 1987 election. With Labour leader Neil Kinnock's attempts to modernise his party coming up against the hard rock of nuclear disarmament, the Tories were almost unchallenged. In October 1987, inflation was at 4.3%, unemployment had fallen to below three million, and the weatherman Michael Fish was so confident that nothing could go wrong he decided not to tell anyone about the massive hurricane heading toward the south of England.

The Great Storm of 15-16 October, just preceding Black Monday, was a portent of rougher times in Thatcher's third and final term. Despite the economic boom, the prime minister was still a deeply polarising figure. Her third term saw her take on education reform under her Education Minister Kenneth Baker who, thanks to the satirical puppet show *Spitting Image*, nobody over forty can now picture except as a slug. The 1988 Education Reform Act brought in grant-maintained schools removed from the control of local authorities and created the first ever National Curriculum, which specified exactly how far behind children should be at each 'key stage' of their school lives.

Outside of Britain, the world was changing apace. South Africa was ending apartheid, no thanks to Thatcher's dogged opposition to economic sanctions, while Gorbachev's policies of *glasnost* and *perestroika* had ended the Cold War and sent Eastern Europe into a dizzying orgy of protest and freedom. On 9 November 1989, the world watched in astonishment as thousands of East Berliners clambered over the wall that had divided their city for thirty years.

Against all the odds and after all those decades of conflict, Germany was finally invading herself. Although supportive in public, the UK privately opposed German unification on the grounds that it was bad enough trying to beat West Germany at penalties, never mind the both of them together.

Thatcher's stance on unification typified her general distrust of Europe. In 1984 she had negotiated a rebate on Britain's contributions to the European Community. In her third term, she fought against the movement toward further political and economic union, in particular the establishment of a common currency. This put her at odds not only with her European counterparts but also her chief allies in the cabinet, Nigel Lawson and Geoffrey Howe, who threatened to resign if Thatcher did not agree to join the Exchange Rate Mechanism, the precursor to full monetary union. In October 1989, Lawson did just that and Howe would not be far behind. Britain ended up joining the ERM anyway in October 1990.

By then, Maggie was busy digging her own grave with her determination to replace local property taxes or 'rates' with a flat charge for all citizens regardless of income. She called it the 'community charge', while the rest of the population referred to it as the poll tax. The last time a government in Britain had tried to impose a poll tax, the reaction had been rather negative, so it had seemed prudent to wait a while before trying again. That had been 1381. The response now was not a great deal better. The Scots were used as guinea pigs for the introduction of the tax, because they had to be useful for something, and they hated it so much it all but wiped out support for the Tories from then on. When it was rolled out in England a year later in 1990, it caused a riot in Trafalgar Square. By the end of the year, as many as eighteen million people were refusing to pay. Thatcher's plan to deal with the crisis by riding out to meet the rebels at Smithfield and slaughtering them on the way home with pikes didn't seem feasible with the modern media, and it seemed incredible that a politician with such an instinct for the popular mood could misread the country so disastrously.

On 13 November 1990, Howe delivered his resignation speech in the Commons. In 1978, Denis Healey had said that an attack by Howe was 'like being savaged by a dead sheep'. By 1990, it had advanced to the level of at least an aging pony. Thatcher's long-term critic Michael Heseltine, the only politician who spent more time on his hair than Thatcher, seized the moment to challenge her to a leadership contest. Though Maggie won the first round of voting, she did not have the support to avert a second round after the bottom candidates had dropped out. It seemed likely that in the second round she would be defeated. On 22 November, she spoke to her cabinet colleagues one by one and appeared genuinely shocked when they proceeded to defenestrate her. The only thing they agreed with her on was that nobody wanted Heseltine to replace her.

At 9:30 am, she announced her intention to resign as prime minister. The same afternoon she carried out her final question time in the Commons where she made mincemeat of Neil Kinnock for one last time. 'I am beginning to enjoy this,' she quipped, her first and only joke in office. Six days later, she gave a final address outside the door of Number 10, her voice tinged with something that might have been a human emotion. Then she climbed into her official government car, a black reinforced saloon manufactured by the recently privatised Jaguar, which had just been sold to the Americans.

The Grey Man

Who was John Major? It was a question that nobody had ever thought to ask before. The son of a comedian and circus performer, who had had five children with four different mothers[*], John had

---

[*] Tom Major-Ball has been called 'one of the most fascinating characters of the century', a description that, it's fairly safe to say, was never made of his son John.

left school with three O-levels and had failed in his lifelong ambition of becoming a bus conductor. Like so many failed bus conductors, he had turned to politics, becoming active in the Young Conservatives. By rights, his colourful background should have made him a breath of fresh air within the staid atmosphere of the Conservative Party. Except somehow it didn't. In 1979, he gained a seat in parliament and from there began a meteoric rise to the top, serving as chief secretary to the Treasury in 1987, foreign secretary in July 1989 and chancellor three months later. At some point, he seemed to have gained his maths O-level.

Winning the leadership election with Thatcher's support, he entered Downing Street on 28 November and immediately bored the economy into a recession. Overseas, George H. Bush had declared war on Iraq after Saddam Hussein's invasion of Kuwait, and Major agreed to contribute 50,000 British troops to the noble cause of liberating the kingdom of Kuwait from its oil fields. On 7 February 1991, the prime minister survived an assassination attempt by the IRA, who fired mortar shells at Number 10 while the cabinet was in session. Luckily, the bulletproof windows of the cabinet office did their job and most of the ministers did not wake up. Despite the grim economy, Major was personally popular with the electorate and, though polls had predicted a hung parliament, the Tories won over fourteen million votes in the 1992 election, the highest ever recorded by a British political party to date. This still meant a relatively small majority of 21 seats, however; and it wouldn't be long before mortars were being fired at Major quite regularly.

The trouble began on 16 September 1992, Black Wednesday, when Britain was forced to exit the ERM after a run on the pound. While investor George Soros famously made a billion dollars by shorting the sterling, the Treasury, which had desperately tried to shore up the pound, lost more than three times that. The humiliation destroyed the government's reputation. Major's refusal to sack Norman Lamont as chancellor for the next seven months only increased the criticism, giving the impression of a leader who was afraid to make the tough decisions. This was somewhat unfair, since earlier in his career Major had had a secret four-year affair with one of his larger than life ministers, Edwina Currie, a decision as tough as any that can be imagined; the image, however, continued to grow over the next two years.

The most damaging blow to his authority was the issue of Europe, which had begun to take on its vital diplomatic role of tearing apart the Tory Party. As European leaders moved toward closer integration at Maastricht, Major successfully negotiated British opt-outs from the social chapter and single currency. While he saw this as winning 'game, set and match for Britain', it was not enough for the Eurosceptic wing of his party who didn't even want to be on the same court as Europe. With Labour tactically opposing certain aspects of the Maastricht Treaty, Tory rebels joined them in voting against ratification of the agreement, defeating the government and forcing a re-vote the following day. Major declared the re-vote to be a vote of confidence in his leadership and eked out a tight victory. But a tie-break was not exactly the way he had expected to win.

By April 1993, Major's popularity had sunk. The press on both sides tortured him on a daily basis, and no matter what he did, he couldn't make them stop. He continued the privatisation agenda of Thatcher, selling off British Rail to private companies in order to improve services for billionaire corporate directors. Then he came up with the idea of the 'citizen's charter', an attempt to make public services more accountable by measuring how many forms they could fill in. Most impressive of all was his Back to Basics campaign, which advocated a return to the upstanding moral values the Conservative Party was renowned for, including toe-sucking (David Mellor MP), auto-asphyxiating (Stephen Milligan MP), fathering illegitimate children (Tim Yeo MP), homosexual affairs (Michael Brown MP), selling arms to Iraq (Alan Clark MP), taking cash for questions (Neil Hamilton MP), and perjury (Jonathan

Aitken MP).

Poor Major became so exasperated with the constant sniping from within his own party he actually resigned as leader while still prime minister, challenging his critics to stand against him in a leadership election. John Redwood, the Secretary of State for Wales, duly stepped up to the plate, supported by *The Sun* under the headline 'Redwood versus Deadwood'. The Deadwood won easily, but his days were clearly numbered. Even if his own party had not chopped him down, there were plenty of axe-wielding maniacs on the other side of the floor ready to get to work. Chief among them were the devilish duo of Tony Blair and Gordon Brown.

New Bling, New Labour

The 1992 election defeat had had a profound effect on Labour. If they could not defeat the Tories in the midst of a recession after ten years of Thatcherism and the debacle of the poll tax, there seemed a very good chance they would never win again. Their new leader John Smith cautiously began a programme of reform to reduce the influence of the trade unions over the party, drawing on the support of two young MPs, Tony Blair and Gordon Brown. Brown was the more senior of the two men, but when Smith died suddenly of a heart attack in 1994, it was the younger funkier Blair who became the frontrunner to replace him. In a now infamous meeting between the two at the Granita restaurant in London, Blair allegedly promised to serve a maximum of two terms in office before handing over power to his friend. He probably never imagined that a Labour leader could really win that many elections in a row, though he had a cunning plan to give himself at least a fighting chance. He wouldn't actually be a Labour leader.

He set out his agenda immediately. Labour would end block-voting for the unions, abolish the Clause Four commitment to public ownership, keep nuclear weapons, follow a pro-American foreign policy, pursue choice in public services, maintain the same levels of income tax, and exercise prudence in public finances. To those critics who questioned how different this made them from the Tory Party they so vigorously opposed, Blair had a confident and coherent answer: "Please, call me Tony."

Communication was crucial in Blair's election strategy. With his two key aides, Peter Mandelson and Alastair Campbell, the Labour Party was ruthlessly kept on message. The aim was to seize the centre ground of politics, pursuing the so-called Third Way championed by Bill Clinton and the Democrat Party in the United States. By 1997, Britain had long since left the recession, enjoying a mini-boom with steady growth and unemployment down to 1.7 million. None of this mattered. Even *The Sun* was on the side of New Labour in the May election, and Blair won in a landslide, capturing 418 seats to the Conservatives' 165. It was the lowest number of Tory seats for over a century. The door to Number 10 was open and Blair was free to redecorate in any way he liked.

12. BRITAIN TODAY (1997 – 2019)

When Tony Blair stepped through the black door of Number 10 in 1997, it seemed like the beginning of something special. The Cool Britannia renaissance was in full swing, with Oasis and Blur fighting it out for the title of Britain's most annoying rock band, and for once it appeared as though politics was on the same wavelength. When Princess Diana died in a car crash, Blair won the nation's heart by publicly humiliating the Queen and that was enough to carry him through four years of dithering into another landslide election win. By 2003, Britain was in great shape with a booming economy, a vibrant culture and a newfound welcome for diversity and difference. Clearly what the country needed now was a war. The Iraq War was a turning point in more ways than one. Suddenly, unity and tolerance were out, and good old British unpleasantness was back. Homegrown terrorism, financial armageddon and Gordon Brown stunned the nation one after the other, opening the door for the Tories to return once more. The Tories set about implementing their own vision for modern Britain by decimating the NHS, gutting public services and forcing disabled people to crawl to the job centre. Then, just when you thought their mission was complete, they organised a referendum to leave the EU. Brexit means Brexit means Brexit, Theresa May proclaimed derangedly. Donald Trump reassured her it was an excellent slogan.

The People's Prime Minister

When Tony Blair entered Downing Street in May 1997, he had had no experience of political office. Luckily, however, this was not a problem as neither had any of his ministers or advisers. In such circumstances, many leaders might have leaned upon the Civil

Service for guidance, but Blair had an instinctive distrust for the musty, moth-ridden bureaucracy that had successfully governed Britain for centuries, preferring to rely on a close team of personal advisers, like Jonathan Powell, Anji Hunter, Alistair Campbell and Peter Mandelson, who were more skilled at coming up with policies[*]. The so-called 'kitchen cabinet' attracted criticism from within and without, but when the other nearby rooms contained people like Gordon Brown and John Prescott, you could understand Blair's desire to keep himself close to the gin and tonic.

The government began with a slew of announcements – independence for the Bank of England, referenda on Scottish and Welsh devolution, a national minimum wage, abolition of assisted places for private schools, a ban on tobacco advertising, entrance into the European Social Chapter, the introduction of Sure Start child education provisions. But, by Blair's own admission, there was a lack of true vision in his first term in office. Labour's famous campaign slogan, for example, that they would be 'tough on crime, tough on the causes of crime' bore little fruit in actual policy.

The biggest event of the early months was, of course, the death of Princess Diana in a car crash in Paris. While the Queen struggled to express her deep and genuine grief at the death of a woman who had last been pictured lying half-naked on a boat with a millionaire Arab playboy, Blair captured the mood of the nation by referring to her as the 'People's Princess'. A mass outpouring of hysterical mourning followed, which quickly turned to anger when the Queen refused to break protocol by putting the flag at Buckingham Palace at half-mast. Blair stepped in to persuade her to return to London from Balmoral, telling her that the nation was modernising and the Royal Family had no choice but to modernise with it. The Queen's private thoughts that of her four offspring, two of them had married attention-seeking floozies, three of them

---

[*] headlines

were messily divorced, and the other one was widely assumed to be gay, so how much more ****ing modern were they supposed to be, were not aired in public, and eventually the feelings of anger subsided. Diana's funeral was a beautiful occasion, and there was unanimous praise for Elton John's inspired decision to sing *Candle in the Wind* so that he didn't have to write a new song.

Blair the Peacemaker

Blair's popularity soared in the aftermath of Diana's death, and he rode the wave of goodwill all the way to the mean streets of Northern Ireland. The negotiations between Sinn Fein, the Unionists and the British government, which had begun in secret under John Major, bore fruit in public under Blair's energetic leadership. After months of wrangling, a power-sharing agreement to formally end the conflict was finally signed on Good Friday in 1998. Even the *Daily Mail* gave Blair a good headline, one of the central policy objectives of his entire administration.

It wasn't long before Blair was intervening overseas again, first with the decision to bomb Saddam Hussein after his refusal to cooperate with UN weapons inspectors and then, more riskily, to send ground troops into Kosovo to stop the massacre of Kosovan Albanians by Slobodan Milosevic. Blair's determination to send in troops was opposed by everyone from the United Nations to the European Union, but his strategy worked, Milosevic caving in before a shot was fired. *The Sun*'s front page blared 'Who Blairs Wins', his best headline yet, and Blair was treated as a hero when he visited Kosovo some weeks later. The Albanians told him how they had lived peaceably for years with the Serbs, only to see their neighbours suddenly turn on them and threaten them with violence. Blair told them he understood because it was just like his situation with Gordon Brown.

The tension with his chancellor had been present from the very start, but by 1999 the rows had become public knowledge. Peter Mandelson, Brown's close friend who had supported Blair in the leadership election, was forced to resign twice after relatively minor scandals, widely suspected to have been leaked to the press by Brown and his team. Policy-wise, there was Blair's support for entering the euro, vigorously opposed by the Treasury, and his promise for more funding for the NHS, which the Chancellor wanted to spend on tax credits and other electoral bribes.

There were other crises too that Blair struggled to deal with. High fuel prices prompted a strike by lorry drivers, who blockaded the oil refineries. As fuel shortages began to bite, there were fears that NHS ambulances would not be able to run and that supermarkets would run out of proper food, forcing people to start eating vegetables. Soon after that crisis was ended, an outbreak of foot-and-mouth disease decimated the cattle industry. In both cases, the right-wing press had a field day, causing Blair's high-voltage press secretary Alastair Campbell to unveil a new strategy for dealing with the media by conducting all of his briefings in swear words.

By the end of his first term, Blair was frustrated he didn't have any major domestic achievements, other than that great headline from the *Daily Mail*. He had wanted to build something concrete, but the only plan of that substance had been Transport Secretary John Prescott's idea of creating a bus lane on the M4. In the end he was left with the Millennium Dome, which was widely regarded as a disaster. Still, it didn't seem to matter. With the Tories in disarray under William Hague, Blair strolled to another landslide victory in 2001. It was time to start getting serious.

Blair the Warmaker

Blair's second term had barely begun when al-Qaeda spoiled his plans for some lovely headlines about NHS spending by flying airplanes into the World Trade Center. Out of the rubble of the twin towers came a new and dangerous menace to world peace: President George W. Bush. When news of the attack came, Bush had been visiting an elementary school in Florida, practising his reading. But when he eventually reached the end of the sentence he was on, it appeared he had already made up his mind about what to do. America would be going to war. Against someone. Anyone really.

For his part, Blair never needed much convincing. In 1999, in the midst of the Kosovo crisis, he had given a speech in the United States setting out his doctrine on international intervention. Democratic states had an obligation, he said, to intervene militarily in clear cases of humanitarian abuse once diplomatic channels had failed (unless of course the humanitarian crisis was caused by Saudi Arabia or someone like that in which case you ignored it). It had been controversial at the time, the Foreign Office chuntering about small diplomatic niceties like international law. But in the aftermath of 9/11 it suddenly assumed massive significance.

Afghanistan was Bush's first target. The Taliban and their *mujahedeen* friends Osama bin Laden and co. had once been allies of the US, armed by the CIA for their guerilla war against the Soviet Union in the 1980s. But they weren't supposed to use those weapons against the West. The allied strategy was to overthrow the extremist Islamic militia of the Taliban with the help of the Northern Alliance, a disparate band of resistance fighters mostly made up of extremist Islamic militia. While the British press warned of an unwinnable war that would suck in troops for years, Blair and his friends were confident there was nothing to worry about. They had a new Afghan leader ready and waiting, Hamid Karzai, whom they knew could be trusted because he spoke with a British accent.

Unfortunately, the press were right and Blair was wrong. Although the Taliban regime quickly melted away and Kabul was liberated, it wasn't long before the fighting resumed. By 2011, there were still 140,000 Nato troops in the country including over 9,000 British. Prince Harry, a helicopter pilot in the British Army, was the best of all of them. As for bin Laden himself, he somehow managed to slip through the careful net the Americans had closed somewhere in the general vicinity and was widely assumed to be living inside a cave, though they hadn't quite figured out which one.

If the Americans had concentrated all of their resources in Afghanistan, the conflict might have actually achieved its objectives. Unfortunately, by 2002, President Bush was distracted by the sudden appearance of a brand new dictator in the Middle East who had only been in power for 24 years. Bush was sure Saddam Hussein was the secret mastermind behind 9/11, given that he had once invaded Kuwait using a number of airplanes. He was determined to put an end to the grave threat Saddam posed to his common sense.

In Britain, rumours of an impending war provoked outrage amongst the general public and deep rifts within the Cabinet. Robin Cook, the Foreign Secretary, talked about the dangers of going to war without a proper UN resolution, urging diplomatic action from the prime minister. Blair assured him that he would speak to President Bush and make him fully aware that Robin Cook had talked about something. The UN resolution hinged on the question of whether Iraq had weapons of mass destruction. The Iraqis claimed they had destroyed all their WMDs years ago, but if that was the case, Bush and Blair protested, why couldn't the UN weapons inspectors seem to find any? It didn't make sense[*]. Blair had the British secret service draw up a dossier setting out the latest intelligence. The dossier claimed that Iraq was actively pursuing nuclear weapons and that it could launch a chemical or biological attack within just 45 minutes. Neither of these claims were rooted in actual intelligence and the Blair administration was widely suspected of 'sexing up' the dossier for their own ends. For the time being, however, it did exactly what the prime minister required. 'Brits 45 Mins from Doom', screeched *The Sun*. 'Saddam Could Have Nuclear Bomb in Year', bellowed *The Times*.

---

[*] really, it didn't

"They don't call us a service for nothing," said the secret service.

By January 2003, war had become inevitable. Iraq produced a 12,000 page document explaining what it had done with its WMDs, but experts argued it contained so many half-truths and obfuscations it could almost have been written by British intelligence. Despite this, opposition to the war was fervent. On 15 February, huge rallies were held around the world. A million gathered in Hyde Park in London; three million took to the streets in Rome. The vote in parliament was on a knife-edge, with Blair's entire premiership on the line.

In the end, the vote to go to war was won. Blair's speech to parliament won high praise in the media, *The Sun* proclaiming that he had won a place in history alongside Winston Churchill and Margaret Thatcher. It was unclear which Blair was happiest to be compared to. The early weeks of the invasion went well, with the Iraqi forces surrendering en masse to the overwhelming firepower of the Americans and British. President Bush flew to the USS Abraham Lincoln and declared it was Mission Accomplished.

It was at this point that the Iraqis decided to start fighting back. Looting in Baghdad was the first sign the mission might not be as accomplished as it seemed. Murders, robberies and kidnappings followed. Blair's impassioned plea to be 'tough on crime, tough on the causes of crime' didn't seem to be much help. Day by day, the situation worsened. The only hope was that Saddam's huge stockpiles of WMDs would be found, but, to everyone's astonishment, it turned out he'd destroyed them all years ago. If only he'd thought to tell everyone that, say in a detailed 12,000 page document. Al-Qaeda terrorists poured into the country to kickstart the resistance, and by the end of the year the best line President Bush could come up with was that at least the terrorists were in Iraq and not in the West.

He was wrong about that too. On 11 March 2004, ten bombs exploded on trains in Madrid, killing 192 people. The Spanish government fell within a week, replaced by anti-war socialists. 'You can't start a war with lies,' declared the new Spanish government. But obviously you could. A month later, there was more shock when pictures emerged from Iraq of the torture of POWs at Abu Ghraib prison. A spread-eagled man wired up for electric shocks, naked prisoners forced to lie on each other in a human pyramid. What little goodwill there had been towards the Americans evaporated immediately. Blair, as their chief ally, was eviscerated.

Scars on My Back

With the mess that was Afghanistan and Iraq dominating the news each day, it was a miracle that the government was able to focus on domestic issues at all. But Blair was determined not to let the conflict in Iraq overshadow his much more important war with Gordon Brown. If the relationship between the pair had been difficult in the first term, in the second it became downright toxic. There were policy battles over whether to join the euro, when to hand over the premiership, whether to increase university tuition fees, how they should reform public services, when to hand over the premiership, how to tackle antisocial behaviour, how much to increase public spending, and when to hand over the premiership. At one point John Prescott even forced the two men to a peace summit at Admiralty House, in which Blair allegedly promised to hand over the reins of power during his third term in return for Brown's cooperation on public service reform.

Public service reform had become Blair's obsession. In June 1999, he had given a speech to the British Venture Capital conference in which he complained that he bore 'scars on my back' from trying to prompt the civil service into enacting reforms. Although the scars were not quite as severe as those on the British soldiers blown up by improvised explosive devices in Iraq, they were quite itchy in their own way. In the second term, Blair set about giving them a good scratch. He introduced a certain amount of private competition into the NHS, establishing Foundation Hospitals which would be mis-run by semi-autonomous trusts instead of the government. He allowed state schools to apply for academy status, taking them out of the control of local authorities, and even flirted with the idea of creating free schools. Gordon Brown managed to scupper the more radical education reforms, fearful that people might learn to understand his budgets, but he permitted massive increases in public spending. This paid for thousands of new doctors and nurses in the NHS and provided renovated buildings for the nation's failing schools, giving local children much-needed new walls to paint swear words on. Tuition fees, meanwhile, provided a boost in the arm for universities, who were finally able to give their vice-chancellors the kind of salaries they deserved.

By the end of his second term, Blair was exhausted. Labour won its third election in a row in 2005, but for the first time it was despite Blair rather than because of him. The Iraq War had tainted him in the eyes of millions, damaging their eyesight so badly they began to look on Gordon Brown as the better leader. It wouldn't take long before they changed their minds, but as Blair walked up to the door of Number 10 once more, it seemed only a matter of time before the venerable old house would belong to someone else.

The Slow Goodbye

It is never a good idea to announce that you might be leaving, either in public or private. In his final two years in office, Blair was determined to tie down his legacy, to bind his successor to the reforms he had fought so hard to push through. He still had a choice, he told himself. He could renege on his promise and remain as prime minister (it wouldn't exactly be the first time) or he could pick someone else to take over, someone whose surname didn't match the colour of his personality. The truth was, however, Blair's choice was rather more limited than that: he could either jump off the cliff or he could get pushed.

The first year of his final term coincided with Britain's presidency of the G8 summit, a position that gave the host nation the huge honour of deciding how to stop anti-globalisation activists throwing mud at the dignitaries' cars. Blair's daring plan was for the G8 to actually achieve something, namely the cancellation of Third World debt. It was the one issue he and his chancellor agreed upon. The summit of 6-8 July began with the news that London had beaten out Paris to be the host of the 2012 Olympic Games, a tribute to the organising team's unstinting efforts to bribe the IOC[*]. The second day of the summit, however, brought news of a rather different hue. A massive terrorist attack on the London Underground, which killed 52 people and injured 700 more. As details of the attack emerged, the news grew even more shocking. One of the four perpetrators came from Buckinghamshire. A home-grown terrorist, the government's worst nightmare. The other three were from a place called Yorkshire.

In the circumstances, the other members of the G8 could hardly refuse Britain's plan to help Africa. A huge aid package accompanied the debt cancellation. It was to be the last major achievement of Blair's time in office. As the rows over his departure date grew ever more heated, there was just time for one more scandal with the government accused of taking cash for honours. Turning lazily in his grave, Sir Robert Walpole wondered how it could possibly have taken people so long to find out. On 27 June 2007, Blair finally resigned. He received a standing ovation at his final PMQs, the tributes led by the new leader of the Conservative Party, David Cameron, the self-styled 'heir to Blair'. His staff wept openly as he made his way down the staircase of Number 10.

Had he been a good prime minister? Without doubt, under his leadership Britain had become a better place. It was kinder, more open and more tolerant, an advertisement for vibrant

---

[*] allegedly

multiculturalism with a newfound confidence in its place in the world and a strong economy to match. Without 9/11, Blair could have been remembered as one of the very best. But events in the United States had changed everything in Britain, as they were often wont to do. As Gordon Brown finally took the helm in the summer of 2007, they were about to do so once again.

Financial Armageddon

Gordon Brown entered office promising change because this is what his polling had suggested he should say. In his short opening address outside Number 10, he used the word 'change' no fewer than eight times before he turned triumphantly toward the famous black door of his new home. Which wouldn't open. It took a full minute before someone finally thought to let him in, with Brown turning alternately from the press ranks to the door and back again. Amazingly, however, it wouldn't be the most awkward moment of Brown's short tenure as prime minister.

The issue from the very beginning of his time as leader was money. The banks had lent too much of it, the government had spent too much of it, and the Americans had lost too much of it. The threat this posed to the British and the world economy would provide both the greatest failures and the greatest triumphs of Brown's roller-coaster ride of a premiership.

The problem, simply put, was this. Since around 2003, the West had been going on a huge borrowing spree, taking advantage of low interest rates and massive influxes of new money from China, Russia and the Middle East. In the US, a lot of this money had been used to finance sub-prime mortgages – zero-deposit housing loans given to low-income families who would not normally have been granted credit. These high-risk loans were packaged together with other forms of debt into hugely complex financial products known as Collateralised Debt Obligations (CDOs). Given AAA ratings by ratings agencies too lazy or too corrupt to attempt to understand them, CDOs became immensely popular with financial institutions in the West. In 2006 alone, over £3 trillion worth were sold, with some investment banks borrowing up to 100 times what they had in capital. As long as house prices in America continued to rise, this wasn't a problem, since sub-prime borrowers could sell or refinance their mortgages if they fell behind on their payments. As soon as prices fell, however, they would start to default and then the whole world was, to use an economics term, screwed. This happened just around the time Gordon Brown was getting locked out of Number 10.

The first signs in Britain that something was wrong were rumours about the building society Northern Rock. The Deputy Leader of the Lib Dems, Vince Cable, had been warning parliament that British banks were seriously over-leveraged and, though the Northern Rock management assured the government they were as solid as the Tyneside sand they were built upon, it wasn't long before Cable was proved right. In September 2007, they were forced to go to the Bank of England for a bail-out. Initially hoping to keep the news secret until the bail-out had gone through, the story was broken on the BBC by Robert Peston. Huge queues followed the next morning as desperate savers tried to withdraw their money, forcing the government into a hasty announcement that they would guarantee all deposits until the crisis had passed. While the panic died down, the crisis stubbornly refused to pass. By February 2008, it was clear that the Bank of England bail-out was insufficient and that the building society would have to be nationalised. It was the beginning of the Great Recession.

Brown dithered throughout his first year in office, unable to find any direction except backwards and sideways. The Tories called him Mr Bean while Liberal Democrat leader Nick Clegg said he was pointless, the ultimate insult coming from a Liberal Democrat. Volatile at the best of times, stories leaked out that the prime minister's fits of rage even had his own protection officers flinching, fearing they were about to be hit in the face. By August

2008, things had got so bad he was forced to bring back his old frenemy Peter Mandelson as business secretary.

Then, on 15 September, came a sudden escalation of the banking crisis and the beginning of Brown's unlikely, and very temporary, burst to global fame. The US investment bank Lehman Brothers filed for bankruptcy having been refused a bail-out by the US Treasury. Overnight, the banking system all but collapsed. Financial institutions stopped lending to each other out of fears of where the next bankruptcy would come. Credit dried up. Stock prices went through the floor. On 17 September, the US government announced the bail-out of the insurance firm AIG, but by then it was too late. Throughout the West, political leaders scrambled to find a solution. President Bush announced a $700 billion bail-out plan called TARP, but even this was not enough to stop the rot. In the end, it was the British government under Gordon Brown and his chancellor Alistair Darling who provided the blueprint others would follow, buying up shares in the most afflicted institutions like the Royal Bank of Scotland and Lloyd's. More bail-outs followed as well as a huge programme of quantitative easing overseen by the Bank of England, which was widely regarded to be a kind of magic.

As companies went bust, jobs were lost and wages were slashed, the anger towards the bankers who had caused the crash, and the politicians who had stood by, was palpable. Worse was to come when the disgraced executives began to award themselves multi-million pound bonuses as a reward for the dedication they had shown in earning their banks billions of pounds of taxpayer money in bail-outs. The government was powerless to stop the culprits walking away with gold-plated pensions, and as usual it was left to upstanding members of the public to take the initiative of vandalising their cars.

I Agree with Nick

By early 2009, the government was beginning to move into

election mode, scheduled for the following spring. But just as it seemed that overseeing the destruction of the entire world economy might be the worst thing British politicians had done for a while, the *Daily Telegraph* suddenly broke the news that they had been fiddling their expenses as well. The scandal centred on the second home allowance awarded to MPs to cover their living expenses while at parliament in London.

At first the stories were all about Labour politicians, almost as if the *Telegraph* had an agenda. Hazel Blears had claimed for three different London properties in the same year. Alistair Darling had switched his second home four times in four years. Keith Vaz claimed for a second home in Westminster despite his first home being just twelve miles away. Jacqui Smith, the home secretary, had claimed for pornographic films her husband had watched on pay-TV, though she swore they were an important part of her government research into how to screw people for money.

The scandal appeared to an all-expenses-paid gift to the Conservative Party. But as the days went by, it transpired that a whole bunch of the Tory MPs were involved as well. The only difference for Tory MPs was that when they decided to claim dodgy expenses, they did it with style. No fewer than five of them claimed for the maintenance of their private swimming pools. Oliver Letwin claimed for leaking pipes on his tennis court. John Gummer claimed £8000 in gardening fees. Sir Michael Spicer claimed for a chandelier and a hedge shaped into a helipad. Sir Peter Viggers, meanwhile, claimed for a duck house, apparently unaware of basic duck living arrangements. Even he, however, could not compete with Douglas Hogg, the 3rd Viscount Hailsham, who claimed for the cleaning of his private moat, which had become uncomfortably clogged up with peasants.

Gordon Brown, as ever, struggled to deal with the fall-out. By the end of 2009, his popularity was at an all-time low and when *The Sun* declared that for the first time in a decade they were officially endorsing the Tory Party, a humiliating election defeat seemed inevitable. The election campaign hinged on the question of the deficit. As chancellor, Brown had significantly increased public spending, though most of this was covered by rising tax revenues (spending as a percentage of GDP remained relatively steady throughout the Labour years). The bank bail-outs and subsequent recession, however, had thrown these figures into disarray. Spending as a percentage of GDP jumped from 40% in 2007 to 47% in 2010, practically doubling the deficit. Brown's attempts to explain the reasons fell on deaf ears, the press encouraging the idea it was good old-fashioned Labour profligacy rather than the unavoidable effect of a deep recession. Under David Cameron and his shadow chancellor George Osborne, the Tories promised to cut hard and deep as soon as they were in power, while Labour warned of the dangers of a double-dip recession if austerity was started too early.

In spite of the hostile press, Brown actually managed to close the gap on the Tories as the election grew closer. His advisers urged him to get out and about with the voters so that they could begin to see his human side, at least in a small enough dose not to notice he didn't have one. This, however, proved to be a misjudgement. On 28 April, he found himself in Rochdale being harangued about immigration by a 65 year-old pensioner named Gillian Duffy. Returning to his car, Brown complained of the 'bigoted woman' he had been forced to speak to, unaware that his microphone was still broadcasting his conversation to the national media. Needless to say, the story didn't play well and on subsequent walkabouts the prime minister had to be assigned extra protection officers, though, given Brown's rage history, they may have been there to protect the other protection officers.

As the weeks ticked down to the election, the major leaders engaged in televised debates, during which Brown and Cameron took temporary leave of their senses and found themselves declaring: 'I agree with Nick,' a phrase that even Nick Clegg seemed never to have heard before. Labour found themselves fearing they might even end up behind the Liberal Democrats in the popular vote. As it happened, however, they did less badly than expected, gaining only 48 seats less than the Tories. The country was left with the first hung parliament since 1974. Despite winning fewer seats than they had the election before, the Lib Dems found themselves in the position of kingmakers. Several days of tense horse-trading followed, the one single constant of the negotiations being that, whichever horses ended up being bought and sold, Gordon Brown's was going to get put down. Eventually, Nick Clegg announced he was teaming up with David Cameron to form the most unlikely partnership since Paul Daniels and Debbie McGee. Most political commentators gave them two years at most. As for Gordon Brown, he left Number 10 much as he had entered it: lonely, confused and out of his depth. The only difference this time was that the door stayed shut.

We're All In this Together

Throughout the divisive election campaign of 2010, the Labour Party had tried to portray David Cameron as a man out of touch with the needs of ordinary people. As though a man raised in an upper-class family in Berkshire, educated at Eton and a member of the exclusive Bullingdon Club at Oxford could not possibly understand what life was like for the vast majority of ordinary working-class people. Cameron retorted that he had in fact experienced exactly how the vast majority of ordinary working-class Britons lived, for he too had ended countless nights staggering out into the streets, drunk out of his mind and vomiting over the pavement. The only difference was that he had been in a tuxedo. Despite Labour's best efforts, Cameron appealed to the full range of traditional Tory voters. The wealthy knew he would take care of their offshore trust funds, since his own father had owned one; the urban middle-classes trusted him to keep their taxes low and their house prices high; and the good folk of rural England were confident they could rely on a man who had shown such a deep understanding of country life that he had once put his private parts in the mouth of a dead pig[*].

Together with his fellow Bullingdon old boy George Osborne, Cameron set about implementing a proper Conservative vision for the state and its citizens. 'We're all in this together,' he assured the nation, as he began to freeze public service pay, gut social care, slash local services, cut benefits, close libraries and cancel school refurbishments, none of which affected members of the Bullingdon Club *that* much. The narrative was that the 'age of irresponsibility' sponsored by the Labour Party was giving way to the 'age of austerity' under the Tories, who were both responsible and bold enough to overturn decades of basic economic thinking which said that cutting government spending during a recession would only make the recession get worse.

In 2011 and 2012, the recession got worse. Britons' real disposable income fell by 1.7 percent in the first quarter of 2013, the biggest quarterly drop since 1987, while the deficit continued to rise as a result of lower tax revenues. As usual, the poor were hardest hit. Food banks took up the slack, with over a million people using them in 2014, a 19% increase from the year before. Most controversial of all the cost-cutting measures was the so-called 'bedroom tax', which reduced the amount of housing benefit tenants could receive if they had a spare room in the house. Almost two-thirds of those hit by the penalty were disabled.

The austerity measures put huge strain on the fragile Conservative-Lib Dem coalition. Five Lib Dems had joined the cabinet as part of the deal, with Nick Clegg as deputy prime minister and Vince Cable as business secretary the most prominent betrayers of everything they had ever believed in. In 2010, the coalition announced they were tripling university tuition fees to £9000, shining a spotlight on Nick Clegg's ironclad election

---

[*] part of an initiation rite at Oxford apparently, though Cameron vigorously denied meeting any pigs at university

pledge never to support fee increases for students unless he was given a really plush office in Whitehall. What little respect the Lib Dems had after going along with the austerity measures vanished with the U-turn on fees, leading to the virtual extinction of the party in the next election.

The economic and financial condition of the country continued to be unremittingly grim as the coalition entered its third year. But there was at least one area of the economy that was continuing to deliver good news: arms sales to repressive states. In 2011, the world had been stunned by mass protests in Tunisia, Egypt, Libya, Syria and Bahrain, as Arab peoples suddenly rose up against the repressive regimes of their countries and pushed for the three basic human rights of freedom, democracy and total lawless chaos. Cameron used the occasion to tour the Gulf states to see how Britain could help the Arab people find their path to freedom by selling advanced weaponry to their undemocratic governments. Inside the coalition, the Lib Dems argued forcefully against this flagrant sacrifice of moral principles, and eventually Cameron was forced to give in to their stringent demands by buying the deputy prime minister a new reclining chair.

This didn't, however, free Cameron from the need to respond to the Arab Spring. In Libya, Colonel Gaddafi had reacted to the threat against his regime by bombing his own citizens. US President Barack Obama was reluctant to intervene, but the British and French felt they had a responsibility to save the Libyan people from Gaddafi's terror so that they could get killed more slowly by Islamic extremists instead. A short bombing campaign reduced Gaddafi's defences to dust, and soon the haughty former dictator was pictured bedraggled and bleeding, surrounded by a howling band of extremists about to shoot him in the head. It was another proud moment for Western foreign policy.

Libya quickly descended into anarchy, with the Europeans quickly deciding their part in the civil war was over. A few thousand miles of desert sand to the east, another civil war was just getting warmed up as Bashar al-Assad's brutal regime in Syria came under attack from assorted opposition groups, separatists and extremists, all eager to brand the country with their own special form of madness. If the situation in Libya had been complicated, the Syrian civil war made it look like a children's television programme. By this time, however, Britain had found itself with its own violent band of separatists to worry about. And these separatists had decided to hold a referendum.

Scots, Hackers and Paedophiles

Ever since the Scottish National Party had gained a decisive victory in the 2011 Scottish general election, a referendum over Scottish independence had become all but inevitable. In March 2013, the Scottish government announced that the referendum would be held on 18 September 2014, a year marking the 700th anniversary of the Battle of Bannockburn, the last significant thing achieved by Scotland. Alex Salmond, the leader of the SNP, appeared to see himself as a kind of Braveheart figure, though with fewer social skills. On the other side of the fence was David Cameron, not gay like Braveheart's nemesis Edward II but just about as unpopular in Scotland.

The SNP's vision of post-independence life was set out in a 670-page document entitled *Scotland's Future*. It described an idyllic Nordic-style paradise of full employment, free childcare and generous cradle to grave welfare. Scotland would join the EU but keep the British pound. It would remain in Nato but discard nuclear weapons. It would maintain links with Buckingham Palace but sever them with Westminster. It would abolish the BBC but keep *EastEnders* and *Doctor Who*. The SNP claimed they would even be able to compete in the Eurovision Song Contest, which was expected to provide a significant proportion of national income. The remaining revenue would come from North Sea oil, which Scotland had decided was all theirs now.

In England, the majority of people were strongly opposed to

Scottish independence on the constitutional grounds that Andy Murray might win Wimbledon again and say he wasn't British. With David Cameron afraid to cross the border for fear of being slaughtered in battle, campaigning for the No side fell to renegade Scots Alistair Darling and Gordon Brown, who managed to resurrect himself from the dead via the occult. The ensuing campaign was bloody, brutal and almost incomprehensibly accented, but in the end the Scots voted narrowly in favour of remaining within the UK. Within six months of the result, a massive drop in world oil prices had collapsed revenues from North Sea oil by 97%, rendering 699 pages of *Scotland's Future* completely void. Scottish songwriters realised they had better get busy.

Back in Westminster, the coalition government was continuing to remind its citizens exactly why the Scots wanted to leave. Andrew Lansley, the Minister for Health, was busy implementing plans to revolutionise the governance of the NHS by abolishing some regulatory bodies, adding some more and doing some other stuff. It may or not have been designed to advance privatisation; nobody could really tell. Waiting lists were growing, though, and that wasn't good. His successor Jeremy Hunt then managed to achieve the seemingly impossible and make himself even more unpopular than his predecessor. He imposed a new contract on junior doctors to push the NHS towards a seven-day week, triggering strikes and widespread disruption. It didn't really help the waiting list situation.

Outside the government, there were scandals galore. The first to hit the headlines was the disclosure that the *News of the World* had been hacking the phones of numerous celebrities, politicians and members of the royal family in order to gain access to details of their private lives. It was a shocking revelation that stunned absolutely everyone who had never read the *News of the World*. Then it transpired that they had also been hacking relatives of deceased British soldiers, victims of the 2005 London bombings and, most chillingly of all, the phone of murdered schoolgirl Milly Dowler. The story horrified every strata of British society, except, of course, the prime minister, who had hired managing editor Andy Coulson as his communications director and who counted chief executive Rebekah Brooks as a personal friend. The *News of the World* was eventually forced to close, but luckily Rupert Murdoch was soon able to announce the launch of a brand new paper called *The Sun on Sunday* which would be completely different from the *News of the World* in that it had a different name. To complete the happy ending, Rebekah Brooks became the CEO of Murdoch's News UK, having successfully persuaded a jury that she had no knowledge of the phone-hacking activities of the newspaper she was editing at the time.

Amazingly, considering the paper's history, the one piece of celebrity gossip the *News of the World* hadn't been able to break was that around 75% of BBC television personalities in the 1970s and 1980s appeared to have been sex criminals. Sir Jimmy Savile was the first to be named and shamed, the allegations coming as a shock to the generations of children who had grown up believing the most creepy thing about him had been his tracksuits. Then came the announcement of a major police investigation into other creeps of the era, including Dave Lee Travis, Rolf Harris, Max Clifford and Stuart Hall. Convictions were secured for these bearded monsters, but other arrests led nowhere, most notably that of Cliff Richard, the raid on whose home was filmed live by the BBC. As the singer threatened lawsuits, the BBC strongly defended their actions, arguing that anything done to publicly humiliate Sir Cliff Richard was obviously in the public interest.

In May 2015, Cameron called a general election. The pollsters, who had predicted a comfortable Conservative victory in 2010, were now convinced 2015 would yield another hung parliament. Ed Miliband, who had murdered his older brother David in order to seize leadership of the Labour Party in 2010[*], had been widely mocked by the media for everything from his mildly left-wing views on corporate responsibility to his inability to eat a bacon sandwich. Yet he had managed to hold steady in the polls, appealing to traditional Labour voters. In the end, however, the pollsters did what they did best: get it totally and utterly wrong. Cameron won himself a majority of twelve seats, while Miliband and Labour were humiliated, wiped out by the SNP in Scotland. Cameron became the first prime minister since Lord Salisbury in 1900 to increase his share of the vote after a full term. The Tories were on top of the world. Surely nothing could stop them now.

If It Ain't Broke, Don't ~

Brexit. This was the only word on people's lips as the world entered the fateful year that would come to be known as 2016. In the election campaign, Cameron had promised a referendum on EU membership if the Tories gained an overall majority in the Commons, a move that he hoped would energise the right-wing of his party and neutralise the threat from a relatively new force in British politics, the UK Independence Party of Nigel Farage. The UK Independence Party, popularly known as UKIP[*], had been formed in 1991 as a single-issue Eurosceptic party, but it was not until Farage assumed leadership in 2006 that it began to gain national attention.

Farage expanded the party's Eurosceptic agenda to feed on wider public fears about immigration and multiculturalism. He blamed immigrants for traffic jams on the M4, claimed parts of Britain were unrecognisable because of the number of foreigners, said he would feel uncomfortable living next to men from Romania, called for immigrants with HIV to be banned from entering the country, and advocated dispatching the British army to put down

---

[*] David claimed he wasn't really dead, but it was difficult to tell for sure.
[*] and several other names that probably shouldn't be printed

an imaginary migrant rebellion in Calais. These statements, however, were positively mild compared to those made by other prominent members of his party. Amongst other things, they argued that Islam was 'a cancer that needed eradicating', that halal food was 'sick, evil and satanic', that parts of London had been 'ethnically cleansed' of white people, that the comedian Lenny Henry should go back to 'a black country', that 'poofs and dykes' should not be allowed to marry, that legalising same sex marriage would be a precedent for legalising incest, that wind farms should be 'blown up' and that, just to make clear UKIP was not a one-issue party, they had the strength to 'kill a badger with their bare hands'[*].

David Cameron had heard all these statements and thought: yes, these are the kind of people we need to bring into the Conservative fold instead. UKIP had already become the dominant British force within the European Parliament and in the 2015 election had managed to gain 12.6% of the popular vote, significantly more than the Liberal Democrats. Only the lack of proportional representation had saved the House of Commons from having Nigel Farage participating in Prime Minister's Questions. For David Cameron and his one-nation Tory allies, the referendum on EU membership was supposed to be the hammer with which he would crush Farage and his cronies forever.

And so we entered the referendum campaign, which would make the Scottish independence campaign seem like tea and crumpets with the Mother's Union. On one side was the Remain campaign, supported by the government, the Bank of England, the business community, the academic community, the City of London, President Obama and the vast machinery of the EU itself. On the other side was Nigel Farage, a couple of Tory politicians called Boris Johnson and Michael Gove, and a big red bus. It was clearly

---

[*] Controversially, however, it was claimed that this was a not an initiation rite into UKIP.

going to be a very close-run thing.

The referendum campaign quickly descended into a bear pit of accusation, counter-accusation, spinning and lies. The Leave team claimed Brexit would free the nation from mountains of restrictive red tape. Britain would open itself up to the world (without letting anyone inside obviously), creating new trade deals with China, India and the United States. She would control her borders to stop the flow of immigrants into her factories, fields, warehouses and cafes, which would become liberatingly free of staff. She would make her own laws and spend her own money, gaining an extra £350 million a week to spend on the NHS. When the Remain side tried to point out the inaccuracies of these figures, to indicate the huge complexities that came with Brexit and to emphasise the disastrous economic implications of being outside the common market, they were accused of scare-mongering. The country had had enough of 'experts', Michael Gove pronounced. It was a group of people the Leave side of the campaign was mercifully unburdened with.

As the referendum date grew closer, the pollsters predicted that, although the result would be tight, there would be a clear majority in favour of remaining in the EU. Thus, it was no surprise whatsoever when the Leave side won. The overall result was 51.9% in favour of leaving and 48.1% in favour of staying. The demographics of the vote showed just how divided Britain had become. While 60% of people over 65 voted Leave, that was true of only 25% of those aged 18-24. Only 29% of people with a university degree voted to leave, compared to 66% of people who had left school at sixteen. 57% of Tory voters chose Leave compared to 31% of Labour supporters.

Within two days of the vote, David Cameron announced his resignation, telling the nation that new leadership was required to clean up the mess he had created. The rest of the political establishment watched in shock as everything they had believed in crumbled around their ears. Britain was not the country they thought it was. British voters were not the voters they thought they were. Everything was different now. There was no hope. The apocalypse was here.

Running Through Fields of Sludge

They were right. Cameron's resignation triggered a feverish leadership election, since a vacuum at the highest echelons of British government was just what the country needed right now. There were three frontrunners: Boris Johnson, the floppy-haired architect of the Leave campaign; Andrea Leadsom, another prominent Leaver; and Theresa May, a quiet Remainer who had promised to cut immigration to 100,000 a year as home secretary but somehow managed to get away with a figure three times that high. As the campaign got underway, Boris abruptly had his legs cut away by his former ally Michael Gove, whose wife had decided she would like her husband to be prime minister instead. Gove's act of betrayal destroyed Boris's campaign but also his own, because if there was one thing the Tory Party couldn't stomach, it was a traitor who hadn't gone to Eton. So then there were two. Andrea Leadsom's platform was based mainly on the idea that she had children and Theresa May didn't, but it turned out this wasn't of primary importance to the country right now. May won easily, quietly turning herself into a committed Leaver with the help of the *Daily Mail*. 'Brexit means Brexit,' she announced grandly, a statement that was the closest thing she would ever get to an actual policy.

Her cabinet reflected the giant pile of manure Cameron's referendum had left her in. There had to be a place for Boris Johnson, the former Mayor of London who had accused US President Barack Obama of having 'an ancestral dislike' of Britain on account of his Kenyan relatives, who had called Obama's likely successor Hillary Clinton a 'sadistic nurse', who had compared the EU to the Third Reich, and who had suggested Turkish president Erdogan enjoyed having sex with goats. May decided he would make a fine foreign secretary. As Minister for Brexit came David Davis, a man so poorly regarded even his fellow Leavers thought he was 'thick as mince' and 'lazy as a toad'. And as chancellor Philip Hammond, a backer of the Remain campaign who didn't bother to hide his contempt for his two most senior colleagues. Together, these three men and one woman had the responsibility of leading Britain through the most complex and fraught negotiations the nation had ever seen. It would be an absolute breeze.

But first, however, there was a problem because Theresa May had realised it had been more than three months since the country had had an election and there was a danger people would forget how to vote. Looking for a political mandate to negotiate Britain's exit from the EU, which a couple of her ministers were in favour of, she called for a general election. Victory seemed certain. Not only was the *Daily Mail* on their side but the Labour Party was being led by a hard-left anti-nuclear socialist who had died in the late 1970s and somehow come back to life. His name was Jeremy Corbyn. Corbyn was widely believed to be a complete disaster for the Labour Party, except by the 60% of Labour supporters who had voted for him. He promised the renationalisation of the railways and water companies, more funding to the NHS and social services, more money for schools and local authorities, free childcare for young children, an increase in the minimum wage, a repeal of the bedroom tax, an end to university tuition fees, a price cap on energy bills, a fat cat tax on banks and corporations and an increase in tax for the highest earners. David Cameron called him 'a threat to our national security, to our economic security and to the security of your family'.

Corbyn offered a different kind of politics. He went out into the streets and spoke to people, vowing to keep his shirt collar open and his politics clean. May, on the other hand, refused to leave her room for fear of bumping into someone she might have to talk to. The closest she came to honesty was admitting her naughtiest ever act, which was running through fields of wheat as a young girl. She conveniently omitted the end of the story in which she and her friends pushed little peasant children into combine harvesters.

Despite the differing quality of the campaigns, May was still expected to win a decisive victory as the polls opened on 8 June 2017. When the results were announced, however, it was yet another huge shock. In spite of all the negative press coverage, the personal attacks and Labour's confusing stance on Brexit, Jeremy Corbyn had managed to pull off a miraculous defeat. His party wasn't wiped out by the electorate. In fact, it increased its number of seats. The Conservatives, meanwhile, lost the meagre majority they had held and had to resort to an alliance with Northern Ireland's Democratic Unionist Party, who, amongst other things, denied gay marriage, rejected global warming and opposed abortion even in cases of rape. Needless to say, the one thing they did support was Brexit.

So Now What?

So, that's pretty much where we are today. Two years after absolutely, definitely, indisputably vowing that Britain would have left the EU by the projected leaving date of 29 March 2019, at the time of writing Britain still hasn't left the EU. The Brexit negotiations didn't go smoothly. The EU's chief negotiator, Michel Barnier refused to even begin talks on a trade deal before Britain had agreed to pay the €60 billion divorce bill that was owed. His British counterpart David Davis, meanwhile, refused to begin talks on the divorce bill before they worked out a trade deal. It made for short meetings, at least. After the eventual resignation of Davis, Theresa May took over negotiations herself, along with her new Brexit Secretary Dominic Raab. This proved a masterstroke, with EU leaders breaking through months of bitter deadlock by sometimes agreeing to let her walk near them on the way to the conference room.

Labour, meanwhile, made their position on Brexit absolutely clear, stating that they were definitely in favour of Britain leaving the EU, unless it turned out it was better not to, but if we didn't leave we should definitely be in a customs union, or was that if we did leave, we're not sure, but freedom of movement is a must, though obviously people shouldn't be able to just live anywhere they want, and as for the European Court of Justice that was definitely something that Britain should probably abide by, unless it was something we shouldn't, we're not really sure what it is to be honest, got that? Good.

As the negotiations dragged on, remainers continued to dream the whole thing never happened. Nick Clegg produced a book outlining how Brexit can be prevented from taking place at all by voting for the Liberal Democrats, whatever they are. The hardline Brexiters, on the other hand, argued Britain didn't need any kind of deal with the EU. We could become a low-tax, high-carbon super economy based on the vast reserves of oil, minerals and precious gems that are bound to turn up soon. The ex-New York mayor Michael Bloomberg politely disagreed, calling Brexit 'the single stupidest thing any country has ever done', besides electing Donald Trump.

Eventually, May and Raab agreed a deal with the European Union that categorically delivered on the results of the referendum which nobody had been able to interpret. Raab then went to parliament and explained that, obviously, he himself wasn't in favour of the deal he had just negotiated on account of the possibility it might damage his future political career which, at this critical stage in Britain's history, was what the people of Britain really cared about. The rest of parliament also comprehensively rejected the deal, and so the prime minister engaged in some deep contemplation and soul-searching and then asked them again about a week later. And again. And again. When they stubbornly and unfathomably continued to reject the exact same deal every time, May finally gave up and went back to the EU to ask for an extension. The new leaving date by which Britain will absolutely, definitely, indisputably leave by is 31 October 2019. Don't forget to let me know what happens.

And that's it really. So as we come to the end of this long winding road, all that is left of this story is a short glimpse of the future, a tiny snippet from a British classroom in the year 2030:

"So, children, let's see if you can answer this simple question. Who is the most influential British politician since the Second World War?"

"Winston Churchill?"

"No, children."

"Aneurin Bevan?"

"Don't be silly."

"Margaret Thatcher?"

"No, children, come on! Think harder!"

"Oh God, it's Nigel Farage, isn't it?"

The End.

ABOUT THE AUTHOR

Dave Rear is a writer and academic who lives and works in Tokyo. He read history at Cambridge University and, out of sheer lack of imagination, almost became a school teacher, until he came to his senses and emigrated. He now lectures in English, history, social science and anything else his students let him get away with. He is married with two children, who occasionally give him five minutes or so to write. His first book, *A Less Boring History of the World*, was published by Vintage Books, Random House UK, in 2012.

54395118R00161

Made in the USA
Middletown, DE
13 July 2019